CW00867074

David Mather

Rome Falls

The Iron Sword Series:

Rome Falls: Book 1

Empire Of White Gold: Book 2

Princes And Kings: Book 3

Rome Falls
is for Rosslyn and Joan Mather.
My dad and mam would have been so proud.

Contents

Map 1 Etruscan and Roman Cities

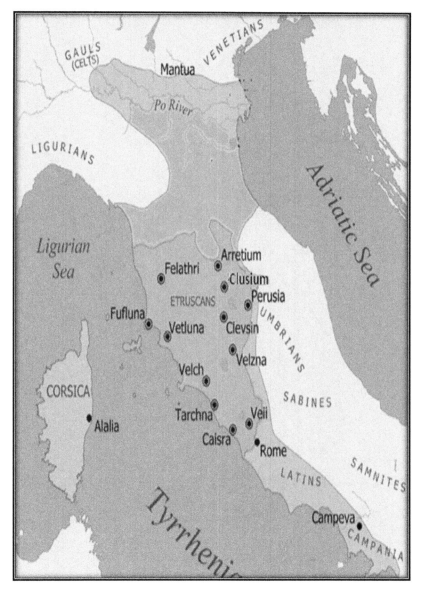

Map 2 Battle Of Allia Roman Formation

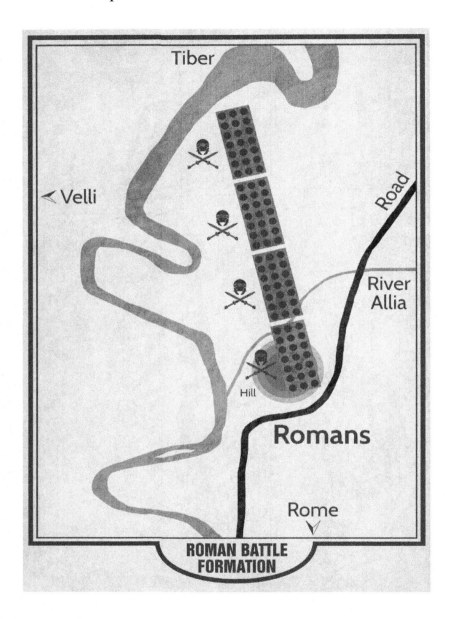

Map 3 Battle Of Allia The Celtic Formation

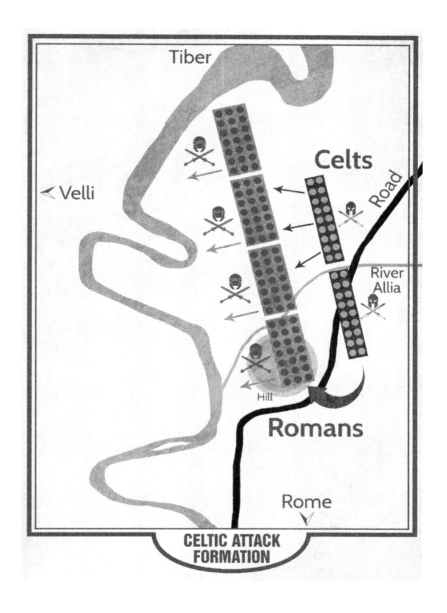

Chapter 1

The Country Villa

Rome May 390BC

Marcus Fabius Ambustus was in the courtyard of the family villa practising his sword techniques with a wooden gladius. He was sparring with Lucius, a high ranking warrior from the Aequi tribe, now one of the many slaves the family owned. The older man stood not much taller than his younger opponent at five feet seven inches. His jet black hair oiled and pulled back into a short ponytail at the crown of his head. His black beard was closely cropped and very neat against his chiselled jawline.

The Hernici tribe, who lived far to the east of Rome, had long since resolved their differences, and had allied themselves with the dominant city for over two hundred years. The Etruscans held a large geographical area, and even had one of their major cities on the northern tip of Rome. They honoured their treaties, not venturing in to the lands considered Roman.

There were two tribes that were persistent thorns in Rome's side. They were constantly waging war, depleting resources and impacting on trade. The first was the Volsci, who had nine cities to the south of Roman territories. The second was the Aequi who constantly attacked from the mountain ranges to the east of Rome.

Lucius was captured in the Aequi's final stand, at the battle of Mons Algidus. The Aequi attacked an advancing Roman army only to be hit from the rear by a second Roman army. They were unable to repost both armies simultaneously, with the end result being defeat. The high ranking Aequians that survived were taken back to Rome to act as slaves to serve Rome's ruling classes. Although now aging, Lucius still possessed the athletic physique and agility of his younger years.

Rome was enjoying a hot summer with the crops growing well, and the slaves talking about an early harvest of the olive orchards. Food was always plentiful for the rich, but even more so on the large country latifunda estate with its mixed variety of agricultural produce, pigs, cows and sheep.

The villa's location was perfect. Its proximity to Rome allowed an easy transportation of crops and livestock to the markets, also giving it protection from marauding raiders. This had become less of a worry these days as Rome was growing in military strength, and had defeated many warring tribes to expand its territory. However, it was still not close enough for its owner who spent most of his time in his single storey domus in the centre of Rome with its marble pillars, statues and detailed mosaic floors. The city house was decorated far more elaborately, with a picture depicting Romulus and Remus at its centre, the founders of Rome who were fathered by the God Mars. It was made up of thousands of tiny coloured tiles that had taken months to lay.

The two had been practicing since early morning in the hot, dusty palaestra of the countryside villa which followed the usual Roman layout of a rectangular court framed by equally spaced columns topped by elaborately carved marble slabs. Adjoining it was a series of rooms used for a variety of functions.

Marcus held a smaller version of an aspis on his left arm. It was half the size and weight of a full size wooden shield, but was still eight pounds in weight. The muscles in his left arm burned as he kept the shield high to block the attacks from Lucius. The young boy was tiring rapidly, but wanted one last attack to succeed. He feigned right, putting all of his body weight onto his right foot, quickly followed by a dart left to expose his opponent's sword arm. This would allow a slash across his right forearm, not a killing blow but enough to make a fighter drop his weapon.

Lucius spun out of the attack, and in a single movement, was behind Marcus in an instant with his wooden gladius at the lad's throat.

'An excellent move, Master Marcus,' Lucius said, but your eyes gave away your move before you had even began to make it. With your permission, may we finish our session for today as your mother gave me strict instructions to have finished by midday, and the sun is already above us.'

Marcus turned around and with a beaming smile, sweat drenching his tunic said

'If you're tiring old man, I think I should let you go and rest.'

Lucius smiled, bowed and gathered up the sparring swords and shields.

Despite the young man's best moves Lucius had easily parried and dodged every one of the attacks all morning, after all Marcus was only fourteen.

The young lad went up the three steps to the first adjoining room off the palaestra. He moved in to the apodyerium, which was merely an area to undress and store clothes. Marcus hung his tunic on one of the wooden pegs knowing that when he returned, a slave would have replaced the sweaty training tunic with a fresh robe.

He energetically leaped straight over the two marble steps that led down to the frigidarium, plunging into the bath. The cold water made him exhale sharply as the shock of its coldness hit his senses. Marcus bathed for a while, listening to the gurgle of water lapping over the sides before entering the warmer bath of the tepidarium.

As he relaxed in the warm water he performed one of his favourite techniques. Filling his lungs with the warm air which had been heated by the bronze braziers that burnt charcoal in each of the four corners of the room. Using the buoyancy from his inflated lungs he let his arms and legs drift up until his whole body was floating on the surface of the water with just his nose, mouth and eyes above the water. The lad had learned this trick at an early age, breathing slowly and deeply, he had discovered that he was able to slip away into an almost trance-like state.

Marcus left the warm tepidarium and made his way to the oven-like caldarium, the hottest of the rooms where its thin mosaic base disguised a hollow floor. Below more braziers were fed charcoal by some of the household slaves. The room was roasting, as the teenager sat on one of the benches he poured cold water over his head from the jugs to the side of the room. The sweat was pouring from every pore of his body as he felt the hot scented air burn his lungs with every intake of breath.

He finally returned to the tepidarium, and lay down on a raised marble slab. Juliana, one of the house slaves, was waiting with a bronze strigil, its curved blade perfectly shaped to scrape his body. Marcus wasn't sure how old Juliana was, but he thought that she was a few years older than him. Unlike some of the slaves, who were purchased, she was born into slavery as her mother was a household slave.

'Which oil would you prefer today Master Marcus?' Juliana asked.

'I have your favourite sweet almond oil, but there is a new one has just been bought from the market. It is a fragrant coconut oil.'

'You decide,' he replied, not really caring in his relaxed state.

The scent of the warmed coconut oil rose in the air as it was rubbed into the young master's body before being gently scraped off by the strigil.

'Will there be anything else, Master Marcus?'

'No thank you, Juliana, but I think you might have just found me a new favourite oil,' Marcus replied kindly. Juliana smiled, bowed and left.

The teenager returned to the apodyerium, and sure enough, the soggy clothing had been replaced a clean linen tunic and a light toga. After he skilfully wrapped the twenty feet of toga cloth around himself, he headed off, in search of food.

Chapter 2

The Celts

Senones Tribal Home, Gaul, May 390BC

Brennus woke up on his bed of furs. The sound of dogs barking outside his roundhouse had woken him from his slumbers. His home was made of stone, which reflected his status as chieftain and had comprised of four rooms. It was much larger than the single roomed wattle and daub roundhouses of his people. Brennus was chief because his father was before him. This was how it was, his senior warriors would have been sons of his father's senior warriors.

Brennus left his sleeping room and made his way in to the central are where a slave tended a large cooking pot. The large bronze container was suspended above the fire on the earthen floor, the straw had burned away from the heat of the cooking area. Smoke was being drawn up through the hole in the conical thatched roof. The room was still very foggy and it was stinging his eyes, making them water. His head hurt from the feast the night before. Even his neck hurt, and he realised he had slept awkwardly on the large gold torque. Brennus ran his fingers through his long shaggy blond locks. He felt pieces of hay from his mattress and tried to remember going to bed.

Celtic tribes loved three things; fighting, feasting and drinking. It was a great honour, and a reflection of your status within the tribe to be invited to the Chief's feast. Not only would you drink your fill and eat the best meats, but you would be showered with gifts. This extravagance served many purposes, it showed that the chief was a wealthy man, and in his service the warrior would also become wealthy. This kept his current men loyal, but also was a sign to others that by joining his tribe there were riches to be made. By accepting the chief's hospitality a man was bound to the Lord and follow him in to battle.

Slowly parts of the night before came back to him, little by little. He had thrown a feast to celebrate the arrival of his cousin from the Silures tribe, far to the north and across the great sea. The lavish meal was in the large rectangular feasting hall with Brennus being at its end, facing the door. Furs were positioned to allow him and three others to sit either side, so that they were able to eat off small tables. Ordinarily the members attending a feast would sit in a circle with Brennus in the middle, but the numbers present did not allow for this formation. Instead four rows of skins stretched lengthways down the feasting hall, enough for twenty warriors in each row.

The banquet raged on all night with more than thirty pigs and ten cattle being slaughtered. Slaves brought in countless platters of meat, hams, hard cheese and blood pudding that were consumed in vast quantities. It was common place for competitions to take place as the lower level warriors tried to advance their status in the chieftain's pecking order. These could be drinking, eating or tests of strength. Only one fight broke out between one of Brennus' men and one of his cousin's men.

'Boy,' Durston yelled, one of Brennus' men.

'That ham in front of you is mine!'

The warriors around him cheered. They knew he didn't really want the ham, he had more than enough in front of him, he was picking a fight.

Dafydd was sat on the opposite row of fur skins, looked up and smiled. 'No, I think you'll find its mine. If you think differently come over here to get it, or will you send one of the sheepherders sat with you?'

Now it was Dafydd's comrades turn to cheer. This was much better entertainment than the bards and poets they had experienced earlier in the evening.

Durston got up off his furs and came over to Dafydd, who was still sat on the floor. He casually reached for the ham and took a big bite from the succulent joint. Durston raised his right leg, pivoted his hips and brought an arching kick down towards Dafydd's head, but he was far too quick for him. Dafydd rolled with the kick, using its energy to sweep him on to his feet. His friends cheered again, but knowing what was about to happen moved cautiously to one side. Dafydd placed the ham on the table, before hitting his opponent with a swift left punch to the stomach, combined with a lightning fast jab to his jaw. Durston was dazed and winded, but not seriously hurt.

'Is that all you've got boy?' Durston taunted.

With a roar he launched himself at Dafydd and gripped him in a bear hug as they both fell to the floor, the small tables smashing under the weight of the two of them. Durston was on top but Dafydd was the bigger man. He put all his weight on one side and rolled Durston on to his back. The roll broke his grip on Dafydd who nimbly moved his body onto Durston's chest, pinning his arms down. This was followed by a hefty left and an almighty right across his face. Durston felt the impact rock through his skull with the taste of iron in his mouth accompanied by white flashes in his eyes. A horn blew and Dafydd looked up, it was a signal that the scrap was over.

Dafydd got up and dusted himself off. He reached a hand down to Durston, who gripped it and pulled himself up, still dazed.

'I told you it was my ham,' Dafydd said.

'Indeed it is, my mistake,' Durston replied and then added 'let's drink!'

Brennus could barely contain himself, roaring with laughter and throwing Dafydd a gold bracelet.

The two fighters spent the rest of the evening drinking, and telling increasingly exaggerated stories of their battles.

When all the smooth imported wine had been drunk Brennus ordered the slaves to bring ale, and as the evening wore on in to the early hours he called for mead. It was the mead that always made his head thump. They were cousins through marriage, as was the custom of the Celtic tribes. By joining Brennus' own Senones with the Silures tribe Brennus had become one of the most influential chieftains of the thirty plus tribes that formed the Celtic nation.

The skin covering the roundhouse door thrust open, and there stood his cousin Arenwen. He was huge, even by Celtic standards, being a good head taller than Brennus. Arenwen must have been at least six foot three, and had learned his trade as a smith from the age of ten. Now at twelve years later, the many years of pounding bronze and shaping metals had given Arenwen a torso rippling with muscle. He not only had the reputation as a fierce warrior, but also as one of the best smiths in the entire Celtic nation. All that time forging weapons, with a mighty hammer, had also gifted him extraordinary speed as well as lightning fast hand/eye coordination. This made him a ferocious warrior, although the scars from hundreds of tiny burns were visible on his tree trunk arms. Both of these statuses were reflected in the detailed horns and winged beasts on the ends of his large gold torque that sat around his thick neck. It was not as large as the one Brennus wore, but it was far more intricate. Unlike Brennus' solid gold torque, this one was made of nine strands of gold chains, wrapped around each other to give a rope effect. Each of the strands was in turn made from nine individual threads of gold making the rope.

'Cousin,' Arenwen said 'you look like you've slept in a hedge.'

'Woman, bring us some porridge and a horn of mead,' the warrior said, ignoring his cousin's comment.

Arenwen had an annoying habit of never having the sensation of a thousand crows pecking inside his head after drinking the night before. Once, just once, Brennus thought he would like Arenwen to experience it so that he might be a little more sympathetic the next day.

'I must admit that I particularly enjoyed the wine last night cousin.'

'Don't speak so loudly,' Brennus said. 'Why, by all the gods, don't you suffer the next day? Do your druids have special potions? If they do, I will give you a chest of gold to take this pain away.'

'Aaah if were only that simple, cousin. All of my family are the same,' Arenwen laughed.

'Ever since my father's father was dipped in a sacred river by a druid when the moon was blood red.'

Brennus chuckled to himself. He liked Arenwen a lot, but he didn't know when he was telling the truth as half of his lies weren't true.

As they sat they ate their breakfast and reminisced about the night before.

'Your man was fast last night,' Brennus said.

'If you think he was fast you should see his sister. She's a little smaller than Dafydd, but lighting fast and deadly with spear, sword and bow. She is my best charioteer,' Arenwen added.

'So why did she not feast with us last night?'

'She meant no disrespect cousin, but one of her horses became lame on our journey here. The druids gave her potions to treat the animal and told her to pray to Epona, the goddess of horses every night.' Arenwen explained.

Both men looked to the door as they heard a galloper ride up and dismount with a heavy thump outside. The guards recognised the man and let him in without challenge.

Bilhild entered the room, he was one of Brennus' senior warriors a tall, lithe man. His red checked cloak, pinned with a silver brooch, was splattered with mud and was a striking contrast to his green checked tunic. A modest silver torque encircled his neck and his longsword was strapped to a belt above a pair of loose brown trousers. Brennus had sent four small bands of riders south and east in search of a prize. They had strict instructions, find it or die trying.

'Lord,' Bilhild said, 'I have found it, I have found the passage through the mountains.'

Chapter 3

The Romans

Quintus Fabius Ambustus lounged on one of the plush red sofas surrounded by his friends. Not only was he an important ambassador, but also a member of the Fabii family who claimed to be descended from Hercules himself.

He would often visit brothels, as most married Roman men did, but this meretrix was more than a common prostitute. She was his 'high class, good faith' prostitute, who loved him, unlike the other men and women he used who, in turn, used him for his money.

Ambrosia wore a brightly red toga, loosely hanging from one shoulder. This was certainly not like the linen stola which 'respectable' Roman women wore. The gold anklet was covered in an array of beautiful jewels, which also distinguished her as a meretrix of a wealthy patron.

She was unlike his pale skinned skinny wife, whom he married for political ambition. She was a tall, tanned Greek with jet black hair and deep blue eyes, who had bought her freedom as a slave using the tools she possessed to part stupid rich men with their money. Those days were gone now and she plied her trade for a small number of rich, powerful men. Perhaps in the not too distant future one of them would leave her enough to see out her days in a comfortable villa.

'Ambrosia, bring me more wine,' Quintus slurred.

He had been drinking heavily all day, which was not unusual. He had received bad news earlier in the month about his political ambition. Although being part of a very high ranking family, it was a very large family with over two hundred members. He had been outvoted as a magistrate in favour of one of his many cousins.

Ambrosia gave a darting look to Gaius Maximus as if to question the request for more wine. Some men get drunk and are harmless, but not Quintus - he was a nasty drunk. He had a foul temper after too much to drink, and this latest setback of not being voted a magistrate only fuelled the anger in him even more.

'Come now Quintus, let's think about heading home,' Gaius suggested.

'No, I will drink until it is coming out of my ears, and if you want to run off home like a whipped dog that's up to you,' came the reply.

'I'm sorry but I will need to go and get more wine,' Ambrosia said, telling an untruth. It was common practice to dilute the wine with water but, by leaving the room, she would replace the beverage with one that was so diluted that it was more water with wine than wine with water. This she hoped that this would bring down Quintus' foul mood. She would also do what she did best, show some tit and open her legs. Men are fools she thought, give them what they want and even the most sensible brain becomes mush, pliable to a woman's manipulation. Ambrosia left to replenish the drinks.

'Why, why did they do it to me, Gaius?' Quintus asked.

'Why didn't enough of the plebs vote for me? Have your men found out the reason yet?'

'My men knocked some doors and knocked some heads,' Gaius replied, 'and from what we can gather your bribes were not as much as they received from your cousin. Not only did he pay more, he promised when he was elected to have a new public bathhouse constructed.'

'The mentula! I will cut off his collones with a rusty spoon, force them down his throat and make him eat his own balls!' However, it was a clever move, why did not I think of that? I must remain a tribune, at least for now, Quintus thought.

Gaius had served time in the army and was used to the soldiers using such foul language, but it surprised him to hear it coming from his friend.

Ambrosia returned to the room and filled Quintus' goblet, taking time to ensure he saw enough of her ample cleavage to move his mind to other matters. She poured Gaius a goblet and spoke softly enough not to be heard by Quintus.

'I have sent a boy to take his horse back to his domus, and summoned a sella to carry him home when he has had his fill.'

Gaius nodded in approval knowing that she had his friend's best interests at heart. Not only could he physically hurt himself by falling from his horse, but it would not look good for him politically riding drunk through the streets.

Gaius drained his goblet to leave Ambrosia to ply her trade.

'I must go, my friend,' Gaius said, 'I have business to attend to, but I leave you in capable hands.' Knowing that his friend would immediately understand the double meaning.

'Off you go then, back to your nagging wife. I also have business to attend to,' as Quintus pulled a necklace from his toga. 'This is for you Ambrosia.'

She took the necklace from Quintus. It was magnificent, the gold links were interspersed with bright green glass every four links until they came to a heavy gold pendant with an etched picture of a woman holding a horn.

'Ohhh this is so beautiful,' Ambrosia purred 'and the goddess Abudantia is so appropriate as she must be smiling on me to bring me such good fortune'

Quintus emptied his cup as Ambrosia got to her knees, raised his toga and received his reward. Men are stupid she thought as Quintus satisfied himself.

Quintus awoke a little later, and noticed it was starting to get dark outside.

'Ambrosia, one more drink, make it a large one and not like that watered down rubbish you gave me earlier. Do you think I'm stupid?'

Ambrosia dutifully served the wine with Quintus holding her hand while she poured to ensure it was full to the brim. She had hoped that his mood would have gotten better, but she could still see the flames of anger flash in his eyes.

'One more drink,' Quintus demanded impatiently.

'Is that wise?' Ambrosia asked, and as soon as she had let the words slip from her lips immediately regretted saying out loud which would normally stay in her head.

'Do not forget your status girl. Don't you know who I am?'

Quintus got up and stormed across the room. He stumbled out of the chamber bouncing off the walls, spilling some of the drink as be descended the steps to the street.

Instead of finding his horse he found two of his slaves waiting by his sella. It was very ornately carved to reflect his status with two long poles straddling a covered chair. He flopped in and pulled the curtains closed. As a slave lifted each end he yelled 'take me to my villa and make it quick before I have you whipped to the bone!'

Quintus finished the drink that he had brought with him from the brothel and continued to simmer at Ambrosia's words. Bitch, after all I have done for her, she would still be opening her legs every hour, on the hour if it wasn't for me! He thought. He must have dozed off again, as before he knew it he was being gently woken by Aesop, the overseer of his household slaves.

'Get me wine and tell my wife and brat of a son that I'm home. They are to dine with me immediately!' Quintus commanded.

'Of course, I shall deal with it straight away'.

Aesop had been in service to the family before Quintus was born. He recognised the mixture of foul mood and drunkenness, knowing that any other answer would provoke a raging outburst.

Aesop sent the house slaves scurrying off with a bark of orders to prepare food for his Master, then went to inform his mistress of her husband's return.

He found her in the garden with her son Marcus.

'The Master has returned and requested you both to dine with him,' Aesop said.

'How is his mood?' Lucia asked, 'is he drunk again?'

'I would say the Master is extremely tired,' Aesop replied very tactfully.

'Thank you Aesop. Inform the Master that I will be with him presently.'

'Marcus, go straight to your room and I will dine and deal with your father.'

Her son knew what this meant. She always shielded her beloved child from her husband's drunken rages.

Lucia joined Quintus around the dining table framed by four couches. She lay on the ottoman to the left of her husband's at a ninety degree angle. The square table in the middle of the four couches had been hurriedly laid by the kitchen slaves, but there was still a very sizable offering considering how quickly it had been prepared. There was a plethora of meats ranging from roast goose to dormouse, as well as an assortment of fresh fruit and vegetables. The food was cut in to bite sized pieces with slaves ready to wash the hands of their masters as they ate differing foods with their fingers. As Lucia sat down she was immediately met by a torrent of verbal abuse by her husband Quintus.

'Why have you taken so long?'

'Couldn't you have made a better effort to look good for me? But no, I suppose not it's been many years since you looked good. Not since that brat sucked all the goodness from you.'

'Speaking of the brat, where is he, I summoned you both?'

'It's late, my love, and he's asleep,' Lucia lied.

Quintus erupted, sweeping the plates of food off the table, the silver patters bouncing off the mosaic floor and food being scattered everywhere. He staggered to his feet and started shouting.

'Brat, where are you brat?'

The fact that there was no reply fuelled his anger even more. He stormed from the dining area and started bounding up the stairs, two at a time. Lucia hefted up her stola in an attempt to keep up with her husband. She harangued Quintus in an attempt to give Marcus some warning of their arrival. It worked as it gave the teenager just enough time to quickly get in to bed and pretend to be asleep.

'Get up!' his father shouted.

'I summoned you to dine with me.'

'I am the law in this household and you will obey the law!' He roared, spittle foaming on the corners of his mouth.

Quintus grabbed Marcus, with Lucia trying to get in between the two of them. Quintus struck her across her face so hard it left a red imprint of his hand across her left cheek. She fell to the floor, but the distraction gave the lad the chance he needed and launched himself onto his father's back. The teenager gripped his father tightly with his knees and with fists flailing from behind to land on Quintus' face.

The older man reached over his shoulder with his right arm, pulled his son off his back and threw him like a rag doll into the corner. The boy was dazed, but stumbled to his feet to attack again, only to be met by Quintus cupping the back of the young man's head with both hands pulling him down as Quintus drove his knee into his son's gut. It dropped him instantly.

The boy lay winded on the floor beside his mother, her left cheek reddened and burning. Even though she was in obvious pain Lucia still tried to protect her offspring in her arms, while Quintus towered above the pair of them.

Aesop edged his way in to the room, and tried to diffuse the too familiar situation.

'I have your favourite wine downstairs Master. Shall I serve it in the dining room or in the garden?'

Quintus seemed to slowly realise what he had done. It was if he had been watching someone else do this to his wife and son.

'Garden,' my father snarled and then left the room.

Marcus watched him leave and thought 'tomorrow I will train harder and every day after that, as one day I will be strong enough to kill you, father.'

Chapter 4

The Mission

'Well cousin, it looks like I have an adventure for you,' Brennus said to Arenwen.

'We have been searching for a path through the mountains for quite some time. I have been told that the lands on the other side are fertile and bountiful. It will be an excellent extension to our nation'

'It will take two days to ready our forces, and we will go through lands both friendly and not so friendly. Go ahead of our main force as our vanguard, agree passage and secure food where you can. I want land where the warmth of the sun kisses my skin, and the winter won't chill my bones'

'Will you do this, Arenwen?' Brennus asked.

He dropped to one knee and said 'as you command, my Lord.'

'Pick twenty of your finest warriors. That will be enough to ensure that the gold you carry will be safe from raiders. Bilhild will be your guide and second in command. I will be following along behind with a horde to conquer and settle the new territory.'

'Your reward will be half of the land we capture, to be shared between you and Bilhild. Be bold, be greedy, be ruthless, but above all bring me heads.'

'Leave me now, go consult with the druids, discover when it's most favourable to begin your quest.'

Arenwen and Bilhild bowed, leaving the chieftain's roundhouse together, but Arenwen noticed that his new acquaintance was weary.

'Go and get some hot food inside you Bilhild, then prepare to move. I'm off to find the druids,' Arenwen said.

He hadn't noticed before how Brennus' village differed from those of his home. Although the hill fort had the same layout with regards to the defensive ditches surrounding the wooden palisade, this was rectangular in shape, in contrast to his home which was built with round villages and towns. The ditches rippled around the hill fort and were designed to slow down any attacking force, whereas the practicality of the wooden fence was more to keep the animals in than attackers out.

But that apart, it was the usual daily life of a Celtic town, women on the looms weaving cloth. They would use it to make woollen garments, which got their colour from various vegetable extracts. He could also see women curing hides with salt to prevent them rotting in the cold wet months of winter. Salt was a multi-faceted commodity, and was very important to all of the civilisations of the world. The women were tanning the skins over a fire so that the smoke would preserve them for even longer.

When ready, the leather would make fine bedding or clothing for the people. In reality, Celtic tribes were self-sufficient, growing their own crops, raising their own animals and producing their own clothes. Gold, silver and bronze were signs of status and a useful bi-product of warring.

Arenwen's first thought was that he would find the druid at the large stone obelisk, located at the entrance to the village. He strode through the central muddy path, and saw the obelisk long before he saw the village entrance. It towered twenty five feet in the air, one solid piece of carved stone. The warrior marvelled at how many men it would have taken to transport the huge stone, and how far away the quarry was as he hadn't seen any during his journey.

As he got closer to the entrance the young children of the village were being shown the art of the sling. Originally developed to be used by a shepherd to kill or scare off wolves, it had become a formidable weapon on the battlefield. The shot was capable of travelling three times further than a spear; not as fatal but the shot could kill with an accurate blow to the temple, even a near miss to the target area would blind or maim the victim. The children were pulling stones from their pouches, placing them in the small leather holder. They whirled the leather straps of the sling several times, in great arcing movements, over their heads. They whipped up the speed until they released one end of the cord and sent the stone flying. The targets were recently severed heads from a raiding war band that had the stupidly to infringe on Brennus' territory. The heads were in different stages of decomposition, having been exposed to the elements, as well as suffering from the attention of hungry birds.

Arenwen could see that even now the youngsters were pretty accurate with only a few shots not finding their mark. This was one of the deadly skills the children would learn; sling, bow, spear, sword and short axe, which would have been thrown or used in close combat where a long weapon gave no advantage over the opponent. They would have to wait longer and become stronger until they were able to wield the long axe, which was capable of splitting a man's skull in a single stroke.

Arenwen approached the entrance to the village and addressed one of the sentries. These were young warriors who, as part of their duties, stood watch at the entrance of the village.

'I'm looking for my druid Bakher,' Arenwen said.

'I saw him go in to the forest a little while ago,' the sentry said pointing in a southerly direction.

The warrior walked through the organised rectangular fields growing wheat and barley. The cattle had been let out of the village to graze on the new greenery that sprung up from the land. He soon came to the edge of the forest and noticed a natural path. He followed it and in a very short period of time found that he was much deeper in, with the light flooding through the branches. The trees were budding and would soon grow a rich green canopy that would give the forest a night time darkness, even during daylight. He ducked below a low hanging branch, hopped over a small stream and continued on the track. There was Bakher, the druid, half way up an oak tree, his long white robe hitched up around his waist to enable him to climb. His hood was draped around his shoulders, with his staff propped up on the mighty oak's trunk. Bakher was quite an old man as druid training would take typically twenty years, and even beginning his instruction in his late teens, the druid would be starting to feel the onset of old age. There were multiple Celtic tribes, each with slightly differing beliefs and ways of doing things, but the one thing that bound them together was the druids. The individual tribes were the warp on the loom, and the druids provided the horizontal weft that bound them together into the cloth of a nation.

'Come down old man before you fall and injure yourself,' Arenwen called up.

'No, I must climb higher. I must reach the mistletoe as Rober has marked this as a special tree; it is truly blessed.'

'In all my years I have only seen this once in my life. The sacred oak tree with mistletoe growing on it,' Bakher continued.

Arenwen's face looked blank.

'Don't you remember the lessons I taught you boy? Rober, the God of oak trees! I shall beat you when I come down from this holy tree,' Bakher chastised his former pupil.

'Please come down now and I will get what you need,' Arenwen pleaded.

Bakher ignored his concern, and continued shuffling further up the tree until he reached his prize. He pulled a knife from his belt and carefully selected handfuls of the oval evergreen leaves, feeling their waxiness on his fingertips. Bakher stuffed the leaves in to his pouch then moved onto the white berries. The druid ignored the ones that were clustered in groups of two, and selected only the berries that were in clusters of six. Thirty berries were carefully chosen and carefully placed in a separate pouch. The druid adhered to the ancient Celtic tradition believing that the number three, and multiples thereof, was a sacred number. The number three represented the three sacred elements of land, sea and sky. Although he could have selected fifteen combinations of two his choice of using the clusters of six berries was more mathematically pure. He put his knife away, and started making his way down the tree. Sitting on the last bough, Bakher edged one leg down and dropped the last few feet to the floor, landing next to Arenwen.

'So, why have you come looking for me?' Bakher asked.

'Your advice is needed. I have come to ask you to foresee if the time is right to advance to new lands.' Arenwen replied.

Bakher unhitched his robe and composed himself. Taking a bag of small bones he squeezed the juice of three newly picked white berries into the bag. He emptied its contents onto the floor, held his staff in his left hand and placed his right palm on the ancient oak tree.

He waited for what seemed like an age, muttering something that Arenwen could not quite make out. Whatever it was, it was in an ancient tongue. He studied the bones and then carefully put them back in his pouch. Bakher looked up and said 'the signs are good.'

Arenwen was pleased with the druid's prophecy, but suddenly heard something, crashing through the trees, a sound between a grunt and a howl. He thought to himself how could he have been so stupid? It was not a well-worn path, it was a boar run.

Arenwen pushed Bakher behind him to protect the old man as he knew was coming.

'Get back to the village,' Arenwen urged Bakher.

The druid started off as quickly as he could. Arenwen could see the boar now, not as large as he had seen them before, but big enough to seriously injure or even kill him. Its rusty brown fur matted with mud and two large tusks. Head down it charged at Arenwen at an incredible speed. The Celtic warrior moved fast, and reached to his side to draw his long sword. He would have to pierce the thick skull, as a glancing blow would only wound the animal and further enrage it. This kill had to be a made with a single thrust.

Arenwen could hear the boar blowing hard as it accelerated at him; it was nearly on him now. He glanced back to see that Bakher was clear. The boar came on so quickly with Arenwen still pulling his sword free. His heart missed a beat as he felt the pommel of his sword hit the tree; there was not enough clearance to pull the long sword free. Closer, and closer the boar came at him at great speed. It was almost on him. He thought that he would be lucky to come away from this alive. He had seen the ravaged bodies of men who had come second best to boars in a hunt, it was not a pretty sight.

Arenwen braced himself for the impact, hoping to use the boar's speed to deflect it to one side, and make his move while it sped past and turned. Arenwen's heart was beating out of his chest, any second now and the boar would be on him. The beast was one foot away when suddenly it jerked sideways to the right, with a high pitched squeal as a spear took it through the neck. A second shaft quickly followed and took it through the boar's left eye socket puncturing its brain; it was dead in an instant.

Deborah came out of the undergrowth laughing loudly. It was Dafydd's sister; standing at five foot ten with her brown cape over one shoulder. Athletically built, but the most striking feature was her flame red curly hair tumbling down over her shoulders.

'How long have you been there,' Arenwen asked, beads of sweat running down his brow.

'I've been tracking that beast for hours, been sat here on the boar run for a good while. Didn't you notice the track?' Deborah smiled.

'Then why didn't you kill it sooner?' Arenwen questioned.

'I was enjoying the entertainment. To see the look on your face when you couldn't draw your sword will be one I shall feast on for all my days,' Deborah laughed.

She put her left boot on the boar's snout to extract the second spear from its eye socket. She then pulled the first spear from its neck, wiping them in the undergrowth to clean off the residue of the animal's blood. Men feared Deborah as a fierce warrior with deadly skills, but they feared her birth skill even more. Some said it was a gift, some said it was a curse. She was a necromancer; she talked to the dead.

Chapter 5

The Iron Sword

Marcus was having breakfast with his mother when Aesop announced that one of his uncles, Caeso, had come to visit. His mother looked flustered, and pulled her headscarf over the red welt left by my father's brutality the night before.

'Show him in,' Lucia commanded.

Caeso came in carrying a wooden box tucked under his arm. His smile quickly faded when he saw his sister-in-law's face. He pushed the scarf back that covered her bruise.

'Did my brother do that to you Lucia?' He asked.

'Yes,' Lucia replied 'but he didn't mean it. It was my fault for not being prepared for his return.'

'I shall have words with him,' Caeso said. Lucia took her brother-in-law by the arm.

'No, please don't. It's done now and it will only make him angry again. Let's just leave it and pretend it didn't happen.' Lucia pleaded.

'Very well, but we cannot let this continue,' Caeso frowned at his brother's actions.

Marcus thought to himself that he will never not forget what had happened, and that when he is older he will be able to protect his mother.

'Will you take breakfast with us?' Lucia enquired.

'No thank you, I have already eaten. Where is my brother, I have something to show him? You too Marcus, this will be of interest to you as well,' Caeso pulled the box from under his arm. He smiled while ruffling his nephew's hair and said 'I hear you're training to be in the military rather than a politician like your father. A legatus in the making no doubt.'

That story worked for Marcus, it concealed his true intention as to why he needed to become an effective fighter.

'Yes, that's right, uncle. Who knows I might command all of the might of the great Republican Roman army one day,' he lied, but it sounded convincing.

'Aesop, go and ask the Master to rise. Tell him his older brother his here,' Lucia instructed.

'Tell him, his older and better looking brother is here,' Caeso added with a smile.

Marcus liked both of his uncles, but liked Caeso the best. He often wondered how his father was so different, wishing that his father was more like the other two.

After a short while, Quintus entered the room. Aesop was at his side fussing and flicking his toga so that it fell correctly.

'What has brought you here at this ungodly hour?' He asked his brother.

'By Jupiter, you have lost half of the day. I have been up for hours,' Caeso teased.

'I have something to show you. I know it will be of interest to you.'

'If you excuse me I will leave you men to discuss your business,' Lucia said looking at the floor rather than at her husband's face.

'Be gone, woman and let my brother and I discuss the business of men – nothing of which should concern the likes of you.'

She left hurriedly, and Caeso sat down at the table with Quintus mirroring his actions.

Caeso placed the box on the small marble table and slowly opened it.

'Is that all?' Quintus demanded of his brother. 'It's a very pretty sword, but that's all.'

'Get a slave to bring your best sword,' Caeso said to his brother.

Quintus nodded and Aesop disappeared, then returned a few minutes later with his master's weapon. Caeso unsheathed the sword he had brought and held it in the air.

'Strike it,' Caeso instructed.

Quintus lifted his sword and struck the new one with a ringing clang, but there was no affect to either blade.

'Hit it again. Harder!'

He brought down his blade with all his might. His bronze sword bent while the new sword was perfectly intact, totally unaffected. It was common for bronze swords to bend as they could easily be straightened. This was preferential to a weapon snapping during combat.

'How?' my father asked, 'this is the best that money can buy.'

'Obviously not,' Marcus' uncle replied with a grin.

'A Thracian slave was recently purchased for my household. I came across him at the stables, and was intrigued by the burn marks on his arms and face. I had him brought to me and questioned him. He informed me that he had learned from his father how to make tools and weapons made from a material stronger than bronze. He called it iron, so I had him make me this sword,' Caeso explained.

'Aesop, have my horse readied. I must see this at once,' Quintus ordered.

'I thought this would be of interest to you. Why not bring the boy along too, it would be good to get him out of this villa for a while,' he suggested winking at me.

'Fine, fine, but if he gets in the way he'll come straight back,' Quintus shot a menacing glance at his son.

They left the front dining room and entered the atrium. It was a bright day with the sun braking through the windows, casting shards of light into the area. When the rain water came it would fall in to the shallow pool within the atrium that contained a beautiful mosaic of leaping dolphins. They continued past the wall frescos heading towards the vestibulum. The long, narrow formal entrance was decorated with another mosaic; a chained guard dog which was to serve as a warning to unwelcome visitors.

Their horses were readied and saddled outside. All three stallions had come from Persia, renowned for their stamina and good temperament. Both of the older men's horses were chestnut brown, but the teenager's was marble white. All three standing at twelve hands high, with their heads being at four feet five, which was not much taller than the lad. They mounted and settled into the four horned saddle as they set off to Rome.

They guided the horses through the numerous olive groves and then past the many fields of golden wheat. All wealthy land owners sold their grain in the markets of Rome, but even with crop rotation and efficient farming methods it was nowhere near enough to feed the bottomless pit of Roman need. Wheat was imported from wherever it could be purchased into the port twenty miles away to the west. The three rode the eleven miles to Rome at a quick pace, Quintus riding alongside his brother and Marcus following behind.

'I must see this new metal being made,' Quintus said impatiently.

'I anticipated you would, so I have had my slave prepare what he needs to demonstrate the process to you. I made sure his every need was met, and had everything built to his exact specification,' his brother reassured.

The mighty River Tiber flowed down from the mountains, where Lucius originated from, was busy with merchants ferrying goods to Rome. The river served many purposes. One as a highway for trade, but also as a natural defence with Rome sitting on the east side of the twisting mass of water. It produced good fish; chub, carp, mullet as well as Marcus' favourite eel. It also powered the mills that crushed the grain to make flour for the endless demand for bread.

The small dots on the horizon slowly got larger and larger, until the small group could make out the outskirts of Rome nestled in the seven hills. Lucia had told her son stories when he was younger of how the valleys between the hills were marshy, and were drained to make the areas now used as markets. Many farms, villages and settlements had sprung up outside the city to provide food and labour to the ever growing metropolis.

The dots became bigger so that they could make out the wooden wall that snaked around the seven hills that made up the city. The ditch in front of the wall had proved itself to be a formidable defence against the neighbouring tribes who had been troubling Rome for decades.

The party crossed the wooden bridge that spanned the defensive ditch and through the tall rampart. Caeso led the way to his domus, he spurred his horse to a canter to go up the steep Capitoline Hill, with his brother and nephew following his lead. As the trio approached the domus they were greeted by some of the Roman's slaves.

'Shall we eat first?' Caeso asked.

'We can eat later. First I must see this metal being made,' Quintus replied.

The domus was much smaller than the villa, but space is far more of a premium than in the countryside. They entered through the door and into the vestibulum, through the atrium with a number of doors leading off on both sides. Passing a statue of Vesta and stepping out in to the courtyard. Here they found the Thracian slave.

'Well I wasn't expecting to find this here,' my Quintus said admiring the setup.

'Your political opponents have eyes everywhere. But even they will not be able to have eyes or ears here,' his brother grinned.

'Thracian, do your work,' Caeso commanded.

A stone circle had been constructed approximately three feet in diameter up to waist height with a bellows at its base. The intense heat could be felt quite some distance away. The Thracian was bare from the waist up, but wore a thick leather headpiece.

'I have prepared the ore and charcoal as you instructed master,' the slave said.

'Good, are you ready to proceed?'

'Yes,' he replied.

The slave pushed his tongs into the white hot furnace, and pulled out a lump of orange mass. He placed it on a long flat stone, repeating the process until the blobs of molten metal were as long as a sword blade. He worked and shaped the globular masses until they merged into one. The slave continued hammering and turning it, sparks flying up off every strike on the molten metal. Some sparks fell on to his arms, but he was impervious to its sting. The Thracian worked and turned, turned and worked the object until it started resembling the shape of a sword. He picked it up with his tongs and thrust it in to a bucket of water; a hiss of steam rising instantly into the air. He pushed the shape back in to the furnace and repeated the process over and over again. Eventually, after cooling it one final time he threw it to the ground and said.

'As you requested master, an iron sword.'

Quintus stooped down to pick it up, but the slave quickly stopped him.

'Forgive me, that is still very hot and you would certainly burn if you picked it up now, it must cool.'

'How many of these could you make?' Quintus asked.

'Given the right equipment and with additional help, as many as you wanted. The raw materials are plentiful, but the process cannot be rushed. Too hot, too cold or the incorrect amount of charcoal will produce a blade that shatters on first contact,' the slave explained.

'I must buy him from you brother. I must have him, and replicate this on a much larger scale at my villa. How much do you want for him?'

'He is a gift Quintus,' his brother said.

'Do you know what this could mean for me?' Quintus asked.

'Fine weapons and tools,' Caeso replied.

'No, my brother, with my wealth I shall have one of these swords made for every member of the Roman army,' he said excitedly.

Caeso suddenly seemed to understand Quintus' intentions. He smiled and said

'And the Senate will offer you the position of legatus, and even to join the Senate itself. Hmmm, Senator Quintus, that has a certain ring to it.

Chapter 6

The Advance Party

Arenwen and Deborah followed behind Bakher with the boar now gutted and skewered on one of Deborah's spears. They carried the spear over the end of their shoulders with the boar impaled in the middle, feet bound with twine. Even gutted the weight of the boar made the shaft bend with each stride they took.

They passed the sentries, still guarding at the entrance to the village, looked surprised at the size of the beast being carried between the two warriors.

'We shall dine well tonight,' one of the young sentries said.

Deborah gave him a darting look and replied, 'we? If you want to dine on boar tonight there are plenty in the forest.'

Arenwen roared with laughter, slapped the guard on his shoulder and said, 'consider yourself told boy.'

The pair continued past the children, who were still practicing with their slings. They hefted the boar off their shoulders, then instructed a slave to skin and prepare the animal for the meal tonight.

'Take your time to cook this well. Your Lord will be feasting on it,' Deborah told the slave. She pulled out the spear that was piercing the boar's body, and wiped it clean in the grass. The slave nodded and dutifully began preparing the fire pit that would be used to roast the boar. Once the charcoal was lit and had started to turn white, the servant pulled out a sharp curved blade to skin the animal, edging the sharpened knife between the outer skin and the flesh below. This was done deftly, and soon all that there was left to do was to ram the roasting spit through the boar's mouth, and out the other end of its body. It was trussed to ensure it did not fall off the spit during the slow cooking process. Finally it was mounted on to the rotisserie spit, with a fire dog supporting each end of the beast. The iron supports were always used when spit roasting larger beasts such as boar or cow. The heads of the fire dogs faced away from the fire with large upturned ears to ensure the spit could not roll off the supports.

The boar would need constant attention to ensure that the meat was evenly cooked, and that it did not dry out during the long cooking process. It would need to be turned slowly and frequently basted to ensure a perfect meal. Arenwen could already feel the heat coming from the charcoal fire pit, and heard a sizzle as droplets of fat dripped from the boar's body onto the heat below. The flames blazed as the liquid fell onto the fire.

'Bakher, would you accompany me to see our Lord?' Arenwen asked.

'Of course.'

They approached the chieftain's roundhouse to find him standing outside.

'My Lord, I have brought my tribe's most senior druid, and good tidings,' Arenwen said.

'I have examined the bones and added the juice of freshly picked mistletoe berries. The signs are very favourable,' Bakher added.

'And even more good news, Deborah killed a wild boar in your honour for you to feast on this evening. It is being readied now, Lord,' Arenwen said, knowing it was his cousin's favourite dish.

'Excellent, you three will all dine with me tonight and bring Bilhild too. Join me after dark,' Brennus instructed.

'As you command, Lord,' Arenwen said bowing low with Bakher offering a polite bow.

Bakher set off to inform his fellow druids of his findings while Arenwen went to look for Bilhild, and to think about who to select to join him on his mission. The warrior found Bilhild fast asleep in his roundhouse. It was nowhere near as grand as the large home of the chieftain, but comfortable enough with sufficient trappings to denote that he was a senior warrior.

It was a single room, with the usual conical roof, and the circular hole where the smoke from the fire could escape. The walls were constructed from wattle and daub. Arenwen thought how long Bilhild had ridden for to look for the passage through the mountains, and decided that he deserved his rest a little while longer. He turned around and left him to sleep, he would return later before the feast. Arenwen would need him to be fresh, but they certainly were not leaving today as the sun was already starting to dip, casting long shadows on the ground.

Arenwen set off to find his men, and had already thought of the ones who would join him in the advance party. He would have to leave some behind with the main force.

It didn't take long to find them, they were cheering loudly as they circled around two of his warriors on the floor. They both lay face down, opposite each other. They edged closer, right elbow on the floor, gripping each other's hand. It was to be a trial of strength; it was to be an arm wrestling match.

As Arenwen got closer he was able to see which of his two warriors were having the contest. He smiled to himself as he should have known which two it would be, of course it was Telor and Vaughn. They were born eight minutes apart with Telor being the first son to their mother and Vaughn following closely behind. Ever since Arenwen could remember they were always at it, trying to prove who was faster, stronger, fitter. The twins, with their shoulder length black curly hair, were now on the ground arm wrestling, no doubt to settle some petty argument that had sprung up. A stranger would say they were identical, but Arenwen had seen them grow up. He could see the subtle differences like the very small scar over Telor's right eye, where Vaughn had hit him with a lump of wood when they were little and also that Telor was fractionally taller than his brother. They were fierce competitors and rivals, but if any man challenged one he would have to take both of them on. The pair were ferocious in battle and would fight side by side covering each other's flanks, but of course seeing who could kill the most enemies. Arenwen had been close to them in battle once, and heard them counting kills to each other while describing how they would despatch their next victim.

And so it began with Vaughn starting with a quick attack; his right bicep bulging with the strain, forcing Telor's arm half way to the ground.

'Not bad little brother,' Telor taunted, knowing that the use of the word 'little' always infuriated his twin. Telor recovered from the quick attack to slowly pull his hand back to the starting position where both men attempted to better each other.

'Is that the best you can do?' Vaughn replied. Both men straining and gritting their teeth.

'I can smell your rancid breath, is that goat's piss?' Telor said.

'No, it's your woman you can smell,' Vaughn smiled.

Then all hell broke loose with the competitive arm wrestling match quickly turning in to a full blown fight, with fists and knees flying everywhere. The others cheered as the two continued rolling on the floor hitting lumps out of each other. Vaughn got in a right hook across Telor's jaw while he replied with a head butt to the bridge of Vaughn's nose, instantly making it spew blood. Telor swept his brother's legs away with a low arching kick, and followed him instantly to the ground fists flailing. Vaughn rolled his brother over so now he was on top raining blows down on Telor.

'Enough, enough,' Arenwen called out over the din.

'Pull them apart,' he instructed his men.

The brothers were dragged apart, and held until they both grinned at each other. It was only then they were released, resulting in the pair hugged each other while laughing.

'You two lumps of cow turd, prepare to move out in the morning.'

The brothers bowed in perfect symmetry; they were Arenwen's first choice. He then went on to select eighteen other warriors who would become the advance party to precede the main force.

Arenwen left his men to ready themselves and returned to Bilhild's roundhouse. He found him awake from his slumbers eating a carrot and turnip stew.

'Good to see you awake,' Arenwen said.

'Yes, I needed that. I cannot remember the last time I had the chance to sleep on my own bed,' Bilhild replied.

'Finish your food then show me the maps you made of our destination. We need to discuss the route and the lands it will take us through,' Arenwen suggested.

Bilhild gestured to his guest to come and sit with him on one of the wooden seats, made from large round tree trunks, and grouped by the wall. Unlike the chieftain's, which were ornately carved, these where just thick sections of the trunk and set about knee height.

Bilhild reached down one of the seats, and began to unravel a hide tied with a leather thong. The skin to revealed a detailed map, placing it on the floor he outlined the journey to Arenwen. It would normally take two weeks, but they would be small mobile force. The main army would have foot soldiers and cattle drawn supply wagons, which would travel much slower so Bilhild estimated that it would be a three week journey.

'Very well, get a copy of that map made for the main force and join me in Brennus' roundhouse after dark. We have a treat for you,' Arenwen said.

Bilhild nodded and started gathering the materials he needed to make a facsimile of his original map. He selected a skin that had been cured over a fire, a selection of charcoal and small bowls of vegetable colourings, so he could mark key landmarks for the main army to follow.

Arenwen left Bilhild's roundhouse, making his way to where he had left the slaves cooking the boar. He could smell it long before he saw it, with the rich aroma filling the air. For the last hour it had been regularly basted with the fermented juice of late apples and Arenwen's mouth was salivating at the smell. The skin had been scored to produce a criss-cross pattern on the crispy crackling.

'I hope that tastes as good as it looks and smells,' Arenwen said to one of the slaves tending the meat.

'Get that to our Lord's roundhouse the minute it is ready.'

'It won't be long,' the slave replied basting the meat again.

Arenwen continued to make his way to Brennus, and saw Deborah coming along an adjoining path through the village. He greeted her with a wave and said 'that was good timing Deborah.'

'Not really, I've been pacing up and down for twenty minutes. The smell of that boar is making me ravenous,' she laughed.

The sentries nodded as they both approached Brennus' roundhouse. They ducked inside to find the chieftain listening intently to Bakher's tales of fairies and the magical acts that they performed.

Deborah and Arenwen did not interrupt, so they sat waiting for the druid to finish his stories. As he did, Bilhild entered the roundhouse carrying the copy of the map he had just made.

'Talk me through the route,' Brennus instructed Bilhild.

'As you know, Lord, there is a mighty river on the edge of your lands, to the east. You follow that as far east as it goes, for approximately three days, and then it turns south,' Bilhild explained.

'Continue following it south for another four days to where the river ends. That is the land of our cousins, the Lingones, they speak our tongue and are sympathetic to our mission. They only ask a small tribute for our passage over their land and offer cattle, grain and local scouts at fair prices,' Bilhild continued.

'That is excellent Bilhild, go on,' Brennus said.

'The local scouts will take you seven days further south to a river they call the Rhone. It is a wide and fast flowing river so they will take you to a crossing that can be made by our army, although we will need rafts,' Bilhild explained.

'They will guide you further west into the lands of the Helvetii, another of our cousins who also speak our tongue. I have spoken with them, and they too will provide provisions. Although they rule the land there are small groups of hillside bandits who raid who they can, when they can. We saw them from the mountain ridges. They will not trouble such large numbers as our army, but you would be wise to be observant when you are in this area, Arenwen,' Bilhild cautioned.

'The Helvetii led us through the mountain ranges with steep climbs, but even steeper descents. High, high, high up you go through the mountain mist and snow. But that view down from the last mountain shows fine pasture land with fertile soil as far as the eye can see. The scouts said a tribe called the Etruscans own this land, but they will only own it until we get there, then it is ours for the taking.'

Arenwen, Deborah and Bakher all sat and listened to the details.

'I am very pleased with you Bilhild,' Brennus opened a chest at his side, picked out a large gold cuff and tossed it to his loyal man.

'Thank you, Lord. To serve you was enough but this gift is truly magnificent,' he said humbly.

'Now, let us eat!' Brennus clapped his hands, and a stream of servants brought in the feast with the boar being the centre piece. The group left the stools and congregated on a circle of furs on the floor, with them waiting for Brennus to eat first. The boar had been butchered into more manageable pieces of meat, with the animal being presented on a large number of silver platters. Whole joints were available with the assembled company needing to use both hands to manage the chunks of meat. The food was plentiful with long sausages curled in a circle as big as a man's hand, filled breads, pies and other pastries. This was all washed down with huge bronze cups filled to the brim with ale.

'So will you be ready to leave in the morning?' Brennus asked Arenwen.

'Yes Lord, I have selected my men, and we will be ready at first light,' came the reply.

'Excellent, I shall be two days behind you. Secure my passage, arrange food, camp sites and scouts. And the omens are in our favour Bakher?' Brennus asked, seeking the druid's reassurance.

'Most definitely, they are,' Bakher said.

The small group ate and drank their fill with Deborah entertaining Brennus by recounting the killing of the boar, which had become embellished even in the short lapse of time since the event.

'You have all done well,' Brennus said. He gestured over to two large chests by the painted wall.

'There is enough gold and silver in these two chests to ensure my journey will be smooth. I have had my fill so leave me now, you all know what is expected of you,' Brennus said.

The four got up bowed and left the chieftain's roundhouse.

Arenwen pushed through the entrance skin and said to the others

'We leave tomorrow, first light.'

Chapter 7

Circus Maximus

Marcus stayed at his uncle's domus the previous night, intending to get up early to have a look around Rome before he had to head back to the villa. The teenager didn't have the opportunity to go to the city very often, spending the majority of his time at the countryside estate. The lad knew he had some time to spare as he had left my father and uncle drinking in to the early hours. His uncle had encouraged him to stay up with them, but Marcus made his excuses, leaving the brothers recounting stories from their childhood.

He quickly ate a light fruit breakfast, slipped out the front door and headed out through the streets. Caeso lived towards the top of Capitoline Hill, which was one of the seven hills on which Rome was founded. It lay between the Forum and the Campus Martius, the field of Mars.

Marcus left the domus and turned into one of the streets to be met by the most hilarious sight. Some innocent passer-by had strayed too close to the gaggle of sacred geese of Juno. The angry birds were chasing the man down the hill, wings flapping and making loud honking noises. Three of the geese were taking turns to launch themselves off the floor to attack the man's head. While one attacked high the other two attacked, their long necks making aggressive snaking movements at the man's feet. He just about managed to make it out of their territory, so the geese stopped chasing him but continued to honk loudly until he was out of sight. Marcus ensured he gave the geese a very wide berth.

The teenager continued down the hill, passing the elaborate temple of the holy trinity Jupiter, Mars and Quirinus. Jupiter being most important of all as he was king of the gods and king of the sky. Mars was god of war, but also an agricultural guardian. The third part of the trinity was Quirinus; god of the spear. Marcus had previously been in that temple and had stood in awe at the sight of the huge marble statues dedicated to gods. He offered his thanks to Saturn as he reached the last of the temples situated at bottom of the hill.

The young lad turned left in to the Field of Mars, an area that was over three miles square. It was the land between the city and the Tiber that served two purposes; outside the Villa Publica was an area where citizens gathered every five years so that the census could take place. The Villa Publica was very impressive with its columns of stone rising forty feet in the air. The census only counted free men, as slaves were property not residents. His father had sent his slave Aesop to represent him a few years ago as Quintus thought it was a waste of his time to stand and be counted. As the census was every five years the vast space was more commonly used as the area where the mighty Republican Roman army assembled for drills and exercises. It was still early morning, so the enormous expanse was eerily empty.

It wasn't any of these impressive temples or buildings that Marcus wanted to see, he had come to witness the majesty of the Circus Maximus.

The massive arena was located between two of Rome's seven hills; the Aventine and the Palatine; and was the place where public games would be held to mark religious festivals or celebrations of triumph. It measured over two thousand feet long, three hundred and eighty feet wide and was capable of holding a hundred and fifty thousand spectators. Many different events such as horse racing, athletics and plays were held there but Marcus wanted to see the chariots, hoping they would be practicing that morning. The chariots would have to do seven laps around the track, which was separated by a large brick spina. This wall was approximately ten feet wide, four feet high and had three columns at each end, which took the brunt of any damage from chariots that went too close while turning at its ends. He would need to get moving if he was to get there and back before Quintus and Caeso stirred from their slumbers.

The young man's daily training had conditioned him well, allowing him to run quickly and at distance. He sucked the cool morning air into his lungs, exhaling warm swirling clouds. The oblong arena towered out in the distance, it was constructed to form three magnificent and intricate tiers. Marcus could just make out some of the countless rows of seats.

As he got closer he could hear the noise of horses, chariots, and shouting rippling through the air. It spurred him on to make one last effort to reach his destination, despite his heavy legs. Marcus hurried through one of the many lower tier stone entrances that led to the heart of the arena, this is where the races would start. The ground floor was topped by two wooden tiers where the Senators and high ranking officials would watch from their private boxes. He preferred to sit at the lower level where you could get a sense of the speed of the chariots as they hurtled by.

Marcus was in luck as there were four charioteers on the white lime starting line, each draped in their individual colours of red, blue, green and black and white. Today was just a practice so there would be no procession of dancers, musicians or priests to entertain the masses as they performed sacred rights before the race. Never the less there was still a large crowd shouting out their favourite charioteer's name while hurling abuse at their opponents and their supporters.

Normally the charioteers would race around seven laps of the circuit, but Marcus could see this would not be the case today as he glanced at the two columns that held the lap counters at the end of the spina. Only three marble eggs and to three bronze dolphins were displayed on the crossbar. This signified the number of laps, but that suited his tight time schedule. An egg and dolphin would be removed after every revolution of the course so the charioteers and crowd would know how many there were left. Dolphins were sacred to Neptune who was god of the sea, freshwater, and most importantly in this case; horses. The eggs were a symbol of twins fathered by a god who had transformed himself in to a swan to seduce their mother. So instead of a normal birth the mother laid a single egg, from which the twins hatched.

The chariots were magnificent, being customised to the driver's preferences. The Black and White chariot was the most striking of the four. On its front was the image of a white eagle with its wings sweeping back around the rear. The tips of the wings tapered down so that it didn't protect the charioteer much more than above his calves. The bird was brilliant white with black stripes and had been ornately carved, then mounted on a small base with a pair of six spoked wheels. The designer had sacrificed protection to driver's flanks in favour of a lighter and more manoeuvrable vehicle pulled by two magnificent horses, one black and one white both draped in black and white livery. The stunningly powerful beasts made the Persian steeds look like a small ponies.

The Red chariot was shaped like a rectangular shield wrapping itself around the driver to waist height, and had larger wheels which gave it a much higher ground clearance. It was pulled by two shimmering bay stallions with red pommels attached to the crownpieces of their bridles.

Green was next with a differing wheel configuration. It differed from the others that had the wheels positioned in the middle of the cart central, immediately below the driver's position. These wheels were set further towards the back of the chariot, behind the driver's standing position. The front of the cradle dipped towards the two black stallions with the driver resting on a skin over the front of his bright green cart.

The Blue chariot was the most opulent. It was waist height at the front and tapered down to calf height at the rear. A handle each side made it easier for the driver to use his weight, and put force on to either wheel while turning. It was inlaid with gold-painted reliefs of the gods, the largest being the face of Jupiter Optimus Maximus on the front. The wheels were central, but most noticeably of all was the thick bronze spikes at the end of each axle, designed to break opponent's wheels or injure their horses. It was powered by two impressive stallions decorated in a blue livery, one black and the other white.

Marcus was standing behind two groups of supporters bombarding each other with insults. The Blues were shouting how they were better, and how their chariot reflected their wealth and power.

'We'll see, we'll see,' shouted one of the Black and White fans followed with a song of

'I will never be a Blue' as a fight broke out between the two groups. The red and green supporters got sucked into the fracas joining the Black and Whites, as no one really liked the Blues.

The scuffles quickly came to a halt as the starting trumpet was blown, the crowd turned their attention to the track and began cheering for their respective team.

The chariots shot off, with the horses kicking up dirt as they strained to pull away. They went off at break neck speed, Black and White fractionally ahead of Red and Green that was neck and neck with blue slightly trailing. Lots had been drawn before the race to decide the starting positions, so the Black and

White charioteer held the inside track with Red next to him then Blue and Green being on the outside.

The crowd roared as the four chariots approached the first turn at the end of the spina. Black and White took the first corner well with Red just behind, but Blue had pulled level with Green. The Blue charioteer leaned on his outside, pushing his team closer to green. The Green driver dropped forward onto the skin at the front of his cart in an attempt to gain additional speed. Suddenly spokes flew in the air as the Blue driver took out Green's wheel with the bronze spikes protruding from his axle. It was a cheap shot especially as it was only a practice run. The Green chariot's axle dipped as it lost a wheel, and dug into the ground trailing a gouge in its wake. The horses were still at full gallop as the cart lurched to one side and catapulted its driver out. He tumbled end over end, completely motionless once his momentum had been expended. Two attendants rushed to the track, lifted him onto a stretcher and got him to a safe area to have his wounds and injuries tended to. The Green supporters turned, jeered the Blues and hurled vegetables and more insults at them.

The remaining three chariots had rounded the first bend, and were thundering towards the cluster of onlookers. Black and White still held the lead, Red half a length behind with Blue making up ground after the incident on the corner. He closed the gap by lashing his horses with his whip, viciously cutting into their flesh. All three rounded the turn in front of the crowd, Black and White still holding the inside lane and rounded the corner cleanly, Red rounded well followed by Blue. Marcus felt the rush of air as they passed, a dolphin and an egg were removed.

Black and White had pulled a full length clear with Red then Blue, its driver still lashing his animals to force every piece of effort from his horses. The Black and White driver was using his smaller cart's speed to his advantage and was pulling even further clear from the other two, who by the end of the next turn were level with each other. Blue tried the same tactic of lunging his cart at Red, but there was enough width on the track for his opponent to swerve out of the way. However, in avoiding the Blue chariot it forced Red to take a wider, slower turn around the bend.

Marcus didn't know if it was the sun getting warmer or if it was the excitement of the race, but it seemed like the morning chill had gone. With Red drifting wide on the last turn Blue had edged in front of him, but was still some way behind Black and White. He was clearly out ahead now as he rounded the corner in front of group for the second time. The driver knew he was clear enough for him to throw the mob a wave, his supporters responded with a roar. A second egg and dolphin were removed.

Blue was now in second place, the driver ignored the Red chariot, still lashing his horses for all they were worth. The marks on their hides and backs were clearly visible as they passed by. Thundering on Black and White took the corner, two lengths in front of Blue with Red trailing in their wake.

Black and White pulled away even further in the final straight punching the air as he crossed the line, Blue was lengths behind with Red coming in a poor third. The final egg and dolphin were removed, it was over. The Black and White charioteer went half a length, slowed his team to a walk, wheeled his chariot around and pulled to a stop in front of the crowd. They cheered and showering him with victor's palm leaves.

It all happened so quickly, but Marcus' heart was racing with the excitement - this is what he had hoped to see and boy, was it good! He decided that Black and White was now the faction he would follow when he returned. Suddenly he remembered that he was supposed to be at his uncle's domus, but savoured the atmosphere a little longer, soaking in the sights and sounds of the Circus Maximus.

He made my way out the same way that he had come in, passing the slave market, and running all the way to the bottom of Capitoline Hill. Marcus smiled to himself as he realised he had been subconsciously humming a tune all the way back as he ran, the tune 'I will never be a Blue' looping around and around in his head.'

He struggled to regain his breath as he started up the steep hill. Normally he would have had difficulty running up it if he was fresh, but having already run quite a distance it would have been impossible. Marcus passed the temples and went in to his uncle's domus.

The teenager went in, crossed the atrium, and then to the dining area where he found his uncle reclining on a sofa eating his breakfast.

'Marcus,' he said with a smile.

'I thought you were still asleep, your father is,' he added.

'I've been worshiping at the temple,' the young lad replied.

Caeso got up, crossed over to his nephew, and brushed his thumb across Marcus' cheek.

'Hmmm, mud. You don't see too much of that in the temples these days,' he laughed guessing where the teenager had been.

'You must visit more often, nephew. There is so much to see in our great city,' Caeso said.

'I would like that uncle, I would like that a lot,' he replied.

Quintus entered the room, the ambience changed instantly.

Caeso returned to his couch, picking up some cheese.

'Come brother, join me. I'm not sure if it is a late breakfast or early lunch. What can I get you?' Caeso asked.

'Wine, and send for the Thracian' Quintus responded sourly.

His brother gestured to one of the slaves to follow his instruction. Quintus lay on one of the couches, and his son a menacing glace as another slave poured him his wine. A short while later the Thracian slave arrived.

'We can't keep calling you Thracian. What is your name slave?' Caeso asked.

'Krasper, master, my name is Krasper,' the slave replied.

'Well Krasper, I have given you as a gift to my brother. You will travel to his villa and do his bidding. You are to make him iron swords.'

'As you wish, master,' the slave said with a bow.

'Make me the finest swords you have ever made, Thracian, and you will be greatly rewarded,' Quintus said.

'His name is Krasper,' Caeso reminded his brother.

'I shall do your bidding master. I will make swords fit for the gods,' Krasper said to his new owner.

'That is what I want to hear, Thracian. Now go and ready yourself to leave. I will send for you when I am ready.'

Krasper bowed and left.

'Are you able to provide me with a horse and cart to ship his tools?' Quintus asked.

'Not a problem, brother, I will send it with a driver so he can return to me when you are done with him,' his younger brother responded.

'Now let us enjoy some food, I don't get to see you or my nephew as often as I would like.'

'Tell me about your visit to the temple,' Caeso winked, ensuring that only Marcus couldn't see.

'Aren't the statues truly magnificent?' He teased.

'Indeed they are uncle,' Marcus grinned, his father missing the private joke between him and his uncle. His only concern was that his goblet was re-filled with wine.

They ate our food, with the servants washing their masters' hands as they switched between differing delicacies. After the trio had finished their meal, Caeso called for the Thracian smith.

'Krasper we are ready. Have everything you need loaded on to a cart and meet us outside,' he commanded.

'Have our horses readied,' he instructed another slave.

The three of them made their way to the front of the domus, and mounted their horses. Marcus reflected on how much smaller they were than the mighty steeds he had seen race in the Circus

Maximus that morning. Krasper sat next to the slave who was steering the cart. The Thracian had all of his tools in the back, ready to work his magic.

They slowly descended the steep Capitoline Hill, leaning back in their saddles to distribute the weight more evenly. The brakes on the cart screeched loudly as they rubbed the wheels, the wagon driver trying his best to maintain an even pace down the sharp hill.

They continued through the city, through the city rampart, and over the wooden bridge with the cart wheels echoing above the deep ditch. The group weaved through the villages and farms that surrounded Rome. They travelled at a much slower pace than their ride in to enable the cart to keep up with the riders. Marcus wasn't too unhappy at the slower pace as it gave his father an opportunity to sober up.

Eventually the country villa came in to view, Marcus could see the slaves getting in an early crop of olives. They carried on until they were equidistant between the olive grove and the main villa.

'This is where you will make my swords, Thracian,' my Quintus said.

'Krasper,' Caeso added.

'I want the best iron sword you have ever made Thrac…, Krasper,' Quintus corrected himself.

'I also want your finest bronze sword. Both swords must be the best you have ever made, fit for the gods, do you understand me? Now tell me what you need'

'Am I to just make two swords master?' Krasper asked.

'Initially yes, but build everything big enough to produce hundreds, no not hundreds, I will need thousands,' Quintus replied.

'Do you remember the furnace at your brother's house?' Krasper asked his new master.

'Yes, I do! A stone circle three feet in diameter at waist height,' Marcus interrupted.

'Indeed, my young master is very observant. I shall need,' but before Krasper could finish his sentence Quintus interrupted by shouting for Aesop.

He came scurrying from the villa.

'Aesop, make a list of what this slave wants. Get his equipment stored away and make sure everything is as he wishes, no expense spared,' Quintus said.

He then headed to the villa, while Caeso gave his goodbye tidings.

'I must head home, brother, send the cart back when you are finished,' he flashed Marcus a smile. The young lad stayed behind, interested in what Krasper would ask for.

The Thracian gave Aesop his list.

'I will need clay bricks, lime, sand, charcoal, iron ore, copper ore, tin, beeswax, ivory and bellows. Twelve very big bellows, the biggest you can get,' Krasper said.

'I'll also need two slaves for each bellow. Starting with six slaves, and then the other eighteen when all structures are built,' he added.

Marcus was very interested, wondering what he would do with the things he had requested. He left them and went into the villa to be greeted by his mother, who rushed up and threw her arms around the one thing that brought joy into her life.

'Oh, Marcus I am so pleased you're back. I've missed you,' she said. Marcus was sure he felt a tear fall onto the nape of his neck.

The evening followed its usual pattern. Quintus got drunk, his son and wife stayed out of his way. Marcus awoke the next morning, and went down to continue his training with Lucius. Today they would be practicing with the pilum. The javelins Marcus had seen thrown in the games were light and designed to travel distance, but not the pilum. The three foot long heavy javelin comprised of two parts. The top foot was a thin bronze shaft tipped with a pyramid shaped barb. This was attached to a two feet long thick, heavy wooden shaft. The combined weight, and the piercing point meant that it could easily punch through a shield.

Lucius picked up the pilum, raised it above his head and drew back his arm. He brought it forward in a snapping movement, releasing the javelin at a human shaped target positioned a short distance in front of him holding a shield.

'You see what can happen if you throw it hard enough?' Lucius said to Marcus.

The young man went forward and saw that not only had the pilum pierced the shield, but it had also embedded itself in the straw target.

'When you are older and you command your men they will be carrying two of these. It is best not to face the enemy phalanx straight on as they just march at you, shields locked, skewering your men with their long spears. Its best, if you can, to attack from the side, but the hoplites are well drilled and can turn, reform and advance on you in an instant. Even if you don't throw hard enough to pierce the man the barb will break through the shield forcing the man discard it. Then holes will appear in their formation, the killing starts, bringing death to the battlefield. The first volley should be fired at the enemy when they are sixty feet away with the second at twenty feet. This will leave many dead, and others tripping over their shields as they try to abandon them. This is when you go in with the sword. Make sure your throw is straight with all the weight behind the tip for maximum effect,' Lucius said.

The pair carried on throwing the pilum at the target, moving it further and further away to enable Marcus to judge the force required for differing lengths. As the day wore on the young lad noticed wagons coming and going until a sizable amount of materials were unloaded in the area where Krasper was to build his furnace.

'Thank you, Lucius, that will be enough for today,' Marcus said.

He had enjoyed using the pilum and had become very accurate at varying distances, but this wasn't the weapon he was going to use to kill his father. The teenager left the courtyard and went over to where Krasper was busying himself by a large pile of clay bricks.

The slave had marked an outline of a large circle in the ground, three times bigger than the one he had made at Caeso's domus. He was measuring one part lime to three parts of the reddish brown sand, adding water to make a material to bind the clay bricks together. Marcus moved closer to the olive grove, sat down under one of the trees and spent the afternoon watching Krasper build his circle until it was waist high. There were three small gaps at the base where he would insert the bellows he had requested.

While the Thracian slave worked, more and more wagons pulled up hauling lumps of dark grey stones, which were as big as a man's hand. There was also a small delivery of green copper and silver tin rocks. A huge amount of charcoal was delivered next and finally the first of the bellows, so big they would need two people to operate just one of them.

By the time all the deliveries had arrived, Krasper had built his very large furnace and called to Aesop.

'Do you see this construction? I need three more, just the same, and please have my tools brought out,' Krasper said.

'Of course, I'll send the slaves who maintain the farm houses. They will be able copy what you have built,' Aesop replied.

The days were long this time of year and Marcus felt an ache in his stomach, he had inadvertently missed lunch as he was transfixed by the comings and goings all day. The teenager thought it must be close to diner time so he headed towards the villa in search of something to eat. As Marcus passed close to Krasper he signalled for the young lad to come over.

'Young master, will you kindly take me to your father?' Krasper asked.

'Of course, follow me,' as he headed in the direction of the villa.

They found Quintus in the garden, sitting on a sella. The legs of the chair were beautifully carved in the shape of leaping dolphins. A large goblet of wine was next to him on a three legged bronze table. Marcus hoped he had not already drunken too much.

'Salve, father. Krasper requests an audience with you.'

'What news do you have for me, Thracian?' He asked.

'I have everything I need master, to make the two swords you ordered,' Krasper informed Quintus.

'I shall start the process in the morning by making the bronze sword as the furnace must be at a much higher temperature for the iron. I will smelt the copper in the morning and add the tin to make my bronze. I will be ready to pour about midday. While that sets in the mould I will move on to the iron sword,' Krasper said.

'Don't bore me with the detail. Just bring me the swords! Make them right and you will be rewarded. Make them wrong and I will have your head. Do you understand?' Quintus glared at Krasper.

'I have diverted slaves from the fields to assist you. Do not make me waste crops unnecessarily clearing land for your work!'

'No master, the swords will be fit for the gods themselves,' Krasper replied with a bow.

'Could I watch you work, Krasper?' Marcus asked.

'With your father's permission of course. It would be my pleasure,' the slave replied.

'Father may I?'

'Yes, yes. At least you won't be under my feet or making that din from the courtyard,' Quintus said as he waved Krasper away.

'Thank you father,' Marcus said.

'Enough now, get out of my sight,' his father replied sternly.

Lucia was having her hair set into curls, held in to place with ivory pins, in one of the small rooms off the atrium. Her long silk stolla was clinched at her slim waist with two elegant belts embellished with beautifully polished stones and pieces of sea shell.

'You look lovely mother.'

'Thank you Marcus. Be a dear, have your dinner and go to bed early tonight. I wish to dine with your father alone,' my mother asked.

'Of course,' he smiled.

'That suits my purpose,' the teenager thought, as he wanted to be up early in the morning to watch Krasper weave his magic. The bruise on her face had turned black and yellow. So that's exactly what he did, he ate, bathed and retired to his sleeping room.

Marcus awoke the next morning, skipped breakfast and headed down to find Krasper was already at the furnace. The Thracian had moulded beeswax into the exact shape of a sword blade, taking care to shape the edges.

'You had better not present that to my father. You know what he said about your head,' the lad said jovially to Krasper drawing my thumb across his throat.

'Indeed, young master, and if you allow me to I will show you some of the tricks of my trade.'

He carefully lifted the beeswax blade and laid it on a slab of wet clay, which was just a little longer than the original. He folded the clay over the blade so it covered the wax completely, pinching the ends to seal it.

'We'll leave that in the sun for a while so the clay can dry out,' at this Krasper moved to the furnace. He took small lumps of the green stones, the copper ore, and put them in to a triangular crucible over the charcoal fire. The slave then took a smaller portion of the silver rocks, the tin, and put it in a separate crucible, covering both with lids.

The two ores were smelted down to their base metals, they popped as bubbles burst inside the containers.

'You must melt the ores slowly at the correct temperature. Too hot or too quickly and the metal will be brittle. A sword that shatters will cost me my head,' he said making a chopping action on his neck.

Krasper put the clay into the fire. It hardened instantly, he removed it after a few minutes later.

'Watch now,' Krasper said.

He carefully sliced the top off the clay, turned it upside down and poured the melted beeswax on to the floor. He cleaned the mould with a long thin brush to ensure that all the wax was removed.

'Hold this for me, but use the tongs,' he said as he passed the clay mould to Marcus.

Krasper removed the lids from the crucibles using a wooden pole. With a shorter pair of tongs he carefully measured the tin before pouring it into the copper. It was now clear to Marcus why the crucibles were triangular, as it allowed for a controlled pour, with the edges acting as a spout.

'Now we have bronze,' he smiled.

'I like to use twelve percent tin to eighty eight percent copper, but some use a ten percent to a ninety percent mixture. I find the twelve percent tin produces an edge that can be sharpened better. I have also heard of smiths using arsenic instead of tin but I've never tried it myself.

'Move closer to me with that clay mould.'

His newly appointed apprentice edged closer and Krasper slowly filled the clay with the molten bronze, tapping the base a few times.

'Releases any air bubbles,' he said, then stood the clay in an upright position in a stand inside a bucket of water.

'We'll leave that to cool for a while,' he added.

'Now this must get much, much hotter before we can make the next sword. Iron ore melts at a much higher temperature than copper'. He shovelled in heaps of charcoal then a layer of iron ore then more charcoal.

One by one Krasper pushed in the three sets of bellows into the gaps he had left at the base of his furnace. The six slaves he had requested were standing in the shade of the olive trees. He summoned them over and gave them strict instructions.

'There is a layer of charcoal, then a layer of iron ore, then another layer of charcoal. You must keep pumping the bellows until the charcoal at the top is white. Anything less will not be hot enough for me,' the Thracian informed the other slaves.

He returned to the clay mould, lifted it out of the bucket of water, quickly touching the side to test the temperature.

'Nice and cool,' he said to himself.

Krasper lay the clay mould on the side, broke it open by tapping gently with a hammer, revealing the bronze blade inside. He took several pre-prepared handles, and selected the finest of them. Using a copper tool he made three marks through the handle, two at the top, and one at the base of where it would be secured to the blade. Next he removed the blade from the handle and went about making three holes with his bow drill. He stopped several times to check the alignment of the handle holes and the blade holes. The two parts became one as he took out three rivets from the fire, ensuring that only one end was heated. Carefully placing them one at a time through the holes, turning the handle over and then tapping the hot end with a small moulded tool. It had the effect of making a rivet head that secured the blade to the handle. This process was repeated until all three rivets were in place.

'How is that charcoal looking?' he called over to the furnace slaves.

'Not white yet,' came the reply.

The bronze sword required very little sharpening as the edges where already moulded in from the beeswax version.

He passed the sword to Marcus, the lad feeling that it had a very good balance. The handle had inlaid bands of gold that gave it extra grip, the end finished off with a square pommel.

'It will need polishing and perhaps some detailed engraving on the blade, but the hard work is done. Now on to the iron sword, but that requires much more effort,' Krasper said with a frown.

He looked at the furnace once more and started reading his tools. The Thracian heaved his long flat stone closer to the furnace. He readied his tongs and hammer then called over to the slaves operating the bellows.

'That's it nearly there, pump faster, pump faster,' Krasper urged.

The slaves responded by quickening their pace. Marcus could see the top layer of charcoal changing from a glowing orange to searing white with every burst of air pumped in from the three sets of bellows. Krasper looked into the furnace and smiled. He pushed his tongs in and pulled out three lumps of orange mass, placing each in a line running the length of his flat stone. He worked and shaped the masses until they formed together to became one. Krasper continued hammering and turning the object, as he had done at Caeso's domus in Rome. This time Marcus saw him fold the outer edges of the mass on itself, tapping the ends to form a sharp edge. The glow of the metal had now reduced so the shape was becoming more solid. Krasper thrust it into a bucket of water then back into the furnace, repeating the process over and over again. Finally he pushed two long metal shafts in ground outside the furnace. The poles were flat at the top and he rested the sword across the poles, approximately ten inches above the heat.

'This is tempering the blade. It increases the toughness of the metal. It must be watched closely as I want it to be the colour of barley. That is when it is removed and watered again. If it turns blue the sword will not be strong enough and will break,' Krasper said.

As the blade was cooled the water hissed, and spat as the heat left the blade. Krasper then attached a temporary handle.

'It will take me several days to carve the ivory the way I want it.'

Krasper placed the sword down and looked at Marcus 'you have studied every move I have made, young master. Would you like to try your hand at making a sword?'

'It looked hard work,' he replied.

'Indeed it is, yes but come and I will help you,' the Thracian slave said.

'As long as it doesn't interfere with the work you must do for my father I would like to try,' the teenager beamed.

Krasper was very patient with his tutee, and insisted Marcus wore thick leather protection on his hands and arms with his body being covered by a thick leather apron. While the slave worked on the two swords for Quintus, Marcus used one of the other furnaces that had been constructed.

The teenager's first effort was very poor, He hadn't worked the blobs of molten metal well, with his first effort looking more like a plate than a sword. As the days wore on the newer efforts began to resemble the shape of a sword blade. By day four Marcus had made his first sword, and he was very pleased with the outcome.

'Let it cool and we will test it,' Krasper said.

They let it cool, then attached a temporary handle. Krasper brought over a bronze sword and told Marcus to strike it with his new creation. He hit the bronze sword as hard as he could, but had to duck quickly as the new sword shattered, with shards flying through the air.

'You did not temper the blade correctly. Come let me show you once more,' Krasper said.

Marcus watched closely as the slave demonstrated for a second time how to look for the right colour.

'You see barley, it must be the colour of barley,' Krasper said.

Marcus spent the next few days practising his sword making with a few more failures, but eventually one, even though it was not as aesthetically pleasing as Krasper's swords, had been made correctly.

A week after Krasper had started, he presented Quintus with two magnificent swords. His master took the bronze one first, and slowly pulled it back from its leather sheath. The bronze had been highly polished so it shone like gold.

'Very good, Thracian, I am pleased,' he said.

Marcus could see the ivory handle on the iron sword. It had carvings of the gods and ended with a pommel in the shape of a lion's head. Quintus took it from its metal sheath, the top being lined with sheep's wool to prevent the sword scraping as it was removed. It too had been polished and shone as the light caught the blade. Quintus judged the balance, and noticed it was much lighter that its counterpart.

'You have done well Thracian. These look like well-made swords and fit for my demonstration. The blades had better be as strong as they are good looking.'

'They are the finest I have ever made Master,' Krasper replied.

'Aesop, prepare my finest toga for tomorrow. I will take my plan to the Senate, but first get me a drink,' Quintus said.

Chapter 8

The Fortress of the Great Bear

The shards of first light streaked across the grey sky as the advance party readied itself. It comprised of two chariots, one driven by Arenwen with Bakher as his passenger, and the second chariot driven by Deborah with Bilhild taking the position at the rear of the cart. The two chariots were virtually identical. The square platform had two semi circles made from wicker that had smaller wicker rods going vertically from the top of the loop to the base of the chariot. These offered little or no protection other than the shield hung over the side. The function of the wicker loops was to serve as a foot or knee hold for the warrior to lock themselves in to a position, giving them a stable platform on a moving chariot so that they could throw a spear while retaining their balance.

There was no barrier at the front or the rear of the base for the driver, or the standing warrior. The driver would sit on the edge of the base with their legs dangling over the front of the chariot, usually straddling the shaft that the horses were tethered to. The looping wicker also acted as handles when travelling at high speed or over rough terrain. A long thin container held three spears on the right hand side of the chariots. Each chariot was pulled by a team of two horses with cheek guards made from deer antler. The two large wheels where pinned to the axle by a pair of bronze linchpins.

There were two riders, both who had made the initial journey with Bilhild, they were his sworn men. The rest of the group comprised of fifteen men on foot including the twins Vaughn and Telor, as well as the new best friends Durston and Dafydd. The total party numbered twenty one, which Bakher insisted upon as it is divisible by the sacred number three. It had been decided to take the majority of the group on foot, so that it would more accurately reflect the speed of the main party, although the main party would be pulling heavy carts as well as walking troops.

Brennus approached the group with two warriors falling in close behind him. Both of the men strained as they each carried a heavy chest.

'Secure one on to each chariot,' Brennus ordered.

The warriors dutifully put one of the containers on Arenwen's chariot, and the other on to Bilhild's, lashing them to the wicker panels with leather straps.

'Remember now, grain, cattle but above all safe passage. We don't want any misunderstanding of our intentions, we are just passing through,' Brennus said to Arenwen.

'Yes, Lord, I will ensure everything is arranged prior to your arrival,' Arenwen said.

'By the gods, do you think I want you to undertake the negotiations?' Brennus laughed.

'No, Bakher will carry out all the negotiations this side of the mountains. You are to carry out the negotiations on the other side. I expect Bakher to talk and you to kill,' Brennus said.

'I will make sure everything runs smoothly on this side,' Bakher said to Brennus.

'The sun is climbing in the sky, the omens are good. Be gone with you, and I will see you over the other side of the mountains,' Brennus said.

The party moved out of the large village, with Arenwen sending two horsemen ahead to scout for any danger or places where the main army might have difficulty navigating.

'How long do you think this will take us?' Bakher called over to Bilhild.

'Seven days until we reach the Lingones tribal capital. It is called Andematunnum,' he replied.

'How interesting calling their capital the fortress of the Great Bear,' Bakher commented to Arenwen.

'Seven days is perfect, it couldn't be better,' Bakher muttered to himself.

'What was that you said?' Arenwen asked.

'Oh nothing particular, but we must be there in seven days' time. I can assure you that you'll be very pleased when we get there,' Bakher said mysteriously.

'Riddles, riddles, why don't you druids just say what you mean?' Arenwen was frustrated.

They turned east and went in the direction of the rising sun, making good progress as the ground was still firm underfoot. The riders returned after a few hours, coming in slowly indicating that there was no threat.

'Report,' Arenwen said.

'We have found the river,' the front rider replied addressing Bilhild.

'Excellent, we will carry on following along the bank of the river as far as it goes. When it starts to turn south we will be a good way to our destination,' Bilhild said to Arenwen.

The party followed the scouts, and were soon at the river. Arenwen could make out a well-worn track. The tract of land between the river, and the heavily forested area on the left was sufficiently wide enough for the main army to easily navigate without getting too bunched up and slowing them down.

The first two days passed without any unusual events, after all they were still in the lands ruled by their chieftain, and very few were reckless enough to impinge on his territory. The third day began just as the other two that preceded it, with the forward party breaking camp, dousing the morning fires, and packing the few possessions they had brought, ready for another days march. Arenwen had been chatting to Bakher and noticed that the long shadows of the morning had become very short. He shaded his eyes with his hand as he looked up at the sun. It was directly over them now, it was midday. Holding up one hand he said 'we'll rest here and take food.'

The party drew to a halt. They were travelling light, not carrying much in the way of supplies like their large cauldrons or roasting spits. The food they had brought mainly consisted of cheese, bread and salted meats, but it was more than sufficient. The horses were unhitched and allowed to wander to the bank of the river to have a drink, and to crop the new green grass sprouting from earth. Most of the party sat cross-legged on the floor while some of the others squatted with them in a circle. A few, including Vaughn and Telor, went to collect some water. Arenwen noticed that the twins had slipped off their boots, and piled their cloaks and tunics on the river bank. They eased themselves leisurely into the water and waded very slowly downstream. The leader was intrigued so went over to the river bank to see what the two of them were up to, then he saw that there was an overhang on the opposite bank. He could make out some shapes of fish moving around the shade. It was one of their safe areas, where they would go at the first sign of danger. This was why the brothers were heading downstream, as fish have one of two options when threatened, swim or hide. Fish were much faster swimming downstream, as they could use the current to their advantage, so if that option was taken away from them they will go to their safe place. This is was exactly what they started to do as the brothers slowly approached them.

Telor moved to one end of the overhang with Vaughn at the other, they had manoeuvred most of the fish in to this area. Vaughn moved first and Telor followed, crouching down, arms out wide and slowly moving his hands into the water. The twins used their bodies as barriers to prevent their prey darting into the open river. They both slowly brought their hands up from the river bed, feeling for the underside of the trout. Telor smiled at his brother indicating that he had made contact, he slowly started tickling it. This would send the trout into a trance-like state, and it would become impervious to the grip of a hand around its body. Sure enough, Telor slowly withdrew his hands from the water firmly clamped on a wriggling silver trout, with its distinctive black spots and stripe of rainbow sheen. He threw it on the bank, far enough away that it couldn't flop back in to the safety of the river. It lay on the bank, mouth opening and closing as it gasped for air.

Telor smiled at his brother and softly mouthed the word 'one' while holding up a finger. He slowly pushed his hands back into the water, and went on the hunt for a second. It was Vaughn's turn to smile now as he got the touch of his first fish. The competition had begun with both brothers throwing their catch onto the riverbank, each mouthing their tally to the other. There were over a dozen fish flapping on the river bank when instead of Vaughn throwing his latest catch on the bank he gripped it by the tail and slapped his brother across the face.

Telor took the slap, already in a crouched position, lunged up at his brother grabbing him by the waist and lifting him up out of the water. They both came down with an almighty splash, spraying water everywhere and scattering the remaining fish in all directions. The pair rolled, tumbled and wrestled in the river until they were both out of breath.

'I still caught two more than you brother,' Vaughn said.

'I have to let you win sometimes, little brother,' Telor smiled.

The two climbed out of the water and gutted the fish on the far bank with their knives. Vaughn went off to a nearby tree, jumped up and snapped a sizable branch. He stripped it of leaves and off shoot branches as he walked back to his brother.

'This will do nicely,' Vaughn said, tossing the branch to his sibling. Telor sharped the end, and went about piecing the fish and sliding them down the branch. He repeated the process until all twelve were skewered. Both twins picked up an end, slung it on their shoulders and waded back across the river to the applause of the men.

As this was going on Deborah and Bakher approached one of the horses. Bakher held its head as Deborah took out a knife, making a small incision into the stead's neck. She caught the warm red blood in a wooden bowl, pinched the cut closed, and rubbed it with a small piece of green moss. She made sure the cut had stopped bleeding before moving away.

'That will be more than enough,' Bakher said.

'Yes that should appease the Aos Si. If we are to take from their land we must give something in return,' Deborah replied.

'I'm glad you remember the ancient name for the little folk. I do prefer it to the new name that people use these days – 'fairies' just doesn't sit right with me,' Bakher said.

The two of them left the horse on the riverbank, and headed into the forest. As they continued deeper they weaved through the dense undergrowth until Bakher saw what he was looking for. It was easy to spot, unlike the other trees that were starting to grow their new spring coat, this tree kept its needle like leaves all year round.

'Here is our yew tree. We shall make our offerings here,' Bakher said.

'Perfect, by the look of things the small people come here often,' Deborah said pointing to small markings at the base of the tree.

'Pass me the bowl Deborah.'

She passed the wooden bowl to the druid, who held it in his left hand as he made slow circular movements around the top with his right. After the third rotation he closed his eyes and said

'Aos Si, with this blood we honour you. With your permission we will only take what we need from your land, for which we give thanks.'

He poured the blood over the base of the tree, both of them standing in silence with their heads bowed in respect for the little folk.

'Hopefully the Aos Si will think it is a fair exchange for what we want,' Bakher said, looking around them.

'I hope so, we don't want their anger or mischief hampering our journey,' Deborah replied.

The two of them nodded and smiled to each other, then moved deeper in to the forest in search for the plant they were looking for.

'I can't see it yet, but I can smell it,' Deborah said. Bakher sniffed the air and replied only with the slightest hint of resignation in his voice saying 'clearly your younger nose will serve us better than mine.' Then he got a waft of the pungent, damp musky smell which was very similar to decaying, rotting vegetables. Ducking under some low-hanging branches, the stench got stronger. Then in a small clearing they saw the unique plant. Growing three feet tall, a cluster of thick leaves at the base of the thick stem with smaller leaves growing the whole length of the plant. The yellow and reddish purple bell shaped flowers hanging heavy with their hairy exterior becoming more visible as they got closer. Deborah could now see the distinctive veins running through the five petals of the flower - there was no other plant like henbane.

'So, we find our prize. Best get on with it as quickly as you can - this smell is making me dizzy,' Bakher said.

Deborah quickly went about stripping some of the plant's leaves. She could feel its thick waxiness, it looked as if had been torn and ripped. Pushing them in to a pouch she turned her attention to the flower. She felt a little dizzy as she gripped the base, so not to damage it, she gently shook it catching the greyish brown seeds in the palm of her hand. Each flower yielded over four hundred of the tiny seeds.

'I only need the leaves of three plants,' Bakher said.

'A wise choice of number,' Deborah smiled.

As they moved further away from the clearing the effects of the plants started to wear off. Bakher took the pouch containing the leaves while Deborah took the one with the seeds. With leaves and seeds safely stored, the two made their way back through the forest to join the rest of the party on the river bank.

Arenwen greeted them 'What have you two been up to?'

'Nothing to concern you,' Bakher replied.

Druids and their mysterious ways Arenwen thought.

'Quickly get something to eat as we're nearly ready to set off,' Arenwen said to the two recent arrivals.

Bakher and Deborah hurriedly ate a small meal of bread and dried meat. The horses were hitched to the chariots, and the two scouts set off on their horses to patrol ahead of the small group. The remaining men gathered around the rear of the chariots with Vaughn and Telor, still very pleased with themselves, carrying their prized catch.

Bakher and Deborah took their places in the respective chariots as Arenwen looked over to Bilhild to check if he was ready. He gave a nod, and Arenwen moved the party out to continue their journey.

The small band followed the river, and were soon at the point when it turned sharply south. The afternoon wore on with the sun passing directly over them, dipping slowly to their right hand side. They travelled mostly in silence even the twins were unusually quiet.

'How much further?' Arenwen called to Bilhild.

'Our destination is in sight - look across the plain. Can you see the hills in the distance?' Bilhild asked Arenwen.

'Yes, I can just about make it out,' the warrior replied.

'Andematunnum is at the top of those rocky hills. I think it will take us three and a half, maybe four days more'.

It was still some distance away, but the men overheard the conversation and broke in to chatter as their spirits lifted. That night they ate a hearty meal of smoked trout, courtesy of Vaughn and Telor. It wasn't a huge amount when shared between them all, but the fresh fish was a pleasant addition when compared to the meals they had been eating since the start of their trip.

Day four dawned just like the others had previously. Arenwen mustered the men, some still groggy from the ale the night before.

'Come on, you bunch of cow turds. We've still only half way to our first town so shake yourselves, there will be fresh meat, ale and women so come on get up!'

'We are now on the edge of Brennus' lands, so we needed to stay sharp,' Arenwen added.

The next three days passed by, marching, camping, eating and sleeping. As they approached closer to their destination the two scouts returned to report.

'We are being watched,' the scout nodded east to two mounted figures.

'Yes I have seen them for some time,' Arenwen said.

One of the watching riders galloped off in the direction of the Fortress of the Great Bear while the other continued shadowing them.

'Shall I follow him Lord?' one of the scouts asked.

'No, that rider will let them know we are coming, and that is just fine by me,' Arenwen said.

As they got closer to Andematunnum Arenwen could see why the Lingones had chosen this location for their capitol. The rocky promontory gave a three hundred and sixty degree view of the valleys, and the plateaux surrounding it.

The hours wore on with the once distant hills becoming very close. The two scouts came galloping in.

'Riders approaching from the town,' one of them announced.

'How many?' Arenwen asked.

'Forty, all mounted and armed Lord.'

A show of force, Arenwen thought. Big enough to cause them trouble, but small enough not to be too heavy handed.

'Shields,' Arenwen called to his men.

They swivelled their shields from their backs, and looped their arms into the two leather straps to secure them. This was precautionary as Arenwen did not expect trouble, but it wouldn't do any harm to be cautious.

The riders soon came into view, but they didn't have any weapons drawn and advanced at a leisurely pace. Arenwen signalled to his men to halt, and he went forward with Bilhild bringing up his chariot to his side. As he got closer a single rider approached them.

'Greetings from my Lord Brennus. We bring gifts and assurances of our good intentions,' Arenwen said as he opened the chest strapped to the side of his chariot, to show the wealth it contained.

'Then you are welcome in our lands,' came his reply.

'I thank you on behalf of my Lord, and respectfully request to see your chieftain at his earliest convenience,' Arenwen said.

'You will be able to see my Lord Galatos as soon as you are ready. He thinks your arrival is a good omen in line with the feast tonight.'

It was not unusual for the tribes to have feasts so Arenwen thought no more of it. His men slung their shields back onto their backs and the party was escorted in to Andematunnum, the Fortress of the Great Bear.

'Are you able to provide my men with shelter, and an area where we can keep the horses?' Arenwen asked.

He had never seen a town as large as this. They were led further towards the centre and shown a large open area that looked like it was normally used for weapons practice.

'Your men can sleep here with the horses, I will bring furs, food and drink for them. You and the druid are to be personal guests of my Lord Galatos,' he was instructed.

'Bilhild, get the men and the horses settled. I want you to stay here to keep an eye on them. I'll be back later for the chests,' Arenwen said looking at the group of warriors. Then he turned and spoke to the men 'if anyone gets in to a fight tonight do not, under any circumstances kill anyone. Are we clear?'

'Yes,' came a resounding reply from the men all smiling and boisterous as Durston nudged Dafydd in the ribs with his elbow.

Bakher followed Arenwen who was in turn following their guide.

'I thought you would be more cheerful than this considering the feast tonight,' Bakher said to Arenwen.

'I always like a feast, Bakher, but my Lord Brennus has put great faith in us to make sure everything is ready for him on the journey. I do not intend a feast to impact on my preparations for him.'

'Indeed he has, but Beltane only comes once a year,' Bakher said.

'Beltane, the feast is celebrating Beltane? Arenwen asked astounded.

'I really do wonder if any of my teachings did stick in that dumb head of yours. How did you not remember Beltane?' Bakher cuffed Arenwen across the side of his head. The warrior agreed, how could he have forgotten about the festival of the bright fire? The signs had been all around him with everything in bud and fresh greenery shooting up everywhere. Now as he walked through the town he saw doors, windows and even women's hair decorated with yellow May flowers.

They were approaching a roundhouse, much larger than the others, so it had to belong to the chieftain. Bakher took two quick strides and moved alongside Arenwen.

'Don't forget what Brennus told you. I negotiate this side of the mountains and you on the other side.'

Arenwen nodded and dropped back behind the druid as they went through the door. It took a few seconds for their eyes to adjust to the dim light inside the roundhouse, but then they saw Galatos.

He was a big man, not as big as Arenwen, but still a tall wide man. He was dressed in black and red checked trousers, was bare chested but wore a black bear pelt over his shoulders. A heavy gold torque hung from his neck, but most impressive of all was the gilt conical helmet studded with gems, that sat on his mass of black hair.

'Greetings, Lord Galatos, on this sacred day. I bring tidings and gifts from our Lord Brennus,' Bakher said.

'I thank you for your greetings, I offer you my hospitality. I have heard of the great chieftain Brennus,' Galatos said as he summoned ale and food for his guests.

The party ate and then discussed their journey so far.

'Arenwen, will you be so kind and fetch the gift from our Lord?' Bakher asked.

'Of course, if you excuse me, I shall leave you and bring the gifts sent as tribute,' Arenwen bowed and made his way out of the chieftain's roundhouse.

While he was gone Bakher outlined the rest of the journey to Galatos. He explained that Brennus was two days behind with ten thousand men.

'My Lord sends assurances of his good intentions, and with your blessing they will merely be passing through. You will see the offerings sent to you when Arenwen returns. He brings food and grain, but would like to purchase as much as you have for sale,' Bakher said.

The door opened with Arenwen struggling with a heavy chest. He slowly edged it down in front of Galatos, dropping it the last few inches, it hit the floor with a thud. Arenwen pulled out the pin securing the clasp and lifted back the lid.

Galatos smiled to see gold torques, gold coins, rings with intricate knot work designs, cloak pins and a necklace supporting a beautifully crafted gold oak leaf. Galatos plunged his hand in to the chest, scooping coins, and letting them fall back into the substantial chest.

'Your Lord is very generous, but tell me of the lands of your destination,' Galatos said to Bakher.

'We have been searching for a way through the mountains for some time. We have had reports for many years that the lands on the other side of the great mountains are rich for farming, trading and have wealth,' Bakher replied.

'Then you shall have your safe passage as well as grain and cattle. I will accept two thirds of this impressive offering. I will not take it all as I will send two thousand of the Lingones tribe with you, I too am interested in these new lands,' Galatos replied.

'That was not the Lord Brennus' wishes. You were to receive the whole tribute for your kind consideration of him passing through your lands but...'

Galatos interrupted Bakher mid-sentence.

'It may well not have been what he wanted, but that is what is happening.'

Bakher was a skilled in negotiations, and knew any further protestations were futile.

'Now make yourselves comfortable before the feast tonight, we will start the celebration at nightfall,' Galatos gestured to a room off the main area of the roundhouse.

'There is more than enough room in there for you two,' Galatos said.

Bakher and Arenwen made their way in to their room for the night as more food and ale was brought in for their pleasure.

Bakher drained his drinking horn and said.

'I have rituals to perform with Gelatos' druids and other things to check to make sure everything goes to plan this evening,' Bakher said to his companion.

'Other things?' Arenwen asked suspiciously.

'Nothing to trouble yourself about,' came the reply.

'Bloody druids,' Arenwen thought, 'never a straight answer.' He finished off his drink and reflected on what a long day it had been. He thought that he would need to slow the pace down in forthcoming days as it was unlikely the main army with the supplies, and general camp accoutrements would travel as far as they had in a day. The warrior lay down on the furs to take some of the weariness away, that way he could be fresh for the evening's merriment.

Arenwen awoke from his slumbers, and for an instant did not remember where he was. He shook off the sleepiness, quickly recognising that he was in Galatos' roundhouse. He brushed himself down, and made his way out to meet up with his men. It was dusk when Arenwen left the chieftain's roundhouse. He passed Bakher with two of Galatos' druids. They were setting light to kindling that would be taken to two bonfires that had been prepared earlier. They were chanting mostly unidentifiable incantations in unison, all he could make out was Cernunnos. He racked his memory, Bakher was right he hadn't been a good student, but then it came to him Cernunnos, the horned god, Lord of the Forest, the Green Man. The druids strategically placed the kindling in the bonfires. Arenwen knew it was best not to interrupt Bakher and strode past the druids, heading for his men. He found them in good spirits, dipping their drinking horns in to a cask of ale.

'They look like they are happy,' Arenwen said to Bilhild.

'Yes they are, but not too drunk at the moment, and still fairly well behaved; I reminded them that they are guests here,' Bilhild replied.

'Where's Deborah?' Arenwen asked.

'Bakher came for her a few hours ago. They went off in that direction,' he said pointing to the bonfires that had started to give off smoke as the fire took hold.

The drums started beating. Arenwen, Bilhild and all their men headed towards the piles of smouldering wood that soon would become bonfires. There was still a little light left, but soon it would be dark. Arenwen could see couples in the fading light. The women's hair braided to reflect the joining of the goddess and the god, the White Queen and the Green Man. He smiled to himself and thought, there will handfastings tonight, as this was the traditional time of year to marry. He also thought that many of them would be bearing their first child at the end of the next winter.

The sun went down over the horizon, and with perfect timing the bonfires burst into life of tall, licking flames. The drums beat louder as the three druids lit torches from the new fire. They took the new-born flames and set light to the great fire arch that joined the spirit world with the earthly world.

Arenwen could see lights in the distance. Groups of men had painted themselves red and were dancing and swaying around the two bonfires. A group of drummers were at the head of the procession, getting increasingly louder as they got closer. The warrior could see the torchbearers coming up behind them, followed by a procession of naked men daubed in blue. They were also carrying torches and were coming through the fire arch, when he saw something, but he struggled to understand. There she was, completely naked, painted from head to toe in white, resplendent in a matching crown of bleached twigs pushing her flame red hair skywards. The crown rose above her head with strands of flowers, vines tumbling down her neck which wound around her body, barely covering her nakedness - it was Deborah. Arenwen was dumbstruck never having realised her beauty until now. The Green Man, old, twisted and gnarled like an ancient tree was leading her forward as she held his left arm. Maidens in white escorted their Queen carrying offerings for the magical elements. The men with their bodies daubed in red danced mischievously, writhing hedonistically and leaving the fires as they entered the earthy world. They danced and performed acrobatics to tempt the white-clad women to join with them in a fertility dance. Arenwen knew the ritual - they would initially spurn the advances, but willingly succumb to them later.

In keeping with the ritual the Green Man touched Deborah's breast and the White maidens made stabbing motions, imitating them killing him for his trespass and sacrilege. The

Green Man fell to the floor, the White women went about stripping him of his winter foliage, tearing at the old wood and brown leaves that were secured to his body. And so the scene played out as it had done for hundreds of years before. Seeing him dead on the floor the White Queen took pity on the Green Man, bent down and kissed him, breathing new life in to him. He got up from the ground, reborn young and virile and ready to start the circle of life again.

This was the moment the onlookers were waiting for. The first animals were passed through the gap between the two fires. The flame and smoke would protect them from evil spirits that could bring sickness and death. As the final animals were led away, groups started circling clockwise around the fires. Others sang, danced, drank and the newly handfasted were testing their fertility in the shadows not lit by the ceremonial bonfires.

Arenwen laughed and drank, he looked up hoping to see Deborah, but all that was left were the drummer's rhythmic beat and the torch bearers. The Red men were dancing wildly with the White women and there was laughing and feasting all around him but he still couldn't find any sign of Deborah. He grabbed a horn of ale and went to join Dafydd and Durston. The Celtic warrior could see Bakher siting in a circle of people surrounding Galatos, they were eating and drinking heartily. Galatos spotted Arenwen and motioned him to come over and join him.

'Duty calls,' Arenwen said to his men.

He strode over to the group and two warriors shuffled apart to make room for him to sit down.

'What do you think of this?' Galatos asked his guest.

'Very impressive Lord, the gods were honoured well tonight,' Arenwen replied.

'What did you think of the White Queen? I am so pleased your druid talked me into selecting her, she was absolutely magnificent. In truth the very moment I saw her flame red hair there was no other choice for the White Queen, and that is completely and utterly beside the fact that I'd like to sow some wild oats with her,' Galatos roared.

'An inspired selection Lord,' Arenwen replied, knowing the chieftain meant no offense.

The evening wore on into the early hours with ale, feasting, wine and song. The festival must run from sunset to sunrise in order to please the gods as well as the fairies. The drums still quietly beat as the flames from the fire died down. It was time for men and women to purify themselves in the smoke and flames of the fires.

Arenwen thought about how much he had drunk, and decided that he would jump the fires later when the flames were lower. The warrior glanced up to see who would be first to jump one of the two fires. He saw Vaughn and Telor stripping off their tops. One going to the bonfire on the right and the other to the left, Arenwen and Gelatos' men got up and queued up behind them.

'Ready?' Telor called.

'On three,' Vaughn replied and started counting.

'One, two.'

Telor didn't wait for the three count, and started running at the blaze. Vaughn quickly realised his brother's intentions and sped at the bonfire. Both jumped into the air simultaneously, and were licked by the flames before they safely tumbled to the ground on the other side. The bothers got up, and ran to grab the other with a bear hug of delight at their daring. This carried on most of the night with the fires slowly dying into embers. Many had passed out from the drinking, others had slipped off to celebrate the fertility feast in other ways.

There were feint signs of dawn appearing as the jet black of night gave way to the light of the morning sun that started to appear on the horizon. The view across the plains and valleys was magnificent. Arenwen could see the fingers of light slowly creep closer to them. 'That's enough for one night,' Arenwen thought and gave his thanks to Galatos who was still drinking and eating while in deep conversation with Bakher.

Arenwen watched the warriors and town's inhabitants' dance on the embers of the bonfires while slaves lit torches. All fires would have been put out in the town houses the night before. The torches passed the flames from the bonfire and onto the new fires in their homes. This would bring them good luck and fertility.

Arenwen felt the warm rays of sun on his face as he made his way back to the chieftain's roundhouse, numerous women were on their knees, scooping up the morning dew to their faces in order to prolong their youthfulness.

Tiredly, the warrior made his way to the chieftain's roundhouse and into the sleeping area. His weariness vanished in an instant when he saw Deborah beneath the furs on the floor, her bright red hair emphasised even more by the jet black furs she was lying on. She threw back the covers revealing that she was completely naked, her pale skin still covered in the white colouring from the festival.

'Don't say anything, just get undressed and join me,' Deborah said softly.

Arenwen didn't need any further invitation, fumbling at his belt to remove his trousers. As he did so Deborah rolled to one side and lit a small amount of charcoal. Above the charcoal a small copper bowl was suspended containing some greyish brown seeds.

By the time Arenwen was fully undressed the seeds had begun to roast. He was already drunk from the night before, but now he looked down at himself and his limbs had turned to wood. His skin had turned green and leafy, he was hallucinating that he was the Green Man.

Deborah took him by the hand and pulled him down to the furs and rolled him on to his back. Arenwen looked up at her to see that she had been transformed. Flames shot from her hair, she was the Goddess, she was the White Queen. He was struggling to focus on what was reality and what was the effects of the henbane seeds as fairies danced all around them. Flames were coming from the both of them, flowers floated past his eyes. Everything was a blur, their bodies were a perfect match for each other, they were a God and a Goddess. Arenwen was soaking in sweat. Steam was rising from his body in the cold morning air of the roundhouse.

He awoke sometime later, rolled over to see that the copper bowl was gone and so was Deborah. He drifted back off to sleep, images flashing before him from earlier - was it real?

'Wake up, it's past midday,' it was Bakher kicking him in the ribs.

'Why didn't you wake me sooner?' Arenwen protested.

'Don't worry, you're not alone. Most of the men were the same, Telor and Vaughn woke up with the pigs. Who knows what they were up to,' Bakher laughed. It was late in the afternoon and Arenwen had considered moving out, but thought that an extra day would give the men the chance to recover. It would also give the main army a chance to catch up, so Arenwen went to find Bilhild to tell him of his decision.

'We'll spend another night here, but I'll make sure they don't drink too much tonight as we leave at first light tomorrow.'

'The men will thank you for that,' Bilhild replied.

Arenwen made his way back to the chieftain to inform him of his plans. Deborah walked straight past him without any acknowledgment, had he dreamt it?

The warrior found Galatos outside his roundhouse talking to Bakher.

'With your permission, Lord, we will take the pleasure of your hospitality for one more day then leave at first light tomorrow?'

'Of course, of course,' Gelatos replied, as long as you like. My men will be grateful for that, especially after last night's celebrations.

'Thank you Lord. I may not have the opportunity in the morning so I pass on my thanks and gratitude now.'

Bilhild ensured the men were well fed that night, but curbed their drinking. As sun rose the next morning the party was assembled. It was slightly larger than when they had arrived, as Gelatos had provided scouts for the next stage of the journey.

The Celtic leader scanned the party, then raised his arm for them to move out of the Lingones' town. The group left knowing that a large part of their journey had been completed. In Arenwen's mind was the description of the huge river Bilhild had told him about. He thought to himself how do we cross the Rhone?

Chapter 9

The Swords and the Senate

Marcus had already bathed and eaten by the time his father had arisen. Quintus came down in one of his finest tunics sporting a narrow vertical red stripe from each shoulder. The style of garment expressed his wealth and rank, as only aristocratic families were allowed to have their clothing finished in this manner.

Lucia came in to greet him 'will you be gone long?' She asked.

'My business with the Senate won't take long, but I intend to stay in Rome for a few days. I'm going to take the boy with me as he needs to learn which families can be trusted and which cannot. However, if he gets under my feet I'll have him sent straight back here,' Quintus said casting a glance at his son. That was just fine by Marcus, he would do what he had to do and stay out of his way as much as possible. The teenager knew there would be plenty of time to explore Rome, and maybe get back to the Circus Maximus.

'Thank you father, I won't be a burden,' he said politely.

'Why not let him take Lucius with you? He will keep Marcus busy with his training and provide him with an escort when you're not with him,' his mother said.

'Fine, fine, anything for a little peace.'

'Aesop, bring me food and drink, I will eat before we leave. Make sure my sella and my son's horse are ready, I don't want to dirty my clothes by riding,' Marcus' father said.

Aesop scurried off to make the arrangements. He was very efficient, food and drink were quickly brought with plenty of wine for his master.

'Let us leave your father in peace,' Lucia said to her son, gesturing to the garden. When she made sure that they couldn't be seen she reached inside her stola and pulled out a small leather pouch.

'Take this with you in case you need to buy anything when you are in Rome, and don't tell your father,' she smiled.

'Be careful when you're in the city it can be a dangerous place and stay out of your father's way, you know what he can be like,' she added.

'I will and I will mother,' Marcus replied with a cheeky smile, before hitching up his tunic and pushing the small pouch of coins in to his loincloth. The pair made their way back into the dining area just as my Quintus had finished his food and, as usual, quite a few drinks. Aesop was dressing his master in his toga, carefully folding the last part of the cloth and draping it over my Quintus' left arm. He did look resplendent, just what was needed to go before the Senate.

'Is everything ready?' my Quintus asked.

'Your sella, the young Master's horse and Lucius are all ready for you as you commanded,' Aesop said with a bow.

'Good, then let's get going,' Quintus instructed.

Marcus glanced at his mother, she smiled and mouthed 'be careful.' he returned her smile with a silent 'I will.'

The journey to Rome was much slower than it had been last time, as Quintus was being carried in his sella, although the two slaves were going faster than the normal walking pace. Marcus' father sat with his two swords on his lap, his son ridding just slightly behind and to his right while Lucius made up the rear carrying shields and practice swords.

The group wound their way through the countryside without saying a word. Marcus was excited that he was going back to Rome as there had been so much more to see and do than there was at the country villa. However, he didn't want to show his father that he was pleased to have been taken along. They eventually made their way into Rome and went straight to Quintus' city domus.

The sella stopped at his house, the two slaves gently lowering it onto its four legs. The slave at the rear moved quickly round the front to help his master out of his seat. Marcus dismounted and Lucius led the lad's horse to the stables. The teenager told him to have some food and join him later that afternoon to continue our training.

Marcus followed his father into the domus.

'Wine, bring me wine,' my Quintus shouted as the pair made our way inside.

They went to the dining area where my Quintus was immediately served his wine. As father and son reclined on the couches they were brought a customary mid-day meal consisting of bread, cheese, boiled eggs and salad.

'I have business with the Senate this afternoon, boy, so you will need to busy yourself' my Quintus said.

'Of course, father, I shall let my lunch settle, bathe and then I intend to continue my sword practice with Lucius,' he replied.

Quintus made his way through the streets of Rome. Heading for the Forum, he was very familiar with the area as it nestled in the small valley between the Palatine hill and the hill where one of his brothers lived. He had that air of authority about him that made the plebeians move out of his way. One of his house slaves was carrying the two swords, and struggled to keep up with his quick pace as his mater strode through the streets.

Quintus was heading for the Curia Hostilia where public, official and religious issues were discussed, debated and decided. He proceeded up the Vicus Jugarius and made his way past the Temple of Saturn, which was being rebuilt following a recent fire. To the right he could see the Rostra where a crowd gathered around a citizen haranguing them about taxes. He continued over the stone flagstones of the Forum, and strode up to the Curia Hostilia. He entered through the huge bronze doors that were decorated with stars and acorns. He was pleased, the curia was nearly full with only a few seats empty on either side of the three tiers of benches in the vast chamber. He signalled to his slave to wait by the door, and took one of the empty seats as the senator in the middle was finishing his speech. Quintus sat in the area dominated by his family and curtly acknowledged with a slight nod.

Several hours went by with debates about the building of new roads, and the need for an aqueduct before Quintus finally got his opportunity to speak. Rising slowly from his seat he took his place in the centre of the curia. He strode up and down waiting for the chatter to die down before starting his speech.

'Senators of the great Republic of Rome, our mighty army has swept away all foes before us,' his family members signalled their approval with loud outbursts of 'yes' and 'quite right.'

'We now stand in a new era with Rome expanding so much that I believe it will become the centre of the world, and the heart of a great empire.' However, as our great republic grows we will meet foes with better weapons than us,' cries of 'never' came from the other families while his own family went quiet.

'I do not doubt the skill and courage of our brave men, but I do doubt the weapons we equip them with.'

Quintus signalled to the slave to bring over the swords. He unsheathed the bronze weapon and brandished it in the air.

'This is what we have equipped our army with since the beginning of time. It has served us well, but our distant enemies have developed stronger weapons.'

He unsheathed the iron sword, and passed both swords to the senators closest to him.

'Feel the weight. Which do you think is the stronger?' He asked.

The Senators passed the two weapons up and down the rows until it was returned to the front. Holding up the bronze sword a senator said 'this one, it is heavier, and so must be stronger.' Quintus smiled, they had fallen into his trap.

'I have recently acquired a new metal, at my own personal expense. The Thracians have developed a stronger metal than our traditional bronze, and I present it to you now.'

He passed the bronze sword to his slave and instructed him to hold the sword up in front of himself. Quintus swung the iron sword as hard as he could and the sound of the contact resonated around the vast roof space of the curia. The slave was pushed back by the force but the end result was what Quintus had wanted, the bronze sword had bent. Quintus took the bronze sword off the slave and held both aloft to the cheers of his family members and the applause of the Senate.

Quintus released his grip on the bent bronze sword and let it fall to the floor with a clang. He held the other sword in the air and said 'it is called iron! I propose to the Senate that we equip our mighty army with weapons made from this stronger metal.'

The Senate erupted in a mixture of cheering and chatter. Quintus skilfully waited for the din to die down before readying himself for the questions that were due to come, especially the one that he had primed his cousin to ask. The questions ranged from ease of manufacture, availability of materials and then his cousin rose to his feet and asked the question he had been waiting for.

'You correctly identified that Rome has paid highly in men and money. The cost to equip our entire army would be a significant drain on the treasury. A drain that Rome cannot afford,' Quintus' cousin said.

'Indeed, my honourable senator you are correct, but I cannot in all good faith, as a citizen of Rome, allow our men to carry this outdated weaponry. My proposal is that I will pay for the new weapons, and also have them made on my estate,' Quintus said.

And so the deed was done, a masterstroke of political manipulation. His cousin waved his arms to quieten down the other senators and spoke

'Fellow Senators, we must vote on this generous proposal. I also ask you to consider why such a patriot is not a member of this esteemed body, and therefore I ask you to vote on Quintus Fabius Ambustus being elected as a senator of Rome.'

Both motions were unanimously passed, Quintus thanked the Senate and left. The sword production would cost him a small fortune, he could afford it and it was worth it to be promoted to the Senate. The offer of manufacture at his villa was not an act of kindness, but it was to control the knowledge of this new metal, and in doing so, he would need to be paid for any other materials that required manufacturing. Feeling very pleased with himself, Quintus decided he would celebrate by paying Ambrosia a visit, and raising a goblet or two to the gods for his good fortune.

Quintus made his way through the town and marvelled at its magnificence. He soon came to his usual brothel and climbed the stairs to be welcomed by one of the serving slaves.

'Please be seated sir. I shall prepare a drink for you and notify Ambrosia of your presence,' the slave said.

She returned quickly with a goblet of wine. Ambrosia entered the room wearing her gold necklace that Quintus had presented to her on his last visit. She took him by the hand and led him to her private chamber. Her long ebony tresses were twisted and held at the back of her head with a gold pin. He could smell the perfume on her hair as she unwound his robe and then moved to sit him down on one of the couches.

'Let me refill your wine for you,' Ambrosia said knowing exactly how to deal with him.

'You read my mind, but be quick I have some excellent news for you,' Quintus replied.

Ambrosia returned with the wine which was immediately drunk to be refilled over and over again as Quintus regaled her with his triumph at the Curia Hostilia. While Quintus spoke, Ambrosia slipped her hand up his tunic and into his loincloth. She knew the time was right so she stood up, went over to the other couch and lifted up the light silk dress she was wearing. He got up and pulled the gold pin out of her hair making it tumble down over her shoulders. It wasn't long before could hear Quintus' breathing getting louder and deeper as he stood behind her. The whore felt his legs tremble then turned around and kissed her customer on the cheek. She whispered in his ear.

'That was magnificent senator,' she was really thinking that men are stupid. His face was flushed, but he could feel his heart beat gradually returning to its normal rhythm.

'I shall go and replenish you wine, Senator?' She had played him perfectly.

Ambrosia returned with the drink and asked if Quintus would be eating with her.

'As much as I am tempted, I must leave you as there is so much to organise after this afternoon's events,' Quintus replied.

The newly appointed senator made his way through the town to his domus. He was greeted by a slave who took his robe, while another went to alert the household of their Master's presence.

By the time he had taken the ten paces into the atrium he had been presented with a goblet of wine. He stood there for a while gazing around at the most decorated room in the house. The ceiling was unlike his brother's as it had no pillars. Although this option was more expensive, Quintus preferred the additional room it gave him. A marble bust of himself stood on a waist high pillar in the corner while his pride and joy was the shallow pool sunken in to the floor with a mosaic of Romulus and Remus, the founders of Rome. Although in reality it was Romulus who had undertaken most of the planning as he had killed his brother in the early stages of founding the city.

His wine was replenished as he stood admiring the trappings of his wealth. He made his way to his tablinum. This office was different from all the other rooms as it was open on two sides, with the additional walls being formed by concertina wooden panels. This substantial office contained busts of some of his famous ancestors - after all, his family were descendants of Hercules. He lay down on one of the couches and admired the wall painting to his right. The light was streaming in through the open window, illuminating the vivid colours. The light bounced off the bronze sword that Quintus displayed proudly, as it had been a prize possession since his grandfather had given it to him when he was just a boy.

The wine was good and the sun was warm. He had the fuzzy contented feeling that wine usually brought to him. He closed his eyes and replayed the visual snapshots stored in his mind of that afternoon in the Senate and then he reflected on how he had given Ambrosia a damn good seeing to. He lay back and rested his head in the couch, thinking that he might drift off to sleep. He was very comfortable and smiled to himself just before his beautiful moment was shattered.

Jumping up from the couch Quintus glared out of the tablinium window in to the colonnaded garden to try and find out what was causing the infernal racket. Of course, there could only be one person disturbing his peace. Quintus had completely forgotten all about his nuisance of a son, and instantly regretted bringing him.

Marcus was in the garden practicing his drills with Lucius and just starting some light sparing when his father burst out of the house. He smiled as his father never came to see him practice, indeed he was very rarely in the villa at all. Marcus quickly realised by the look on his father's face that he had not come to watch him practice.

'What is all this noise?' Quintus shouted as he thundered towards his son.

'I'm sorry if I disturbed you father, I had not realised you had returned. I thought I would practice my sword skills before your return,' he replied sheepishly.

'Sword skills! Sword skills! You know nothing boy. You spend hour after hour and day after day with this slave and you think you have sword skills. Be in the atrium tomorrow at mid-day and I will show you sword skills. You are old enough now to learn what it is all about,' his father snorted.

Quintus span around and stormed back into the domus determined that he would teach the boy a lesson for disturbing him. Marcus made sure that stayed out of his father's way until the next day, but saw quite a few people come and go from meetings.

The teenager went to sleep that night wondering what his father had in store for him. Next morning he had my usual morning meal, and stayed clear of anywhere where his father might be. It was approaching midday without any sign of Quintus and his son thought he had forgotten about the day before, but then he appeared in the Atrium, pacing up and down slurping yet another goblet of wine.

'You took your time boy,' Quintus said.

'I came as quickly as I could father. May I ask where we are going?' Marcus asked.

'To begin your real education, boy. Now follow me.'

'You had better come along Lucius, it would keep my mother happy. The gods only know what he has in store for me now,' the lad said quietly.

'As you command,' Lucius replied with a bow.

The bronze door clanged as it closed behind them as we made our way on to the street. As they went Marcus began to get his bearings, recognising Capitoline Hill where one of his uncles lived. Soon he saw the Palatine Hill and he wondered if his father was taking him to the Circus Maximus. The lad's heart sank as they veered right, away from the direction he knew the Circus Maximus lay in.

There was a very unpleasant smell in the air, and Marcus noticed that the crowds were increasing in the narrowing streets. Quintus noticed the uncomfortable look on his son's face and slurred.

'The beautiful aroma of the Tiber and the meat market.'

Meat market, why on earth was my father taking me to the meat market? We were now part of a large crowd that was funnelling down the streets when suddenly we spilled out into a large square.

'And so your education begins boy. Do you see the temple to the right? That is the Temple of Portunus, the God of keys, grain and livestock. He protects the warehouses,' Quintus said pointing to the different buildings.

Marcus glanced right feigning interest, but it was actually an impressive construction. It was rectangular in shape and elevated off the floor on a podium. This meant that the worshiper had to climb the steps that lead up to four columned facia. The building was supported all the way around with columns of limestone. The teenager could see that once you had mounted the steps you would need to take a number of further steps, under the roof, before coming to the huge bronze door.

'Do you see the small round temple, with Corinthian pillars, straight ahead towards the river? That is the temple dedicated to our ancestor Hercules. It is on that very spot where he slew Cacus, the fire breathing giant and son of Vulcan. Hercules slew the human flesh eating beast for stealing eight of his cattle,' Quintus said.

Quintus raised an arm and shouted over to a familiar face who was sat on one of the raised platforms; it was his friend Gaius. Marcus followed his father over to the platform where he saw one of the billboards that were dotted around the square. It read 'in celebration of his election to the great Senate of Rome, Quintus Fabius Ambustus presents three pairs of gladiators as thanks to the gods for bestowing him with good fortune.'

At the bottom of the billboard was the ominous statement 'sine missione' or 'without release' meaning all contests would be a fight to the death. It was common place for the losing gladiators to be spared, but Quintus must have negotiated this grisly option with the organiser. There would be no raised finger signalling a losing fighter's acceptance of defeat, there would be no mercy.

The newly appointed senator took his place of honour in the middle of the platform, his son taking a sat in a row behind him. Quintus completely ignored the lad as his friend handed him a goblet of wine. There were additional platforms either side of the one they were sat in, filled with invited guests and family members. The three platforms faced the Temple of Hercules with the other three sides of the makeshift arena being marked out on the floor with white limestone. These three sides where surrounded by the plebs of Rome and traders plying their wares.

Horns sounded to the right as six gladiators entered the makeshift arena. They paraded themselves around before forming a line in front of their benefactor. In unison the shouted

'Hail, those who are about to die salute you.'

Rome was not short of gladiators due to its military successes. Captives were resigned to one of three fates, work in the mines, be sold as household slaves or as many captured soldiers chose take their chances as gladiators. Becoming a gladiator offered them a respected trade, regular food, somewhere to live as well as the faint possibility of fortune and fame. Many considered it a better life, or even better death than the other two options.

There was a good mix of gladiators presenting themselves before Quintus. There were four Samnites with their large rectangular shields. Their helmets had a plume of horse hair and a visor that covered most of their faces. They all carried their weapon of choice, the short sword. The only thing they wore was a loincloth, and a thick brown leather belt covering their midriff. The gladiators had a leather greave guard edged with bronze on the left shin, which protected them against any potential slashes to their leading leg. Their right arm was bound with furs to protect the sword arm.

A Thracian carried his curved short sword which was designed to stab its victim or to maim an opponent's unprotected back. He gripped the leather straps of his rectangular shield, which was on his left arm. It was larger than Marcus' practice shield but smaller than the Samnite one. He had a bronze shin protector on both shins, which had padding to protect the tibia from attack. There was leather quilting over his sword arm which continued up to cover and protect his right shoulder.

There was one hopomachus who held much smaller round shield. He was much more heavily armoured than the other two types of gladiator. The bronze arm guard had overlapping plates down the whole of his right arm, fastened on with leather straps. His bronze helmet was decorated with a plume of feathers in the middle with a single feather on either side. His waist was protected by a thick bronze belt. He had heavy padding on his legs, but was shoeless with his weapon of choice being a spear and a short sword.

Quintus accepted their salutes and four of the gladiators left the makeshift square, leaving the remaining pair to move to the centre. The first pair were both Samnites who now faced each other, rotating their arms to warm and limber up their muscles.

The fight soon erupted into action with one of them rushing his opposite number, smashing his large rectangular shield into the dented bronze boss of his opponent. This forced the man back several paces while the first gladiator continued his attack by raining down heavy blows, all of which were being blocked. The defender's shield was already starting to show signs of damage. The fight was very one-sided with the attacking Samnite cutting his opponent at will, opening a gash through the furs that protected his sword arm. Another strike, smashing the heavy shield down onto his opponent who lacked the speed to attack the unprotected midriff. The weaker of the two retreated with every attack, my father was unhappy as he drained his wine. He glanced over to his guests and family members who were muttering to each other. The attacker planted his shield down, and with one sweeping movement knelt and stabbed at his opponents shin, slicing through the leather greaves. The crowd were getting restless. The lanista came on to the arena, his job was to whip reluctant fighters and animals. He lashed the defending man across the back and the gladiator started begging for mercy. The crowd were not happy with the performance and cried 'Iugula! -Kill him!'

This clearly was not the actions of a true gladiator, they were to die in silence. Another blow smashed his shield away, and he was now scurrying away from his attacker on all fours. The dominant gladiator saw his opportunity and drove his sword through the ribcage of his opponent, spraying blood in the air. Holding his opponent down, with one foot, he removed his sword and wiped it clean on the losers arm. The winner looked to my father to signal the killer blow. He stood up and addressed the crowd.

'This man does not deserve an honourable death. He fought like a dog and shall die like a dog.'

The victor stepped away from his victim as two of the attendants, who would normally carry away the bodies, entered the arena with wooden mallets. They set about the man on the floor first by breaking his ribs. The defeated gladiator screamed and tried to roll away from the blows without success. The attendants casually tore off his helmet and grieves. They broke both his legs and then set about beating him around the head, taking care not to make him unconscious. The crowd were being whipped up into a frenzy as the man haemorrhaged blood from the wounds, but could not move away. Finally an overzealous blow to the head caved in his skull.

Quintus raised his goblet above his right shoulder for a slave to refill his drink. He lent in to Gaius and whispered 'get down there and tell the promoter that if the next two fights are not to my pleasing I will have him in the arena.' Gaius nodded and went in search of the event organiser.

There was a short interval before the next fight was to start and four criminals were brought on to the arena, hands bound behind their backs. They had been sentenced to death as they had all been convicted as murderers. The four had been stripped naked and had their heads shaved to further humiliate them. The crowd jeered the convicts, throwing stones at them as they were lined up on their knees before my father. One by one, the executioner stood behind them and expertly swung his sword to their necks. Three were cleanly decapitated but one, where the stroke had not completely severed the neck, had the head still attached to the body by skin and muscle. It lopped over the convict's shoulder.

Gaius returned just before the start of the next fight. The remnants of the murderers had been cleared away, and sand had been thrown down to absorb the blood. He spoke to Quintus.

'I have expressed your displeasure of the last fight. He offered his sincere apologies, and said the losing man was a late replacement covering an injury to one of his other men. He sends his assurance that you will not be disappointed.'

'I had better not be,' Quintus replied.

The horn blew and the second pair entered the arena, the hoplomachus and another Samnite. They gave their salutes, receiving the signal to start.

The pair cautiously attempted to outmanoeuvre each other as they moved in a clockwise motion. The hoplomachus was feigning throwing his spear, with his Samnite opponent making small adjustments just in case the spear would be launched at him. There was one last feint of a throw, but the hoplomachus skilfully caught the end of the shaft as it was released. He now used a new tactic of spinning, and using the length of the spear to attack. The attacker was not concerned by the Samnite opponent as the long length of the spear kept him out of reach of his opposing combatant. Spin, whack, spin, whack but the Samnite just used his large shield to expertly deflect all of the vicious blows.

Clearly this tactic wasn't working for the hoplomachus. He lined up the Samnite and launched his spear, it was easily brushed away by the Samnite using his large shield. The crowd cheered as the hoplomachus moved forward with his short sword to do the up close and dirty fighting.

Now it was the Samnite's turn to attack. If this had not been a death match he would certainly be scoring more points, but points were irrelevant in this contest. He attacked high and low, but the heavily armoured hoplomachus used the armour plating on his arm as a shield to deflect the blows. The Samnite attacked and was parried, the hoplomachus glanced over to where his spear lay, but the Samnite was between it and him, and he retreated a step after each blow. Then the hoplomachus saw the slightest of a gap between his opponent and his shield. Using his small round shield as a weapon he drove it through the gap and twisted it at the last moment. He smashed the shield up rapidly in one smooth movement to catch the Samnite squarely below his chinstrap, lifting him off the floor. The Samnite fell onto his back, gasping for air as his oesophagus had been crushed. The crowd cried

'Habet, Hoc habet! -He's had it!'

The victor looked up to Quintus, he stood up and gave the signal, thumbs down. The hoplomachus stood over his defeated opponent, took his sword in two hands and thrust the tip downwards. The Samnite's body convulsed as the blade was driven through his chest, puncturing his heart. The victor removed his sword, bowed and left the arena to the cheers of the crowd.

The two attendants rushed on, this time carrying a litter. The body was placed on it then removed from the arena with more dignity than the last wretch who had died earlier. The horn sounded signalling the customary break in the proceedings. This was the time that the traders enjoyed the most as the hungry, thirsty crowds bought their food and drink at slightly inflated prices, after all it was a matter of supply and demand.

Quintus discussed the last bout with Gaius as they were served food and drink. He chatted about his success at the Senate, and Marcus knew he wouldn't be missed if he took the opportunity to slip away to spend some of the money his mother had given him.

'Just going to relieve myself,' he said.

Quintus didn't even look around so his son made his way down the platform to find Lucius waiting patiently.

'Let's go get some food,' the teenager said.

'As you wish young Master,' he replied with a small bow.

The pair went behind the platform, and pushed their way through the crowds to examine the different stalls that had been set up. Marcus couldn't quite see what all the stalls were selling, but he could smell the fresh fish. He knew what he wanted and was determined to find it, with all these stalls there must be at least one selling what the young man was hankering after. Lucius followed behind and he could see his master trying to glimpse peeks of the stalls as gaps opened and closed in the crowd.

'Are you looking for anything in particular?' Lucius asked.

'Indeed I am Lucius, I have dormice in my mind. Dipped in honey and sprinkled with poppy seeds,' the teenager said trying to control the urge to salivate.

Lucius was taller than Marcus, and could easily see the wares on the stalls.

'I see what you desire young Master. Could you be so kind as to follow me,' Lucius said. Marcus nodded and Lucius moved in front of him, gently parting the citizens of Rome as he made his way through the crowd. They moved towards a stall and waited their turn as a man in front of them was being served. As he moved forward Marcus tucked in behind him to quickly fill the gap at the front of the stall. Lucius had chosen well, the dormice Marcus had wanted were there as well as fresh bread and fish.

'What can I help you with sir?' The stall holder asked.

'I'll take four dormice, two skewers of fish and a small loaf of bread,' the teenager replied, reaching inside his tunic for the pouch of coins his mother had given him. He shook a few on to his palm, and offered them to the stall holder. The trader beamed a toothless smile at the sight of the coins. Lucius shot him a menacing glance.

'Oh Master, that is far too much. Do you have any smaller coins?' The stall holder asked.

Marcus shook the rest of the pouch on to his palm to see that they were all silver. Lucius stepped forward.

'This is young Master Marcius. His father is Quintus Fabius Ambustus, patron of these games.'

The smile slipped from the stall holder's face as what he had been told sunk in. He quickly recovered his sad domineer and painted a false smile.

'Why did you not say sooner? There is no charge for my meagre wares to the son of such a great man. Please take what you will,' the stall holder said.

'The dormice, fish and bread will be sufficient,' Marcus replied.

Lucius gathered the food and whispered in my ear.

'It would be wise to put such a large sum of money away young Master. In a crowd as big as this you are guaranteed to have pickpockets and thieves.'

The lad took his advice, quickly putting the coins back in the pouch. He tucked it back in to his tunic and gave it a tap to reassure himself of its location. He followed Lucius as the slave made his way through the crowds.

'Give my thanks to your father and tell him of my fine food,' the stall holder called as they moved away.

Lucius headed for an area away from the hustle and bustle where his master could sit down to enjoy his food. Marcus sat down and Lucius placed the food on a cloth on the ground.

'Please join me Lucius,' the young lad said.

Lucius sat down, cross legged on the ground, I don't think he quite understood what Marcus meant. His master took the bread, tore it roughly in half and placed it at his feet, quickly followed by two fish skewers and two honeyed dormice. Lucius opened his mouth to protest, but Marcus raised a hand to silence him.

'I bought this for us,' he told him.

'As a thank you for your kindness and tutorship toward me.'

'I am your family's slave and ask for, nor deserve any thanks,' he replied.

'If that is the case, I command you to eat,' Marcus said with a kind smile.

Lucius returned the smile, and they both started on their tasty lunch. First they ate the fish and fresh bread, saving the sweetness of the dormice until last. Honey trickled down from the side of Marcus' mouth as he bit into his second sweet tasty treat. Lucius laughed and wiped it away with a cloth. They had finished their food and made our way back through the crowds to the platform. As they got closer a horn sounded a long blast signalling that the third fight was about to begin.

Marcus left Lucius at the base of the platform and climbed the steps to take my seat behind his father, who was still engrossed in conversation with his friend Gaius. He hadn't noticed his son returning, Marcus wondered if he had even noticed that he had gone at all. Slaves tidied away the remnants Quintus' lunch, cleaned then removed the debris of food on the floor. Quintus signalled and another blast of the horn was sounded, this one much shorter than before.

The two remaining gladiators entered the area. The excited babble in the crowd died down to an expectant hush. The Samnite and the Thracian removed their helmets, held their weapons to their chests and honoured their benefactor, who raised his hand. The two warriors retreated from each other, put on their helmets and prepared for the deadly contest. They both moved in a circular motion, eyeing up their opponent in an attempt to spot a weakness.

They edged closer and closer until they locked shields in a trial of strength. Neither yielded an inch while they slashed at each other with their short swords. Marcus knew from his sparring that fighting was exhausting. The victor was usually the person with the greatest stamina as opposed to the warrior with the greatest sword craft. The Thracian managed to get a glancing blow on the side of the Samnite's helmet. The crowd heard the resounding clang as the curved blade hit the bronze helmet. The Samnite had been dazed by the blow and the Thracian took one step back from the pushing contest making the Samnite stumble forward. The Thracian saw his opportunity, rolled forward on to his shield, and propelling himself up to his feet behind the Samnite to strike. The Samnite was still dazed, but managed to fling his shield arm out to block the lethal strike. This is what repeated training did for you, drill patterns and muscle memory could instinctively take over despite being incapacitated.

The two locked shields for a second time giving the Samnite the opportunity to gather his wits. The push-pull contest continued, Marcus could see the sweat coming from both fighters from their huge exertion. The Thracian stepped back again, hoping to repeat his previous advantage, but the Samnite was ready for it this time and also took a step back. They continued circling each other, sword crashing down on shields. Attack, parry, defend, attack, parry defend. The Thracian had his back to the raised platform enabling Marcus to spot that the gladiator was loosening his grip on the two leather straps of his shield. Stepping quickly forward the Thracian hooked his shield under the Samnite's sword arm, forcing it in to the air. Letting go of the straps he flicked his sword from his right hand in to his left in a single movement. The Samnite's ribs were exposed as the Thracian drove his curved blade under the Samnite's ribcage, exiting at the base of the spine. The blow severed the spinal column as it came out of the small of his back. Blood gushed from the exit wound, more tricking from the Samnite's mouth. He slumped to the floor with his legs still twitching. The crowd cheered as the Thracian savoured their adoration, and lifted his sword in salute to Quintus. In return he turn tossed a gold coin to the victor as a reward of a match that the people would talk about for quite some time. The Thracian gratefully took the coin, worth more than a year's toil to the common citizen. The gladiator bowed and left the arena as Marcus' father rose to take the applause from the crowd who chanted 'Quintus, Quintus, Quintus,' in appreciation of the entertainment he had paid for them to watch that afternoon.

The body was removed on a stretcher and taken to the tent behind the makeshift platform. The Samnite's body would be honoured, and he would receive a respectful burial. Despite his obvious demise, his throat would be slit, like all of the losers today, to ensure they were truly dead.

Quintus swigged his wine and nudged Gaius.

'You and I have business in town, my friend,' Quintus said.

'I thought you had dealt with that business earlier?' his friend replied.

'I feel like continuing that businesses,' Quintus smiled thinking that he would make a second visit of the day to Ambrosia.

'We cannot take the boy,' Gaius said as he turned round looking at Marcus.

'He'll be fine. He has a slave with him. You know you're way back to my domus don't you boy?' Quintus said rhetorically.

In truth, Marcus knew exactly where he was. It was a very similar journey to the one he took to the Circus Maximus, apart from the turn down to this square. The teenager was quite sure that he knew his way back. All he had to do was simply retrace his steps through the square, find the road that led from Capitoline Hill to the Circus Maximus, turn left and from there it was all familiar. Gaius looked concerned and checked with his friend's son.

'Are you sure you know the way?'

'Yes, I'm sure,' Marcus replied following his father and Gaius down the steps. Quintus stopped briefly to enjoy the adoration of the crowd one last time before moving on to complete whatever business he had. Lucius started to follow expecting Marcus to go in the same direction.

'We're to head back by ourselves, Lucius. I know the way,' the teenager said.

The crowd started to dissipate, heading off to wherever they called home. The traders were discounting their remaining wares, and closing their stalls for the night. Marcus spotted the gap in the buildings where he had entered the square earlier that day, and headed towards it. He was being swept along with the crowd heading in the same direction as different streams of people made their way to other exits that surrounded the square. Lucius tucked in tightly behind the young lad, not wanting to lose him in the crowd. They moved very slowly, a half a step at a time as they edged closer and closer to the exit. The road was not wide enough to handle such a large number of people, but Marcus knew they would soon be out of the narrow streets and on to one of the huge arterial vias that kept the city moving.

They were crushed into the restricted space of the street, packed tightly as they were funnelled down the high walled thoroughfare. Marcus was unable to take full steps as there was not enough room, so he shuffled along the stone flagstones. The teenager was a head height shorter than most of the people around him. The air he was sucking in was hot, Marcus struggled to breathe. He could feel Lucius straining his body in an attempt to shield his young master from the immense pressure of the crowd all around them. It seemed like an age, but Marcus could see the end of the street. Not long now he thought, straight over the next street and then left onto the much larger roads.

They came to the end of the first street when Marcus saw to his dismay that the majority of the throng were turning right. To complicate matters further another mass of people came from the left, forcing the teenager down the street on the right. It was pointless trying to do anything other than be swept along by the crowd, it would be like trying to swim against a raging tide. Marcus glanced back at Lucius, the slave was getting increasingly more separated from him, but the lad could still see his sword tutor as he struggled to get closer. The crush pinned Marcus between the man in front of him and the one behind. He felt feint as he struggled to catch his breath, white dots flashed before his eyes.

Slowly but surely the multitude eased as people took their respective left and right turns off the road that Marcus had been forced down. He looked around but I was unable to see Lucius, so kept going straight, unsure of location. He figured that by taking the next left, straight up and left again he should be on the road he wanted. The sun was on the wane with long shadows being cast up the side streets. The teenager turned left and made his way down what he thought to be a small road. Marcus was twenty paces in before he realised it was an alley with a dead end. He hadn't heard the footsteps behind him.

Then the youngster heard a voice, one that he recognised.

'That's the one I told you about. A money pouch that will make us wealthy men.' It was the toothless trader with two other men, they were all holding daggers.

'Throw me the purse of silver, boy, and we will let you live,' the trader said. Marcus knew he was lying, he was able to identify him and the trader knew who his father was. If the lad was lucky they would kidnap him for ransom, but it was more likely that they would slit his throat. Marcus scanned the narrow alley looking for an escape route, but could not see anywhere to evade the three rogues. His next instinct was to look for something he could use to defend himself with, again there was nothing with which he could hurt the robbers.

The three edged closer and closer, but there wasn't enough of a gap between them for Marcus to slip through. The teenager resigned himself to the fate of the gods, he wondered if his mother ever get the opportunity to burn his body, or would he just be another dead boy in the wrong end of the city?

They were very close to him now, the thug on the right scraping his dagger down the alley wall.

'Throw me the pouch boy,' the trader repeated.

Suddenly there was movement from the shadows. The man on the right dropped his dagger as his face was smashed into the wall. Thank the gods, Lucius had found his master. The second thug lunged at the slave with his stiletto blade only to receive a swift elbow to the nose. Lucius wrestled the man's arm behind his back, Marcus heard the snap of his humorous. As the bone in his arm broke the second assailant dropped his dagger, the teenager instinctively bent down and picked it up. Lucius glanced at the second dagger on the floor and then to Marcus, he understood his dilemma. The slave looked again, and received a nod of confirmation from Marcus. He quickly picked up the nine inch blade.

The first man got up off the floor, blood streaming from centre of his face of what was his nose. He looked around, quickly deciding that he had had enough and ran for his life.

'Keep an eye on him,' Lucius said pointing at the man on the floor cradling his broken arm.

Lucius flicked the knife to the throat of the store trader. These weapons were designed to puncture rather than rip. There was a drop of blood of the tip of the blade as Lucius touched it under the trader's jaw. The merchant was on his tip toes trying to relieve the pressure of the blade. Any effort to speak would move his bottom jaw onto the weapon so he stayed silent. Lucius stepped left, the trader followed as he tried to stop the knife piercing his skin. Lucius stepped right and the trader followed once more, shuffling on his tip toes.

It was like watching a cat toy with a mouse, and then it was over in an instant. Lucius thrust the blade through the trader's jaw bone, through the soft palate of his mouth and into his brain. The stall owner remained there still impaled on the knife until Lucius withdrew it, allowing the dead body to slump to the floor.

'What do you want to do with him?' Lucius gestured to the one Marcus was guarding.

The attacker was now blubbering his apologies, his tears made snot from his nose run into his mouth and out again as green bubbles.

'Mercy Master, mercy,' he pleaded.

'Do you want me to finish him?' Lucius asked.

'No, I've seen enough killing for one day,' the teenager replied.

'Thank you Master,' the wounded man said. He struggled to get up, but was met with a vicious kick to the ribs, severely bruising them if not breaking a few to add to his snapped arm. The man collapsed on the floor. Lucius threw his blade to the far corner of the alley and wiped the blood off his arm on the dead trader's tunic.

'You know I could be executed for picking up that knife, Master Marcus,' Lucius said.

'I do Lucius, but in doing so you saved my life. We will keep this incident between the two of us, never to be spoken of again. Now let's get out of this shithole and get back to my father's domus.'

Chapter 10

The Rhone

It had been three weeks since the advance party had left the comforts of the Lingones tribe. Arenwen was still unsure about that night with Deborah, though she had not mentioned it so he thought it best to stay clear of the subject.

They had been led south by the Lingones guides, and they now led the advance party east. The leader guided his chariot over the rough terrain while Bakher sat on the floor behind him. Bilhild and Deborah were on the second chariot, with the rest of the party in an orderly line behind them. They were travelling at a walking pace to ensure that the main army did not fall too far behind. One of the mounted guides trotted up next to Arenwen and said

'We will soon be at the great river.'

'Good, you and another rider go ahead to secure what we need,' Arenwen replied thinking that they would need to secure some form of craft. The guide nodded, kicked his heels the horse's flank and sped off, calling to another rider to join him as he went. When they reached the river one guide would go upstream and the other would head downstream. Their purpose was to purchase boats or rafts to get the small party across the raging river, but also to secure transport for the large army. They would be interested in anything that would safely get the sizable army and supply carts across the river. Even the smallest of boats could be lashed to others to form a substantial base. Then a wooden platform could be secured on top to carry large numbers of warriors or the baggage carts.

The group of Celtic warriors arrived at the river and Arenwen could see why the scouts had brought them to this spot. Scanning up and down the river he could see that this point had the shortest distance between the banks. Although this was the narrowest crossing point, there was still a significant body of water to traverse. Arenwen calculated that it must be about half a mile between the two banks, and he could see tree debris shooting downstream at a rapid pace. This one made the first river they had followed look very tame in comparison. There was a downside to the shorter crossing as the water was channelled into a narrower passage and flowed much faster. Arenwen called to the small party 'we'll wait here until the riders return.'

They sat down next to the river bank and ate a light meal. No fires were lit as they knew that the guides would be returning shortly. They also knew that once they had crossed the river it was less than a day to their next taste of Celtic hospitality that would be shown to them by the Helvetii tribe.

The warrior chatted to Bilhild who explained that the river was an important trade route between the Celtic tribes, and that the scouts would have no difficulty in finding the craft the party needed to cross the river.

The rider from upstream returned first, dismounted next to Arenwen.

'I have found a merchant who has what we need. I offered to buy his boats, but he prefers we hire them and for us to return them to him after our crossing. He did not have anywhere near enough for the army, but the hire would include his services to navigate Lord Brennus across the river if we found suitable transport. He should be here within the hour,' the guide said.

Arenwen nodded his approval as the second rider rode in to the small camp.

'I have secured everything that is in the immediate area, but it is not much. It will take our main force weeks to cross in small numbers,' the second guide said.

'I'm sure you have done your best, it was always going to be unlikely for us to get everything we needed to get the troops across. However, I have a solution,' Arenwen smiled and looked at the thick forest on the far side of the river.

Bakher overheard the conversation and joined Arenwen.

'Yes indeed, the gods have provided once more,' Bakher said realising that there were more than enough timber to provide the materials they needed to ferry the large army across the raging river.

The boat owner came into view from upstream with his cart horse towing six large boats complete with oars and two long poles. Alongside the big cart horse was a young girl of about eight or nine years of age. Her long black hair had been plaited with one plait hanging over each shoulder. She wore an ankle length tunic, predominantly blue in colour, but with a beige check running its entire length. The boat owner waved as he got closer, calling to the guide he had met earlier.

'Bring him over,' Arenwen said.

The scout mounted his horse and went to escort the boat owner into the camp. He was led in, tethered his horse at the riverbank with the boats still attached to its harness. He scanned the party and spotted Arenwen's gold torque which identified him as the leader. He walked towards Arenwen and threw open his arms.

'Lord, my name is Idocus. As a humble trader I have navigated these waters for many years and am pleased to be your servant'.

Arenwen and the merchant negotiated a price to hire his boats, along with his services. Once they had completed the transaction the trader went about his duties.

'I will lash four of my boats together in pairs to transport your chariots. The remaining two boats will be more than sufficient to transport your men. I will need six of those trees chopping down from the copse behind us. Once they have been felled they must be split in the middle. Twelve lengths will be enough to cover the boats,' Idocus said.

'Bilhild, split the men in to two groups. Fell three trees each, and then half the logs at the midpoint,' Arenwen instructed his second in command. He raised his voice so that the rest of the camp could hear.

'There'll be extra ale for the team that brings their six lengths of logs first,' he said.

The men cheered and started organising themselves in to groups. The twins purposely chose opposing teams, this was going to be another competition which they would hope to win and therefore have bragging rights. The two teams grabbed their axes, and ran towards the copse of trees. Arenwen turned towards Bilhild and said 'let's go watch the entertainment.'

Arenwen could see that Bakher and Deborah had made their way to the small wood. They were well out of the way from the tree cutting, but Arenwen could see them making offerings to the fairies for taking the trees.

The two teams of lumberjacks approached the task in different ways. The team Telor was in started on a single tree, as one man raised his axe the man on either side was striking the trunk. The other team with Vaughn in were using a different approach, they had split in to smaller sub teams, each chopping a tree. Both teams shouted abuse at the other as they copped at the trunks with their axes.

Arenwen flicked back his light cloak and reached in to his trouser pocket. He pulled out a leather pouch that jingled in his hand. He playfully threw it in the air and caught it again. The warrior undid the leather strap and took out a coin, small and round with the image of a horse but clearly gold.

'How about a small wager?' Arenwen said to Bilhild.

'A gold coin on Vaughn's team,' he added.

Bilhild assessed the situation, Telor's team had nearly finished cutting down the first tree. The team were working well together, and he could hear a rhythmic chopping sound as chunks of wood flung through the air with every chop.

'I'll take that wager,' Bilhild replied.

There was a shout and the first tree came crashing to the ground. Telor's team cheered, pulled it clear from the stump, immediately setting about the second. The other team were systematically working through theirs, but not one of the three smaller teams were close to felling their individual tasks.

Once again the rhythmic chopping sound could be heard as Telor's team set to work on their second tree. Their axes chewed through the soft wood, and quickly a shout went up again as the second of their three trees fell crashing to the ground. The men were sweating heavily and extremely parched, but determined to win the contest. They ran to their third and final tree.

'Easy money,' Bilhild chuckled.

Vaughn began singing a war song, quickly taken up by the others from his team. Durston and Dafydd sang with their deep baritone voices and all three of the sub teams picked up their pace. Then in a quick succession one, two and three of their trees came down. It was their turn to cheer now, but their cheers didn't last long as Telor's third tree hit the ground.

Vaughn paced out the length of one of the trees to calculate the mid-point while Telor did the same. Vaughn called over to Durston and Dafydd 'measure and mark the other two.'

Both dashed up the other two horizontal trunks, and made marks at the mid-point. Telor didn't see this and measured then marked all three trunks himself. Vaughn had gained a slight advantage, as he marked the first tree his team started cutting at its centre with the other two sub groups quickly following.

Telor had measured his three then his men began chopping.

'It's going to be close, you watch Vaughn's team and I'll watch Telor. Raise an arm when they have finished,' Arenwen said.

'Agreed,' Bilhild replied.

The two groups chopped furiously, but it was too close to call.

Both teams were working as fast as they could, gasping for air as their muscles burnt as they craved more oxygen. Arenwen glanced back and forth between the two groups and was then interrupted by a shout.

'Stop, we have a winner,' Bilhild called.

Vaughn's team had won, but there was only less than a few seconds between them. Arenwen could see that two of Telor's trunks had been cut and the third was a few strokes from completion.

Vaughn dropped his axe and ran over to his brother, grabbing him in a headlock and rubbing a hand full of grass in his face.

'Extra ale to the winners,' Arenwen called.

Then he went over to Bilhild, slapped him on the back and added 'and a gold coin for me I believe.'

The warrior let the men gulp down some water and regain their breath before getting them to finish off the task. The six trees were now twelve lengths of long logs. They were lashed together in to two groups of six, wide enough to create a platform for the chariots. The lengths were dragged onto the boats that had been bound together. This made two secure floating platforms that could each carry a chariot, a horse and a few men.

The guides led their horses on to the rafts first. Then the chariot horses were unhitched from their harnesses and led on next. Finally the chariots were dragged on. Telor and Vaughn pulled Bilhild's chariot on while Durston and Dafydd helped heave Arenwen's chariot on to the floating platform. The remaining men got into the other two boats.

Idocus secured his cart horse to a log next to the riverbank and spoke to the young girl. She unhooked some pots from the horse, and sat down on some furs she had thrown down. Idocus then jumped on to Arenwen's raft to guide the small flotilla across the raging river. He picked up one of the long poles, that he had brought, and pushed the craft away from the riverbank. He called over to the others to follow him and shouted 'do what I do, when you see me push, you push, when you see me lift my pole, you do the same. Do you all understand?' Idocus said.

They moved away from the tranquil river bank and into the torrent of swirling water. Idocus skilfully guided the raft across the river, taking care to avoid the swirling whirlpools, using the eddies which were formed by the huge rocks strewn across the river bed. The other raft and two boats followed in close proximity to the first.

Suddenly Idocus' raft hit the fast flowing water while leaving an eddy. It pitched up and down in quick succession. One of the guide's horses became agitated at the sudden movement and strained in its reins. The mount started moving its hind legs from side to side, the guide struggled to secure the powerful beast.

'Grab his bridle,' the guide called to Durston.

Durston looked uneasy, Dafydd could see something was wrong, was he scared of horses? The scout called again and Durston edged his way to the spooked animal and gripped the bridle with both hands. He used all his weight to pull the horse's head down in an attempt to prevent it from moving any further. The craft pitched again, the horse reared making the guide lose his grip on the reins. Durston was pulled up into the air with his hand twisted in the bridle straps. Another dip and the horse panicked, it jumped off the raft taking Durston with him.

'Let them go, they'll just be washed down stream. He'll have a horse and will be able to catch us up in a day or two,' Idocus called over the din of the raging river.

Dafydd looked on in horror as the horse trashed in the raging water with Durston's hand trapped in a loop of the bridle. The stallion twisted over itself, and went down beneath the water which dragged Durston with him. They were gone under for quite some time and then to the relief of them all surfaced again. Durston was screaming something, but it was difficult to hear over the crashing water.

'What is he saying?' Dafydd asked the men around him.

'Can't something,' Arenwen replied.

Durston and the horse went under again as Dafydd ran different combinations of words through his mind and then it clicked. The missing word was swim, he can't swim.

'The stupid sod can't swim,' Dafydd said as he dropped his weapons, pulled off his cloak and boots. Wearing nothing more than his trousers he dove in to the raging river.

Dafydd was a strong swimmer, and he was going with the current so it took little effort. The contrast was between the two men was striking. Dafydd was confidently gliding through the water while Durston was flailing his one arm trying to get a grip on the bridle that trapped his other hand. Slowly but surely Arenwen could see that Dafydd was getting closer and closer. The remaining men shouted encouragement to Dafydd as he got closer and closer to Durston, he was almost in reach of his target. Durston raised a smile when he saw his friend approaching, but this disappeared quickly as the horse plunged them both back under the water.

Dafydd grabbed the horse by the mane and pulled himself closer to his friend. That was the last that Arenwen saw of them as they were swept around a bend in the river and out of sight.

Idocus had not been distracted by the goings on of his passengers. He methodically guided his raft across the river shouting instructions to the others that followed closely behind. They reached the far bank without any further incident. The horses were led off the rafts and then the chariots were off loaded. Bilhild came over to Arenwen and said

'Do you think they will be alright?'

'Knowing those two, yes. I expect them to meet up with us in a few days, and no doubt will have concocted some tale to tell around the camp fire' Arenwen replied.

The warrior went to his chariot and undid the leather straps of the money chest. He called Idocus over and gave him half of the agreed payment.

'Wait here until the large army comes. It will be about two days behind us. Use your skills to guide them over to this side of the river, then you will receive the rest of the payment,' Arenwen said.

'But these two rafts won't be enough for such large numbers, Lord,' Idocus pointed out.

'Don't worry about that I have a plan. Just wait here,' Arenwen instructed the trader.

'As you command, Lord,' Idocus replied.

Arenwen gathered the remaining party together, leading them off behind one of the guides. The rider who had lost his horse joined the men walking behind the chariots. Arenwen turned around to the guide and asked 'how long until we reach the town?'

'A few hours at an easy pace, Lord,' he replied.

Arenwen weighed up the options. The party hadn't eaten for a while but the promise of hot food, a warm bed and Celtic hospitality outweighed the rumbling coming from his stomach.

Although the path ahead of them was starting to rise it wasn't yet a steep incline. However, Arenwen saw the massive snow-capped mountains towering before him, and knew they would be going up soon. Would these monstrous mountains be the ones they had to cross to reach their destination?

The road in front of them soon started to get steeper and steeper. Arenwen could feel the horses straining to pull the chariots that weighed them down. He knew some men who would use a whip to drive their horses on but this wasn't Arenwen's way, he would encourage them with small clicks from his mouth and at most shake the reigns.

They climbed further into the mountains, passing great lakes with small settlements surrounded by crystal clear blue waters. The air was getting thinner and the temperature had dropped. Arenwen was a little light headed, and rubbed his eyes to check what he was seeing. He thought he saw a town floating above a lake. It was their destination, it was Aventicum.

As the party got closer to the town Arenwen could see that the houses weren't floating above the lake, but were actually suspended on stilts. A small band of riders approached, and pulled up next to Arenwen's chariot.

'My Lord Felix offers you his welcome and invites you to join him in his house to dine.'

The messengers wheeled around and split in to two groups which formed a well-drilled escort flanking the small party on both sides. The town was getting nearer, this was unlike any other Celtic town Arenwen had seen before. There were several clusters of buildings around the edge of the lake which were framed with the obligatory wooden fence. The dwellings were rectangular rather than the traditional round houses, but the biggest difference was that two of these clusters had long wooden walkways which led to a stilted platform in the middle of the lake. The platform had four houses on it, much larger than the ones around the lake.

The party pulled up at the edge of the water, with the men being directed to an area where they could spend the night. The chariots were unhitched from the horses and Arenwen, Bilhild and Bakher were led to the wooden walkway.

'Just one moment,' Arenwen said to their escort.

'Telor and Vaughn, bring my chest from my chariot,' Arenwen called to the twins.

They were led over the wooden walkway. It was well constructed, wide enough for two people to cross shoulder to shoulder, and elevated fifteen feet off the ground. Arenwen could see that it had been manufactured in sections that were bound together which gave the impression that it was one complete walkway.

As they crossed, the warrior also noticed that the houses were a different style to the roundhouses he knew. The roof was much bigger than his traditional round house, and had an inverted 'v' shaped roof coming down to about four feet off the floor on both sides of the building. The front and back had walls made from horizontal logs, and had a wooden door in the centre.

They were led in to the largest town house and introduced to Felix, their new host and leader of the Helvetii tribe. The Helvetii tribe comprised of four pagi or subgroups. Each pagi had its own chieftain, but they all recognised Felix as their principal nobleman. The tribes occupied the territories from the lowlands of the Alps right up to the great plateau they were on now. Unlike other Celtic tribes, the Helvetii lived in large towns which were heavily fortified. Felix was a tall, thin man, although not quite as tall as Arenwen. He had long black hair, a well-kept moustache and wore a two-horned helmet trimmed with gold. He was dressed very well, with his thin frame wrapped in furs to keep the cold of the mountains at bay. Arenwen made his introductions and indicated that Telor and Vaughn should put the chest on the floor.

'That will be all for now. Return to the others and get some hot food,' Arenwen said to the twins.

Felix had some stools brought up for his guests.

'Please sit and tell me about your journey,' their host said.

Turning to a slave he added 'bring our guests food and drink.'

The four men sat down on the stools. I will need many of your men to leave at first light to chop down a large number of trees. These trees will form rafts that our army will use to cross the river the following day. Arenwen got up and walked over to the chest. He undid the leather straps, removed the pin from the clasp and flipped open the lid.

'I am honoured by the wealth your chieftain Brennus offers me but I have no need for gold. Look around I have as much gold as I need, my rivers run with two things, water and gold,' Felix laughed softly.

'I can indeed see that you are a very wealthy chieftain,' Arenwen said.

'Let us eat and drink and see if there is another form of payment you can tempt me with,' Felix offered.

Arenwen returned to his stool as food and ale was brought in. He was racking his mind as to what could tempt his host to help them in their quest. Without Felix's men to cut down the trees on this side of the river there would be no fleet of rafts to transport the army. It could take weeks for them to find a suitable land crossing. The army was well stocked from their stop at the Lingones capital but adding extra weeks to their march would put a great strain on their resources. The conundrum weighed heavily on Arenwen's mind as he had given his word to Brennus, because as it stood he thought that he had failed his cousin. He had to think of a way to get Felix to support Brennus or their mission could fail.

Chapter 11

The Etruscan Ambassador

Marcus awoke the next morning, his bedding soaking wet and his hair stuck to his head from sweat. The teenager had tossed and turned all night, dipping in and out of sleep as his mind replayed the events of the day before.

He made his way downstairs to ease the deep aching feeling in the pit of his stomach. The young lad had gone straight to bed the previous night without eating. He craved food, any food, to fill his empty belly.

As he got half way down the stairs he heard Aesop arguing with a man in the entrance hall. Marcus went down the rest of the way and went over to the house slave.

'What is it, Aesop?' He asked.

'This man wants to have an audience with your father,' he replied.

Marcus looked the man up and down. He was dressed well, but from his attire he could see he was not from Rome.

'Who are you and what business do you have with my father?' The teenager asked the man.

'He doesn't have an appointment,' Aesop chipped in.

'Has my father risen yet?'

'No and I have told this visitor that my Master is not available.'

The man had his hair greased back into a ponytail at the top of his head. He had a thin black beard, but no moustache. He was quite a scrawny man who rubbed his hands together, and hunched his shoulders forward as if he had spent many years bent over a writing desk. The bottom of his clothing was splattered with mud, which would suggest he had travelled a long distance.

Marcus was the son of a very prominent Roman who had just been promoted to the Senate. The lad had also spent time in the capital so his confidence, despite yesterday's ordeal, had grown sufficiently enough to question the man as to the reason for his visit.

'As our overseer has informed you, my father has not yet risen,' he told the man.

'Who are you, and what business do you have here?' the lad added.

'My name is Camar and I am a camthi or as you say 'an ambassador,' the man replied. His Latin was perfect, but he clipped some of the words when he pronounced them, giving away that it wasn't his first language.

'And what business do you have here, you have no appointment?' Marcus asked.

'You are quite correct, I don't have an appointment, but we have heard of the great service your Father is providing to the magnificent city of Rome. I have been sent as an ambassador from the Etruscan League of twelve cities. I have travelled from the city of Clusium to pay tribute to Senator Quintus Fabius Ambustus,' Camar said.

'Aesop, show our guest to the dining room, and arrange for food and wine to be served while he waits for my father to rise. Then return to me,' Marcus instructed.

Aesop held out his arm and gestured Camar in the direction of the dining room. The slave would make suitable arrangements for the ambassador to have refreshments, but Marcus needed him for another purpose.

He returned from the dining area having ensured the uninvited guest was well tended to.

'How else may I be of service young Master? Aesop enquired.

'What do you know of the Etruscan League of twelve cities?' Marcus asked.

'It is probably easier to show you (Map 1) than tell you. If I may take your leave for a short while I know of a map that will explain,' Aesop replied.

The teenager agreed to Aesop's request, and he went scurrying off to Quintus' office. He quickly returned with a parchment tucked under his arm. Aesop rolled out the skin and placed a weight in each corner to keep it flat on the table. He explained that several hundred years ago the Etruscan empire had been large and powerful, even controlling Rome. The balance of power had tipped about a hundred and fifty years earlier, and after many years of war the Etruscans relinquished their claims on Rome. Both sides had agreed that the river Tiber would be the border between their two lands. Now after a hundred and fifty years of peace between the two peoples they had both settled in to a mutually beneficial pact as allies.

Aesop pointed out the area that the Latin League controlled with its capital being Rome. Then he moved his finger on the map that showed the lands to the north that the Etruscan League controlled and its capital Clusium.

This made things much clearer Marcus' mind. The Etruscan's were a barrier between the Latin alliance and any faction who would attack from the north. Equally Rome and its allies were a buffer to any attack on the Etruscans from the south. Both sides offered each other mutual protection, and it was logical to have a peace treaty between the two nations. There was always a threat from the mountains to the east, but both nations were stronger together.

The slave began to roll up the map as they heard a voice from upstairs that they both knew well.

'Wine! Aesop where are you and where is my wine?'

Quintus had risen from his slumbers, and his first thought was always of wine.

The newly appointed senator had left his son following the gladiatorial games he had paid for, and headed for a second visit of the day to his kept prostitute. He had been drinking until the early hours of the morning, but couldn't remember getting home.

However, that wasn't unusual as he regularly had memory gaps from the night before.

Aesop rushed upstairs to attend to his master's needs. Marcus heard his father grumbling about something, but couldn't quite make it out. After a little while Quintus came downstairs with Aesop following several steps behind him.

'We have an unexpected visitor,' Aesop said to Quintus.

'Show them away, I am in no mood for visitors.'

'As you wish Master, but this is an ambassador from the Etruscan League who has a tribute for you,' Aesop expanded on his first statement.

'Why did you not say that sooner? Where is he?' Quintus demanded.

'It was remiss of me not to mention it, Master. He is in the dining area on the off chance that you would grant him an audience,' the slave said with a bow.

'I will go to my office. Bring me wine,' Quintus snapped.

Aesop went to fetch wine and goblets, then returned to Quintus in his office. The senator took a cup, and held it out for Aesop to pour. The pounding in Quintus' head didn't subside as he drank the first goblet, and held the drained vessel out again for it to be refilled. Aesop knew that he should stay there until his master instructed him otherwise. Quintus slowly was able to focus on objects around him, the waves of nausea passing with the third goblet of wine.

'Bring him in,' Quintus instructed the slave.

Aesop headed for the dining area to fetch Camar, who was ushered into the office where he found Quintus sipping from a goblet of wine.

'My most beneficent host. My name is Camar, and I offer greetings and salutations from the Etruscan League of cities,' the ambassador said with a low bow.

'Yes, yes, let's skip the formalities. What matter of urgent business do you have coming to the house of a Senator unannounced?' Quintus demanded.

'May I offer you my deepest apologies for not arranging a formal appointment, but matters seem to have come to fruition so quickly,' Camar apologised.

'Firstly may I offer you a gift from the Etruscan League in tribute to your recent promotion to the Senate? A much long overdue promotion, if I may say so,' Camar said.

He clapped his hands and two of his slaves brought in the gift. Camar presented the offering to Quintus, it was an Etruscan urn. Terracotta in colour with two large handles. Each arm was partially formed so that a ladle fitted inside them perfectly, and became the top part of the arm. The urn was the size of a man's torso with the limbs curving down by the side to look like a large bust of a man. It was topped off with a life size head cast in bronze.

Camar clapped his hands again, his slaves carefully removed the bronze lid and immediately Quintus smelt the sweet aroma of Etruscan wine, the finest that money could buy. Camar had obviously done his homework as to what would please

Quintus. Even with Quintus' thirst this would last months before they would see the bottom of the urn.

'May I?' Camar asked as he took the empty goblet from Quintus.

The senator released his grip on the goblet as the Etruscan ambassador used one of the arm ladles to scoop wine from the urn and into the cup. Camar handed Quintus the drink with a smile that exposed his yellow teeth. Quintus took the cup, and in his customary fashion drank the whole goblet in one.

'That wasn't bad,' Quintus said casually.

'This is the first of many,' Camar said.

'You have presented your gift, now what else do you want?' Quintus asked. Camar described how the news of the new type of metal had come to his capital. He also described how the Etruscans thought it was a magnificent gesture to equip all of the Roman army with this new weapon, and that it was to be financed by Quintus.

'You use a thousand words when you could use one, get to your point,' Quintus said impatiently.

'Your most regal senator, you are both wise and talented. Indeed I will truncate my conveyance to not waste any of your precious time. We have thought that all those swords will each need a scabbard,' Camar said.

'Of course they will, and the craftsmen of Rome will make them,' Quintus replied tersely.

'That is my secondary mission after passing on our congratulations. I am here to offer the best price on the manufacture of these items. You tell me how much the lowest Roman price is and I have the authority to better it,' Camar said.

Quintus thought this offer was somewhat suspicious, but he played along. He suspected that the Etruscans were concerned that this new weapon would tip the balance of power in their alliance, giving Rome the advantage on the battlefield. Quintus knew how much he had been quoted for the scabbards, and saw this as an opportunity to test the ambassador's true intention. Quintus halved the lowest price he had been given by the Roman craftsmen. Camar didn't even batter an eyelid when Quintus proposed the ridiculously low amount.

'That is a fair price. On my return to my capital I shall instruct them to be manufactured and dispatched. Shall we say five hundred units per week to be delivered to your villa?' Camar suggested.

'To be delivered to the armoury in Rome if you please,' Quintus replied, not giving away his suspicion.

Camar ladled Quintus another goblet of his fine wine, and thought that Quintus was a drunken fool. He thought that he was about to catch him in his elaborate web. Quintus may well have been a drunkard, but he was no fool.

'That is a most generous offer from our Etruscan friends,' Quintus said.

'It would be our pleasure to help our long established allies. I understand that the swords are being manufactured at your villa,' Camar said leaning his head to one side.

'That's correct but why do you ask?' Quintus asked, still playing the game.

Not too quickly now, tease it out,' Camar thought. He looked at Quintus as he drank another wine and said 'I travel very closely to your villa as I return to my capital. I will, with your permission, take one of the new swords to ensure the scabbards are to the correct dimensions.'

And there it was, just as Quintus had guessed, they wanted a sword. They would either take it to test against their swords, or even try to reverse engineer the entire process. No doubt Camar would have a good look around his villa and to the pits where the new metal was being smelted.

'Yes, a sword to ensure the correct dimensions is a great idea,' Quintus agreed immediately. Camar tried his best to hide the pleasure in what he had just heard. That had been his mission all along; to acquire one of the weapons made from the new material his spies had told him about.

'You are most wise,' Camar flattered his host.

'But there is no need to go to my villa. I have what you want right here,' Quintus said.

Camar's primary objective was to get a sword. He had been instructed that, if he had the opportunity, he was also to find how they were made but the main priority was to get a sword.

'There is one here? That is very fortunate for me senator, but it is no hardship to head home via your villa,' Camar said.

'No don't put yourself out, not even by an hour,' Quintus replied.

Camar knew better than to push to visit the villa, and was pleased that he would get one of the new swords.

Marcus heard his father call him.

'Boy!' he yelled.

His son ran to his father's office to see what he had in store for him now. He wondered if his education was to include a visit to twelve cities of the Etruscan League, or maybe just to their capitol Clusium?

'How may I be of service, father?' the lad asked.

'I want you to go and fetch your sword,' his father replied.

'My sword father?' Marcus asked, not sure what he meant.

'Yes boy, your sword. The one you use with your slave,' he replied staring intently at his heir.

The lad did as he was told and left the office in search of Lucius. Marcus found him in the kitchen having his midday meal.

'I need one of our gladii.'

Lucius put down his bowl, and went to his shared quarters to fetch the training swords. He returned and handed both of them to his young master.

'Just one is fine thank you,' he said to Lucius.

The lad took one of the swords and returned to his father's office. He handed it to him and Quintus held it in the air. Looking down the blade checking it was straight and true. Satisfied that the weapon was good he flipped it catching it by the wooden blade. He offered the sword to Camar.

'But this is a practice sword Senator,' Camar said in surprise.

'Indeed it is, and it is the exact specification you need,' Quintus smiled.

'Now if you excuse me, I have other matters to attend to. Aesop, show the illustrious ambassador the way out,' the senator said triumphantly.

Camar bowed and knew that any protest would be futile. He had underestimated Quintus, which had been an elementary mistake to make. He had been outwitted and out played.

'What was that all about father?' Marcus asked.

'Just another lesson for you to learn, boy,' he replied.

'I don't understand what I was to have learnt.'

'The lesson is boy, that an ambassador has two other names that they never go by,' Quintus said.

'And what are those other names, father?' His son asked inquisitively.

'Spy and assassin,' he smiled as he replied.

Chapter 12

Sink or Swim

Dafydd gripped the horse's mane and pulled himself closer to his friend. He held onto the hair tightly with his right hand as he worked on his friend's trapped hand. Durston was still conscious, but had swallowed a lot of water.

'When I push this part of the bridle up, you pull you hand free,' Dafydd shouted in Durston's ear as the sound of the crashing water made it difficult to hear. Durston nodded, and grabbed the bridle with his free hand.

'Now,' Dafydd said as he pushed the leather up, loosening the loop that had trapped Durston's hand. His friend had been in too much of a panic to realise this was the best action. The more he had pulled at the headgear, trying to release its grip, the tighter the loop got.

The first part of the rescue had been completed. Durston now had both hands free and was hanging on to the bridle. His body mass was on one side of the horse's head, and was panicking the gelding, as the additional weight pulled its head deeper in to the water. They were being swept further down river. Dafydd glanced back, but they had been pushed around a bend so the rest of the advance party were out of sight.

'Grab my neck, slide down my body, and then grab on to the horse's tail,' Dafydd said to Durston.

There was a flash of panic in Durston's eyes at the realisation of what his friend had just told him to do.

'It will be all right, just do as I say,' Dafydd reassured his friend as the water surged all around them.

Durston took a deep breath and did as his friend had instructed him. He let go with one hand and transferred it to Dafydd's neck. Durston released his other hand from the bridle, and clamped it vice like on Dafydd's shoulder.

'That's fine. Now just use the force of the water to help you slide down me,' Dafydd said.

Durston let go of his friend's shoulder and slowly slid down his body. He first slid to his comrade's waist, then down to his legs and finally to his ankles. The speed of the water meant that the two of them were being pushed horizontally to the horse. The gelding calmed as the unwanted weight had been removed from its head, and it was able to concentrate on swimming. One last manoeuvre would have Durston in the position his friend had told him to get to. Durston reached out for the horse's tail with his right hand. His extended arm was pushed way from the tail by the huge pressure from the river, and Durston quickly re-attached himself to Dafydd. He tried again, this time allowing for the force of the water to influence his reach. Aiming further to the left than he had previously he extended his arm once more. This time he was rewarded with a firm clump of horse tail. He was now suspended between Dafydd's ankle and the horse's rear. He released his grip on Dafydd and was spun in the water as the raging river tossed him around like a rag doll. He had done a full twist under water, and had felt his short throwing axe slip from underneath his cloak. The warrior blindly grabbed in the location of his other hand, and was relived to feel the touch of the coarse horse hair. The warrior pulled himself further up the horse's tail until his head was clear of the water.

Dafydd looked back and was pleased to see his friend was securely attached to the horse, he didn't fancy having to try and rescue his flailing friend without the aid and the buoyancy of the horse. Dafydd moved from the horse's neck, and took a hold on the bridle. Moving an arm underneath the horse's head he now had one hand on each side of the headgear. Dafydd slipped his legs under the gelding's neck, and felt the power of the river pushing him into the horse.

Dafydd simultaneously pulled the horse's head to the left while kicking his legs. The horse responded by edging left, closer to the bank. He repeated the actions, each time guiding the horse and its baggage closer to the bank until they were in the relatively calm area of the river bank.

Dafydd smiled at Durston 'OK, you can let go now,' Dafydd said.

'But I can't swim,' Durston replied.

'I know that, but I do know you can stand,' Dafydd said as he stood up to reveal that the water was now only waist deep.

'You arse,' Durston said.

'That I may be, but I'm the arse who just saved your life,' Dafydd replied with a grin.

Durston waded out of the river and collapsed on the riverbank while Dafydd led the horse out of the water and walked it around until it got steady on its feet. He secured the steed to a nearby bush and returned to his friend. He slumped down exhausted and burst out laughing.

Durston raised his head and asked 'and what is so funny?'

'The look on your face when the horse took you under,' Dafydd laughed. Durston burst out laughing.

'Yes it must have been an amusing sight. I never had the need to learn to swim, but after this experience I'll be learning soon enough!'

The friends gathered their breath for a few moments before moving. Durston was soaked through, and hung his cloak on the bush next to the horse. Both men's woollen trousers hung heavily on them as they had absorbed water from the raging river.

'We need to take stock of what provisions we have,' Dafydd said.

'You mean what I've got as you have nothing but a pair of trousers,' Durston said slapping his friend on the back. The inventory didn't take long:

Durston was fully clothed with Dafydd just in his trousers.

Weapons; one sword.

Food; none.

Drinking water; plenty from of the river and of course, one horse.

'So what's the plan?' Durston asked Dafydd.

'Well as I see it we have two options. We follow the river north, find the point at which the others landed and pick up their tracks. If we do that we will always be behind them, and it may take a day or so to catch up.

'And the other option?' Durston asked.

'We travel north east and we should be with them much quicker, but we don't really know where we are.' Dafydd said.

'Hmmm, a safe and boring option or one with a risk and opportunities,' Durston said.

'We are agreed then, we go inland. Food, clothing and catching up with the others are our priorities,' Dafydd said.

The pair set off in a rough north easterly direction, hoping to come across the trail of the other party. The hoof prints would help identify the unit, but the tracks of the two chariots would easily reveal that they had come across the right group.

They had both been riding the horse at the same time, and had been travelling for a few hours when they came across a wood. As they started going deeper in it was clear that it was impossible to remain mounted. They both slid off the horse and led it through the dense undergrowth.

'What shall we do with him,' Durston asked.

'It's just going to slow us down in this thick wood,' Dafydd said.

'Set it free?' Durston suggested.

'It will be a lucky find for someone,' Dafydd replied.

So with a firm slap on its rump it was sent back in the direction that they had come from. The friends were glad of the shade from the sun as Dafydd had no protection from its warm rays. The leafy trees made sighting the sun much harder, with only a few occasional breaks in the dense canopy. Dafydd noticed Durston glancing up in an attempt to keep them going in the right direction.

'What are you doing?' Dafydd asked.

'Tracking the sun so we don't get lost,' Durston replied.

'Can't swim and can't navigate in a forest. Were you taught nothing as a boy?' His friend teased, remembering how Bakher had taught him such crafts as he was growing up.

'See the moss on the tree,' Dafydd said.

'Yes, I see it,' Durston replied.

'Moss grows on the north side of the tree, as the fairies always plant their seeds on the side that is damper and gets less sun,' Dafydd explained.

'So if the moss side is north, we keep a little to the left of that and that will be north east,' Durston said.

'Exactly, with no need to keep glancing up at the trees and tripping over roots,' Dafydd said.

He could see that Durston was very pleased with himself, and let him lead the way with his newly acquired skill. They continued through the dense undergrowth until they climbed a slight rise. As they reached the ridge of the small incline, they looked down and saw it was one side of a wide track that went in a west to east direction.

'Do you think we should follow the path?' Durston asked.

'It doesn't go in the exact direction we want, but I say we follow it. It will be much easier going than through the forest and if it doesn't turn more after a while, then we'll head back into the trees,' Dafydd replied.

Durston nodded his approval, and the two set off along the track. The going was certainly easier than the rough undergrowth of the forest, and also much easier going for Dafydd who was barefoot. The pair strolled along and chatted about the river incident. The woods on either side became less dense, and Dafydd wondered if they were coming to the end of the wooded area. The path had started going in a more northerly direction. They were hoping that it might intersect with other tracks where they might see the tell-tale signs of chariot wheels.

A horn blew and the pair looked at each other. Instinctively they climbed up the small bank on the side of the road, and lay flat on the ground. They peeked over the edge of the bank and down to the trail. They heard sounds of rapid hooves and barking approaching from the west end of the path. Then they saw a magnificent stag hurtle past them as it shot down the clearing, pursued by two huge staghounds. The beast and dogs were followed quickly by three riders. The lead rider couldn't have been much more than eleven years old, but he was riding his horse with a rare confidence, and whooping as he pursued the stag. The boy was spurring his horse on, and holding a spear in his right hand. The young lad didn't have the spear in a throwing position yet, as there were low hanging branches that might impede the spear's flight. It was unusual to see a young boy ride such a powerful horse, but from the brief glance of his attire he was certainly part of a wealthy family.

There were two others following closely behind him, but they were clearly struggling to keep up through the path's twists and turns. Dafydd watched them as they galloped past, and could just see that there was indeed an opening up ahead as the stag burst through, followed closely by the three riders.

Durston nudged Dafydd in the ribs.

'Let's go watch the sport.'

Dafydd grinned and the two of them got up, slid down the bank, and sprinted towards the forest's exit. They ran along the trail, pausing at the edge of the trees as the hunter's path led out on to a large open green field.

They could see the hunt, the stag was clearly tiring as its tongue was hanging from the side of its mouth, with great clouds of steam as it exhaled. The dogs were closer now as the animal darted left and right in an attempt to shake them off. The boy was up in his saddle with his arm cocked and ready to release the spear. Dafydd and Durston heard the boy call the dogs back with a high pitched whistle. They responded immediately, stopping dead in their tracks.

The young lad tore past the static hounds, closely followed by the two riders. The stag had turned and was heading back towards the entrance to the woods, but it was slowing rapidly. The magnificent beast thought it was safe as the dogs we no longer snapping at its heels. The boy launched the spear, it flew through the air, taking the stag through the neck. It stumbled but continued to run only for it trip again, blood pumping from it with every heartbeat. Its front legs folded while the rear legs thrashed one last kick of defiance before it flopped onto its side.

The boy reined in his mount, bringing it to a stop. Putting his hands on the horse's neck he vaulted off, landing next to the felled stag. The two accompanying riders dismounted next to the boy. The lad pulled out a knife to slit the stag's throat to ensure it did not suffer any more. He then went about gutting the animal, tearing open the chest cavity, ripping the beast open with a sawing action. As the innards and guts spilled out on to the grass he called the dogs with another whistle.

The hounds came bounding over to the dead stag, where they knew they would receive their reward. The dogs stood waist high to the boy, and were strong powerful beasts bred for stamina. Quick kills didn't happen on a hunt so dogs just bred for speed would quickly fall behind, but these well-bred staghounds could run and run for hours. The young boy spilled more innards onto the grass, now red with blood, clicked his fingers then pointed to the guts. The hounds responded, and moved in greedily eating their prize as their grey muzzles turned crimson red from the stag's blood.

A branch snapped to the right of Dafydd, both men looked automatically in the direction of the noise. They scanned the area looking for signs of movement, but could not see anything. Then Durston saw a flicker of a shape to their right, and as he focused he spotted three others. He tapped his friend on the shoulder, pointing to where he had seen the men. Dafydd followed his guide until he too saw the four men.

An arrow flew for the wood which struck one of the two escorts in the shoulder. The man dropped to his knees as the other bodyguard grabbed his shield slung on the side of his horse, drawing his sword as he did so. Another arrow loosed, but fell short of its target and landed in the ground a few feet in front of the boy.

The man with the arrow in his shoulder got back to his feet just as a second arrow took him through his right eye. The four assailants burst from the trees with a fearsome war cry clearly intent on plundering any loot they could get. Dafydd turned to Durston and said 'shall we?'

Dafydd smiled and replied 'it would be rude not to.'

They too burst from the cover of the woodland, but without making a sound. The boy and the remaining guard thought they were part of the raiding party until they saw that Dafydd and Durston had caught up with the slowest of the four. Dafydd dived at his legs wrapping his arms tightly around him so he fell to the floor in a heap. Durston quickly followed up by ramming his sword into the back of his neck.

Dafydd picked up the assailant's shield and an axe. He pursued the other three men who were oblivious to that fact their comrade had been killed. Now fully armed, Dafydd and Durston roared threats of a violent, painful and most ignominious death to the remaining three. They were caught in two minds to fight or run, but they didn't choose wisely. As they turned to face the two friends the remaining escort launched an attack on the three men with Durston and Dafydd joining in the affray.

Dafydd struggled to riposte his opponent's attack as the short axe he had was primarily a throwing weapon, or to be used in confined spaces where a long sword would be a hindrance. He used his shield as an extra weapon battering his opponent repeatedly, so he wouldn't know if he was going to be smashed with the shield or have to defend against the axe.

Durston was having more of a success with his opponent as he was a good head taller and far more muscular than the short, stout, fur clad attacker. He flicked his sword and slashed at will, the other man was only able to put up a weak defence. Finally after a gash across his sword arm, the attacker turned and ran. Durston was about to make chase, saw his friend was in a good position, but having to do a lot of work because of his short weapon.

Durston attacked Dafydd's opponent from the side, instantly running him through. Dafydd glanced left and saw that the remaining escort had been bested by his attacker and was drawing his sword out of the dead man intent on attacking the boy. The assailant lunged at the young lad who stepped deftly out of the way of the clumsy assault. The boy's dogs were snarling and baring their teeth to the raider who lunged once more, but then fell forward landing face down into the grass with an axe firmly planted in the back of his skull. Sticky, crimson blood oozed from the back of his head onto the previously coloured green grass. As Durston had Dafydd's opponent skewered on his sword, Dafydd had turned his attention to the remaining attacker and launched his axe with deadly accuracy. He strode over to the man with the hatchet in the back of the head and rolled the body on to its side, the axe preventing the body turning completely over.

'Friends of yours?' Dafydd asked the boy.

'Certainly not,' the lad said missing the sarcasm.

'By their looks and clothing I'd say they were tribesmen from the mountains. They don't normally come down this low,' he continued.

Durston joined the two others and said 'what's your name, boy and what village are you from?'

'I am called Tir and I am from a town not far from here,' the boy replied.

'Can you take us there so we can get provisions?' Dafydd asked.

'It is sad we lost two men, but when my father hears that you have saved my life you will be greatly rewarded with provisions and much more,' Tir said.

Durston and Dafydd stripped the attackers of anything useful, Dafydd taking one of the furs to cover his body as well as a pair of boots. The two escorts were put on the rear of their horses, with space enough for Dafydd and Durston to ride their mounts.

'What shall we do with the stag?' Tir asked.

'It would offend the fairies if we did not take it. Slide back and we will put the animal over the centre of your horse so it can carry the weight easier,' Dafydd said.

So with the stag and the dead bodies suitably positioned, Durston and Dafydd mounted the other horses and followed Tir and his dogs to his town. They accompanied the young lad through the fields, ever climbing upwards. Several hours had gone by with the party picking their way through rocky paths and Dafydd was glad of the fur and boots he had taken from one of the attackers, as the temperature was dropping rapidly,

'I thought your town wasn't far away,' Dafydd called to Tir.

'It's not, just to the top of the ridge and then we will nearly be there,' he replied.

The group urged their horses up the steep slope, and came to the top of the ridge. Tir waited for Dafydd and Durston to pull up beside him and look down on to the town below.

'I told you it wasn't far. Here's my town,' Tir said.

The dogs were getting excited by being so close to home and ran ahead of Tir, then waited for him to catch up to them. The small group edged their horses down the slight incline towards the town that had opened up in front of them.

Tir led them to a cluster of buildings where there was a stable housing many other horses. The young lad dismounted and Dafydd noticed how the men were respectful to the boy. They obeyed his instructions without question which confirmed his previous thoughts about his status. The dead escorts were lowered from the horses along with the stag. Tir addressed the men at the stables 'I must speak to my father immediately.'

'Follow me,' Tir said to Dafydd and Durston.

The young boy started out across a wooden platform, Dafydd and Durston falling in behind him. They could see that the raised platform led to a cluster of larger buildings, the young boy was obviously in a hurry to speak to his father as he went at a very fast pace.

Tir approached the largest of the houses and opened the wooden door. His father was there with three men that he did not recognise. The four men were sat on stools chatting, eating and drinking with a large chest of gold open next to his father. Dafydd and Durston followed in behind Tir and they saw three men that they did recognise.

'Sorry to interrupt father, but I have urgent news for you,' Tir said.

'Go on, my son,' his father replied.

'I was attacked in the low meadows. I'm afraid we lost two men,' Tir told his father.

'Attacked by who?' His father demanded.

'By their clothing and weapons, I would say mountain people,' Tir said.

'What!' His father exploded.

'I have left them alone for far too long and they see that as a sign of weakness, but this time they have gone too far. I will hunt them out of their mountain caves and kill every last one of them,' his father said angrily.

'We were attacked while we were hunting father, but these two men came to my aid and without doubt saved my life,' Tir said pointing to Dafydd and Durston.

'Then they shall be suitably honoured. Name your reward and you shall have it,' Tir's father said forgetting his other guests for a moment.

'Ahhh, but where are my manners? We should make proper introductions. Arenwen, Bilhild and Bakher, this is my son Tir,' his father continued.

'And Dafydd and Durston, this is my father Felix,' Tir responded.

Arenwen looked over to his two men who were both beaming grins towards their leader. They knew that they had done well as they had saved the life of the chieftain's son. They both went down on one knee and said 'it is good to see you, Lord.'

'You know these men?' Felix asked.

'Indeed Lord, they are my warriors - two of the sorriest creatures you will ever know, but they are loyal to the death,' Arenwen said as he winked at his men.

'Then we have already completed our transaction, full payment has been made. My son's life is a fair exchange for safe passage and hospitality through my lands,' Felix said.

Arenwen bowed

'You are most gracious, Lord. I will make sure my Lord Brennus hears of your unrivalled generosity.'

'As for you two rogues, you can take a handful of gold from the chest over there, and head back across the footbridge to join the rest of the men,' Arenwen said to Dafydd and Durston.

The two men looked at each other and couldn't believe their luck. They knew that they would be entitled to a share of any new plunder, but a handful from this chest would be more than they would have hoped for during the whole campaign. They both choose wisely picking up a gold cuff and a small number of gold coins. They gave their thanks and turned away to exit the building. As they were nearly at the door Dafydd turned and made his way back to the chest. He bent down and picked up a single gold coin.

'We have a horse to pay for.'

Chapter 13

Rafts and Mountains

Arenwen had had a good night's sleep, having slept in one of the log houses on the floating platform. He had expected to feel the cold during the night, given the significant drop in temperatures he had experienced when they had started the ascent into the mountain range. However, he was pleasantly surprised to find that the wooden lodges provided much better insulation than the wattle and daub houses he was familiar with.

Arenwen stretched, yawned and kicked back the skins that had been covering him during the night. He looked around the room, desperate to relieve himself, but didn't see any copper pots. He went in to the next room to discover that Bilhild had already found what he was looking for. He went over to where his second in command was emptying his bladder, undid the leather cord holding up his trousers and pulled them down over his thighs. Bilhild shuffled over so they could both use the receptacle the same time. The urine was dark yellow and smelt of a combination of ammonia and a hint of the ale they were drinking the night before.

'Bakher finished the negotiations with Felix last night. Felix agreed to send four hundred of his warriors to make rafts for our main army to cross the river,' Arenwen said.

'That should certainly be enough, and they won't have to go far for the wood as there are ample trees very close to the river,' Bilhild replied.

Both men finished, shook away the remaining drips and pulled their trousers up.

'I am going to carry on the route ahead, but I want you to go with Felix's men and ensure that they are making good progress. I don't want Lord Brennus to face any delays when the army reaches the river,' Arenwen said. Bilhild nodded, understanding what was required of him.

'Come and catch me up as soon as you are happy that everything is going to schedule. We'll be maintaining our slow pace, so it shouldn't take you long,' Arenwen added.

He reached inside his tunic and pulled out a leather pouch. He threw it to Bilhild and said 'as long as the boat trader keeps his word, make sure he gets this to pay for his services.'

'It will be good to give the horses a run, they have been getting restless with all this walking we have been doing. I'll make sure Idocus does a good job for us,' Bilhild replied.

With that Bilhild left the wooded stilt house, pulling the door firmly shut behind him. He noticed the plume of breath coming from his mouth as he exhaled and thought, if this is spring did it ever get warm in these mountains? He pulled his cloak tighter around him as he set off across the platform in search of his men. He needn't have worried as he soon saw that his men had risen and were having their breakfast.

As the warrior crossed the last part of the platform he saw the mass of Felix's men, whom he was organising in to smaller groups. Some of the groups were carrying great coils of rope over their muscular shoulders while others were carrying large axes. The axes were as long as the two headed axes his men used but, only had one cutting head like Celt's close combat axe.

Felix saw Bilhild crossing the timber walkway, and strode over to greet him. Bilhild picked up his pace to meet his host, as he stepped off the platform he felt his boots crack some thin ice in the soft mud.

Felix came up to Bilhild, slapping him on the shoulder.

'What do you think of my fine men?' Felix asked proudly.

'They are truly impressive Lord,' Bilhild said. His comments weren't just to flatter his host. The men standing before him were truly superb and Bilhild thought he would be happy to have them under his command.

'Could I have the honour of accompanying them to the river, Lord? I wanted to see if there was any sign of our army,' Bilhild lied. His true purpose was to ensure the rafts were being built quickly enough, but a small white lie was far more diplomatic than the truth.

'Of course,' Felix replied slapping Bilhild on the shoulder again.

He gathered his men together and informed them of the plan. They were to finish their food, and be ready to move on as soon as Arenwen and Bakher returned from the stilted platform.

Bilhild's chariot was made ready, and brought to him on the edge of the lake. Bilhild saw young Tir play fighting with Durston and Dafydd, each tapping the boy on the back of his head as he turned away from them. Tir saw the chariot and came running over to stand in awe at the magnificent vehicle. Bilhild was giving his thanks to Felix when the boy came running over to them.

'Is it true you're going back to the river?' Tir asked Bilhild.

'Yes, I wanted to see if there were any signs of our great army,' Bilhild replied.

'Father, father can I go? I would love to see what it is like to ride on one of these,' Tir pleaded.

'Can we add this to our agreement?' Felix asked.

'Of course Lord, you have been more than generous, it would be my honour to have your son accompany me,' Bilhild replied. He called over to Deborah

'I'm going back to the river. Go on with Arenwen and the rest of the men, I'll pick you up shortly,' he said.

'It will be good to have a walk, riding in a chariot all day is for old men,' she laughed.

Bilhild climbed on to his chariot with Tir hopping up beside him. Felix's men set off to the river crossing with Bilhild and Tir following closely behind them. The boy turned and waved excitedly to his father as they went. Felix waved back to his son, immensely proud of what a young man he was becoming. Bilhild tousled the boy's hair which made Tir turn around.

'I hear from my men that you are undoubtedly a confident rider,' Bilhild said.

'I am not bad,' Tir said modestly.

'Do you fancy trying to steer these two?' Bilhild said gesturing towards the horses pulling the chariot.

'Ohhh could I?' Came the exited reply.

Bilhild demonstrated the art of using the two sets of reins to guide the horses, and how it was important to get the team to work together. Tir took both sets of reins and started moving the horses slowly left and then right. Bilhild was surprised how quickly Tir picked up the subtle movements required to get the horses to respond - he was a natural.

They had travelled for a few hours when the path opened up in front of them, with a slight slope leading down to the river. It wasn't anywhere as steep as it had been, and there was plenty of room to safely pass Felix's men. Tir was still at the reigns of the chariot.

'Fancy giving the horses a run?' Bilhild asked Tir. The young lad didn't even reply to Bilhild and with a quick movement made the reins ripple along the horse's backs, with a snapping sound. The horses responded immediately and broke into a gallop. They tore past Felix's men, who shouted encouragement as the chariot flew swiftly past them. Bilhild held on tightly to the wicker loops of the chariot as they sped down the slope. After all that's what the loops were there for, to hold on to during rapid manoeuvres as well as somewhere to strap your shield.

The right wheel hit a small rock, bouncing the vehicle in the air with a jolt. Bilhild shifted his weight to the right to compensate for the chariot being unevenly balanced. Tir however, just rode the imbalance by adjusting his knees and savoured the experience by making whooping sounds.

The horses were now at full speed which was amplified by the slight slope down towards the river. Bilhild wanted Tir to enjoy the experience, but the river was coming up on them very quickly, too quickly Bilhild thought.

The boat owner had been waiting patiently for them and had set up a small camp just to the side of the river. He looked up and saw the chariot hurtling down the hill, directly towards his small makeshift camp. He started grabbing his meagre possessions and scrambled out of the way of the chariot's direction. Bilhild was getting very concerned, and was about to grab the reigns when Tir pulled firmly on the reins of the left horse. The animal responded immediately with the horse on the right being pulled in the same direction. The geldings came to a grinding halt as the chariot swung round behind them into a skidding stop. They were just a few inches away from the small camp, and a few feet away from the river.

Bilhild breathed a sigh of relief as they came to a stop, and Tir jumped lightly off the chariot. He ran around to the horses, stood in front of the pair and rubbed both horses' necks, and they responded by stamping their hooves and snorting their appreciation of the attention they were receiving. Bilhild thought that his horses had never responded to him in that way. He looked at the boy and could see why his father was so proud of him. Bilhild thought of his children at home. The gods had blessed him with three daughters, but he thought that one day, if he was to have a son he would like him to be just like Tir.

Two thirds of Felix's men had stopped at the tree line of the last slope. They had enjoyed looking down at Tir's exploits, but now had work to do. The men had heaped their furs on a pile and were organising themselves ready for the task ahead. The other third came down the slope hefting their coils of rope.

There was a good supply of trees and the teams quickly set about their task. Bilhild realised he needn't have to worried about how long it would take to manufacture the rafts. The men worked in perfect harmony, their great one faced axes sliced through the trees with ease. They worked much quicker than Arenwen's men, but it was a combination of better tools and also that they were experienced at felling trees. Their whole town would have been built by such an endeavour.

The teams were quickly felling the huge pines, stripping the branches and rolling the trunks down the slope. The gang at the bottom dragged the logs towards the river bank and began lashing them together with the coils of rope, expertly measuring the required lengths and cutting accordingly. Once they had secured three logs together, they lifted the early part of the raft onto two other logs which raised it from the ground.

Bilhild thought the purpose of lifting the logs gave them access to the bottom making the assembly much easier. This was partially true, but Bilhild soon saw the other reason as the first raft was rolled into the river. The craft was secured a little distance upstream to allow plenty of room for the other rafts that were yet to be constructed.

Idocus came over to Bilhild and said 'they are very impressive. They'll have all we need very quickly.'

'Indeed are, they make my men's efforts look like complete beginners,' Bilhild replied with a laugh.

Trunk after trunk was rolled down the hill, being eagerly gathered up at the bottom of the slope. The raft manufacturing process went on seamlessly.

'I had better take the first raft over and see my daughter,' Idocus said.

'How are you going to get all these over to the other side of the river?' Bilhild asked.

'I will take this raft over and wait for your men. I'll bring twenty back on the first trip, showing them were to avoid and when they need to push as hard as they can. The twenty will then follow me back guiding their own rafts. I will then bring twenty more over and so on and so on until there is a constant flow of one hundred rafts back and fore like a column of ants,' Idocus explained.

'How long do you think it will take to ferry everyone across the river,' Bilhild asked.

'Given the good weather I would estimate no more than four hours,' Idocus said scanning the sky.

In a short period of time there were a significant amount of rafts tethered to the river bank with no sign of the production line slowing down.

'Before I cross over to the other bank, may I address a delicate matter?' Idocus asked.

'And what would that be,' Bilhild replied, already knowing what the trader was referring to.

'I was just wondering how the people I am to ferry know that they are to pay me my balance due, and actually how much it is,' Idocus said.

Bilhild smiled and replied 'very good questions, but it has been already attended to. I was to wait until you had completed your side of the bargain. However, I can see everything is in hand here so I am happy to give you your payment now.'

'Thank you for your trust,' Idocus replied, with a small bow. Bilhild whistled and two of Felix's men looked up.

'Of course I trust you, but just in case see those two men there?' Bilhild said.

'Yes,' Idocus replied.

'They are under strict instructions to kill you, very slowly, if anything goes wrong,' Bilhild said.

Idocus couldn't tell if Bilhild was serious or not, so just nodded. The warrior went closer to Idocus and handed him the pouch of coins. He had done well from the transaction, but he was an essential part in ensuring that both the army and provisions had a smooth transition from one bank to the other.

Tir came running up to Bilhild - he had been waving to the girl on the far bank who either couldn't see him or was ignoring him completely.

'Are they your men?' Tir asked.

'What men?' Bilhild replied.

'The six riders further down the river, on the far shore. Can't you see them?' Tir asked as he pointed downstream to the far side.

He strained his eyes but couldn't get a focus, his vision had deteriorated gradually over the past few years. Then he saw movement as the six riders came in to view. Bilhild used a technique that he had been taught by a druid. He clenched is right fist, only leaving a small gap about the size of a pin hole. He brought his clenched fist up to his right eye and looked through the tiny hole while closing his left. The vision in his right eye quickly became sharper and he recognised them as Brennus' advanced scout party. That meant that the main body of the army could only be a few hours behind.

'Now I see them, and yes they are our men. That means we must move quickly to ensure all preparations are made for them,' Bilhild said to Tir.

The six riders were now on the opposite bank next to Idocus' daughter. Bakher waved to them, one of the mounted riders slowly waved back in recognition. It was unlikely that he could see Bilhild, more likely that he recognised his chariot but either way Bilhild was pleased to see that the plans were falling into place.

Bilhild made for his chariot and Tir fell in closely behind him. They both hopped up on to the chariot's platform, with Tir looking at Bilhild expectedly. Bilhild knew what he wanted and didn't mind him taking the reins.

'Take it steadily on the way back. These horses can run at a good pace for hours, but there is a steep incline back to your father's town and I need them to go on from there,' Bilhild said to the young lad.

'Don't worry I won't tire them out,' Tir replied, with one of his beaming smiles.

He guided the magnificent pair of jet black horses back up the route they had come from. The ground was not frozen here, the horses threw up great clods of earth as they pulled the chariot back up the slope. The incline would soon become a hill, then become the foothills of the mountain.

Tir noticed how these horses had much more muscle than the ones he rode back home, and they were much taller. Tir was driving the pair very well. He slowed their pace as the terrain became steeper, firmer and icy.

The countryside was green at the river, but as they climbed it was noticeable that the landscape was changing as they ascended to the lower mountain area. Bilhild hadn't seen the change previously as they had travelled at a much slower pace. But now they were moving much quicker it was easy to identify the difference from the river area to here. The lush green vegetation was slowly having the colour drained from it the higher they went. Winter was trying to keep its icy grip on the land as long as it could.

The horses pulled on, with steam erupting from their flaring nostrils. Tir was in his element with the wind blowing through his hair. Bilhild saw riders approaching them and quickly recognised them as the guides from Andematunnum. The Lingones guides had fulfilled their task and could head back home. Bilhild called to them as they went past 'head back to where we crossed, there are rafts there to take you over.'

The riders waved their acknowledgement as they passed and quickly disappeared.

'There's home,' Tir said. Bilhild still couldn't see the town that Tir was referring to, but with both hands firmly clenched on the chariot's wicker sides he didn't want to use his fist technique. So instead he trusted his younger companion that he could see their destination, after all this was a new land to Bilhild but Tir had known it all his life.

'Ah yes, we should be there in no time,' Bilhild lied as he still couldn't see it.

'Yes, not long now,' Tir said as he increased the speed of the horses as they had nearly reached the edge of the plateau. One last push from the horses and the terrain would become much easier for them. The animals had plenty left to give and they responded to Tir's encouragement. Bilhild could now see the lake as well as the outline of the large stilted town. The plateau dipped slightly and acted as a natural basin to catch all the water from the surrounding hills to form a spectacular blue lake, the sun bouncing rays off its crystal clear waters. Bilhild raised his right hand so that it could form a visor against the bright pale blue, brilliant light that hurt his eyes. Tir seemed oblivious to the effects of the light and focussed on two dark shapes racing from the village.

Bilhild did not know how Tir's two hounds had sensed his approach, but he too could now see them race towards the chariot with the horses closing the gap between the dogs and their Master. The dogs yelped in excitement as the chariot got closer to them. Their yelps bounced off the mountains around them and came echoing back. As the hounds got closer Tir reduced the horse's speed, taking them to a trot and finally a slow walk. The dogs were but yards away now, when Tir pulled on the reins to stop the chariot and leapt off the back. Both dogs launched themselves at Tir bowling him over onto the firm ground. He rolled on the floor laughing as his dogs licked at his face and vigorously wagged their tails.

Tir let the dogs expend their excitement before they eventually calmed down. He got back to his feet, and the dogs automatically sat waiting patiently for their turn of his attention. Bilhild looked down at the boy and wondered what god had blessed him as he was adored by both man and beast. Tir gave both dogs one last fussing and hopped back onto the chariot.

Bilhild took the reins and glanced behind him to ensure Tir was holding on. He clicked the reins and the horses pulled off at a trot with the dogs instantly following. Tir was hanging over the side of the chariot egging the dogs on to try and lick his hand.

The chariot was rapidly approaching the town with Tir still hanging over the side having fun with his dogs. Bilhild had seen that they had been spotted and saw a guard running across the wooden walkway to inform the chieftain that his son was returning. By the time they finally got to the houses at the edge of the lake, Felix was there to greet them.

'I hope you find that my men were up to the task,' Felix laughed.

That threw Bilhild off guard, as he suddenly realised Felix had guessed his true reasons for accompanying the raft party. Bilhild quickly recovered himself and replied 'I am pleased to inform you that the advance party of scouts have reached the far river bank. My Lord Brennus will be here by nightfall.'

'I must also compliment you on the efficiency of your men. It was a pleasure to watch,' he added.

Bilhild thought that he had got away with it as he didn't want anything to go wrong with the main army ready to cross the Rhone River. Felix laughed again and slapped Bilhild on the shoulder with both men knowing the true intention, but happy that it had been dealt with diplomatically with no loss of face for Felix in front of his men. Turning to Tir Felix said 'and you son, did you enjoy riding on this wagon?'

'It is called a chariot father, and yes, I did. Not only did I ride on it I steered it for quite some time,' Tir replied.

Felix did not say anything to Bilhild, but gave him a subtle nod that could have easily been missed. It was a nod from one father to another that showed he was very pleased for pandering to his son's wishes. Bilhild approached Felix thanking him for his generosity and hospitality.

'With your permission I will press on and catch up with my men,' the warrior said.

'Your men gave me the life of my son. You and any of your tribe will be always welcome here,' the chieftain said warmly.

Bilhild gave one last ruffle of Tir's hair. This was met with his usual beaming smile as Tir looked up at Bilhild. With the formalities done Bilhild stepped back on to the chariot, and took up the reins. He urged the horses on and followed the trail left by the small band of men who had left earlier that day. The ground was much harder here, but the tracks were still clearly visible. Bilhild glanced back and still could see Tir in the distance waving like a loon. He waved back and then turned forward. He thought that Tir would make a good son for one of his daughters. He had served Brennus for many years, and knew that he could bet his life on what Brennus had promised him. Half of the new lands were to be divided between Arenwen and himself. He would not have as much gold as Felix, but if the land the other side of the mountains was as fertile as he had been told then he would be recognised as an equal. Bilhild nodded to himself as if in agreement, conquer the new lands, agree his share, recruit men then return home to bring his eldest daughter to present to Felix. With no son, his daughter and Tir would rule both lands after him, and also increase the family bond between two Celtic tribes. Bilhild smiled to himself as he followed the tracks and thought, 'yes that is what I will do.'

He eased back the horses' pace as they were blowing heavily at the increase in gradient, they were certainly in the mountains now. He knew that he would soon catch up to the others as the men would be finding the terrain hard going on foot. A small flurry of snow blew from the white tipped mountains higher above and Bilhild thought he could make out the small party ahead in the distance, but they disappeared again as another flurry filled the air before him.

The temperature had dropped again, and it was getting colder and colder as the chariot followed the track left by the small group ahead. The imprints were becoming more difficult to follow as the small snow swirls covered the floor with a thin blanket of white pulled down from the mountain peaks.

Bilhild was relieved to see the shapes of the rest of the party ahead of him. He could see a large clump of shapes, but the thing that identified them the most was that one figure was much taller than the others - this had to be Arenwen on his chariot. He was still climbing steeply and Bilhild was tempted to urge his horses onto a faster pace, but then thought better of it. He knew he was travelling quicker than those on foot, but he did not know how much further they would have to go once he had caught up with them.

Slowly the outlines became clearer as Bilhild got closer to the small party of men. The wind had dropped, so no more clouds of tiny white daggers were flying down from the peaks. The sun shone brightly, but there was no warmth in it. It was supposed to be spring, but this was as cold as the winter back home. He got closer and could see that the men were shuffling along, keeping together in an attempt to shield themselves against the elements. Bilhild was holding the reins in one hand now as he kept the other hand under his cloak. When the feeling came back in the protected hand, he plunged the other into the warmth of his tunic.

At last Bilhild had caught up with the others. The wind had picked up again and was blowing in their faces. The small party hadn't heard Bilhild approach, as he was downwind from them. Normally he would have been spotted quite some time ago, but the men had their heads down so that they could shield themselves from the biting cold. He was right behind them now, it was Deborah who noticed him first and shouted to Arenwen a few feet ahead of her.

The men parted to let the second chariot through. As he passed, he signalled to Deborah and she jumped up on to the rear of the chariot. Bilhild steered through the men and drew up alongside Arenwen. He could see Felix's two replacement scouts up ahead that he had kindly provided for this stage of the journey. Bakher was huddled at the back of the chariot, doing his best to use Arenwen's bulk as a wind break.

'This is grim,' Bilhild called to Arenwen over the howling wind.

'You're telling me,' he replied.

Then suddenly the cutting wind stopped, and while it was still cold it was no longer bitter. One of the men lurched and threw up. Arenwen thought it was just him suffering from the headaches, dizziness and feeling like he wanted to be sick, but it appeared to be most of them.

'Is this an omen?' Arenwen asked Bakher.

'No, I spoke to the Helvetii druids and they told me this would happen. They said that the higher we go, the thinner the air gets,' Bakher replied.

'Did they give you anything to cure it?' Arenwen asked desperately.

'Yes they did, but they told me that I was to wait until the men were ill before administrating it, or they wouldn't feel the benefit,' Bakher replied.

Arenwen saw that the path up ahead widened, and was sheltered by some large rocks that had broken away from the mountain above. He called to the scouts and waved them to the fallen rocks. Arenwen led the small party into the shelter, and helped Bakher down from the chariot.

'Come closer,' Bakher called to them.

The druid took some yellow, fan shaped leaves from a pouch. They were about two inches long and had been picked from a tree found lower in the valley. He gave a leaf to each person.

'Chew this very slowly. I know it smells like vomit, but it will help ease the symptoms you are experiencing,' Bakher said.

Each of the group took a leaf, and sat down behind the shelter of the rocks to chew. Arenwen waited until everybody else had taken a leaf before accepting his then joined the rest of the party in chewing. The two scouts declined the offer from Bakher as the altitude did not seem to affect them, but they still sat down with the others. The group sat in silence slowly munching the leaves and gradually the symptoms became milder. The headaches had gone as had the sickness feeling, but Arenwen was still a little light headed. It was if as if he had drunk three horns of ale.

'How much further?' Arenwen asked one of the scouts.

'It is not as bad as it looks, we have climbed most of what we need to and the path will weave its way through the mountains. We will not be going anywhere near as high as those,' the scout said pointing up at the snow-capped peaks to his right.

'So how long?' Arenwen asked again.

'About a half an hour. We round these rocks and then a final bend before the track levels off. From there on its flat and much easier going,' the scout replied.

Arenwen relayed the good news to the rest of the group. He could see that the report and Bakher's leaf had lifted their spirits, and they once again resembled the hardy bunch that they were previously before the ascent.

Arenwen let the warriors rest a little longer before rousing them back to their feet. Bilhild mounted his chariot with Deborah joining, him while Bakher climbed onto the chariot with Arenwen. As he was about to pull away when a trickle of small stones fell down from an area above him. He glanced up looking for the source of the disturbance, but couldn't see anything so he just put it down to the elements.

Up until now, the track they had followed had been steep but quite wide. The trees had thinned out to leave only few gnarled pines that refused to give in to the wind. As the party left the shelter of the fallen rocks, Arenwen noticed how the layout of the trail was changing. Previously the track was symmetrical with an even amount of land on both sides. The incline had certainly reduced and was not much more than a slight climb now. This continued until the track became very one sided with a rock face on the left and a sheer drop on the right. The path was very straight when one of the scouts came next to Arenwen, pointing out the final bend about a mile up ahead.

Arenwen was pleased that the track was wide enough to accommodate the ox pulled carts of the main army. The large force that followed behind would need those of supplies until it could secure more on the other side. Only another half a mile to the highest point and they could begin their descent.

Another shower of small stones fell in front of Arenwen's chariot, and he looked up just in time to see an arrow that had been aimed at his head. He ducked as it whistled past him.

'Shields!' Arenwen roared as more shafts flew down onto the party. One struck and lodged itself in Bilhild's shield that was slung over the side of his chariot.

Arenwen glanced back to see everybody had their shields raised high, and angled to give the best protection from above. More and more missiles came raining down on them as Arenwen did his best to protect himself and Bakher.

'Keep moving,' Arenwen shouted as he peered above the shelter of his shield, trying to get a glimpse of the assailants.

He ducked quickly as more arrows thumped into his shield. The men edged their way forward as a new weapon was unleashed on them - large rocks rolled down from the hillside above them.

'Brace!' Arenwen called as the boulders came rolling down at a terrifying pace. Several of them smashed into the party and knocked two men to the floor. Others grouped around them, helped them up and protected them from more arrows.

'I've had enough of this,' Arenwen said to Bakher, holding his shield high while scanning ahead for any opportunity to get higher. Then he saw what he was looking for, a ridge that cut up from the track that looked like it would take him further into the hills. Arenwen called back to his men.

'Vaughn, Telor, Dafydd and Durston, when I move, follow me.'

The four men nodded as more rocks and arrows smashed down on them. He noticed Deborah was returning arrow with arrow, popping up from behind Bilhild's shield to fire off a shaft at the hidden enemy, before ducking down behind the cover to notch another arrow to her bow string.

'Here, take the reins,' Arenwen said to Bakher.

'I don't know how to steer one of these,' the druid replied with a look of sheer terror on his face.

'Don't worry, the horses won't go near the edge, and you won't be steering them for long,' Arenwen smiled.

The Celtic chieftain grabbed two spears that were held in a leather holder on the side of his chariot, and deftly ran down the wooden cross bar that attached the horses to the chariot. In a swift movement he straddled the horse on the left and grabbed hold of its bridle with his right hand, while his left clenched the two spears tightly. The horse on the left would give him more shelter from the arrows, but it would make him more susceptible to the falling rocks.

Arenwen dug his heels into the animal's flank, and it immediately responded by breaking into a gallop with the harnessed horse on the right matching its speed. Bakher clung on to the reins for dear life, unsure if he was guiding the horses or if they were guiding him.

Arenwen squinted a little, and could now see the area he was focussing on come up rapidly.

'When you see me ready to jump off, pull the reins back with all your might,' he called back to Bakher.

'I'll do my best,' he called back, marvelling as Arenwen brought his legs up from the side of the horse and pulled himself on his knees into a crouching position.

The warrior pulled back hard on the horse's bridle and shouted 'now!'

Bakher pulled the reigns and as the horses skidded to a stop, while Arenwen leapt off the gelding's back, rolling on to the ground in one smooth, perfectly executed movement.

'Keep going to the next bend,' Arenwen called as he started up the ridge.

The barrage that had rained down behind them seemed to slow as Vaughn, Telor, Dafydd and Durston ran panting past Bakher. Vaughn and Telor had swords drawn in their right hands. They had two spears carefully tethered behind the shields they were carrying on their left arms. Dafydd and Durston however, were hoping for some close up killing, and had left their swords in their scabbards. They carried their short, close battle killing axes and were looking for hand-to-hand combat.

'Up that ridge to the left,' Bakher called.

Dafydd raised his axe above his head in acknowledgement as the four disappeared behind the ridge following where Arenwen had gone just a few moments earlier.

The four men caught up with their leader, and found him quite a way up the ridge peering between a large bolder that had split and eroded over time.

'There they are, about ten of them,' Arenwen said pointing to a group of men fifty feet below them.

'Twelve,' Telor corrected.

'Mountain men,' Dafydd said.

'How do you know?' Arenwen asked.

'They are dressed the same as the ones who attacked Felix's son,' Dafydd replied.

'He mentioned that they had become braver recently, or as I think; more foolish,' Arenwen said.

'Foolish?' Durston questioned.

'Yes, foolish, this will be the last straw for Felix when he hears of this attack. He will make them curse their parents for bringing them into this world when he brings his men up here,' Arenwen said.

'The odds seem a bit unfair,' Vaughn said.

'What are you talking about, there are only twelve of them,' Telor replied.

'That's what I mean, they should have more,' Vaughn chuckled.

Arenwen shot them an icy glance, he liked their confidence but this wasn't the time for merriment.

'Keep the noise down and let's get to the task in hand,' Arenwen said, outlining the plan as the twelve mountain men were obliviously firing arrows and rolling boulders down on their victims below. They stopped hurling rocks as the party had passed beyond their trap, and were nearly out of range, now bitterly disappointed that their ambush had not yielded anything for their efforts. The last few futile shots were being taken as the mountain men cursed their misfortune.

The five Celts crept closer and closer to their prey, they were well within spear range as they edged even nearer. The first the mountain men knew that the Celts were there was when two of the brigands tumbled over the edge with shafts lodged firmly in their backs, Vaughn and Telor having laid their swords aside, and taken a lethally accurate aim with their spears. Before the mountain men could react, another two of them were sent over the edge by the remaining spears carried by the twins. As soon as the shafts had left their hands, the twins picked up their swords and turned to each other and simultaneously said 'two.'

The Celts must have seemed like demons as they ran screaming down the hill. Panic spread through the remaining eight attackers as their only exit was the ridge currently occupied by five screaming madmen. The mountain men were not equipped for a hand to hand fight and were lightly armed, having planned to easily kill their prey below in an ambush. They had not even entertained the notion that they might need any weapons other than their bows and a short knife to slit their victims' throats.

Two of the mountain men quickly came out of their panic induced trance and picked up their bows. Their hands shook as they tried to notch arrows – only one succeeded and managed to loose a shot at Telor, it thumped harmlessly into his shield. The second man was not quick enough to fire his shaft as Dafydd smashed the bow out of the way with a sweeping movement of his axe, neatly taking the man's right arm off at the elbow. The man's cry of intense pain was short lived as the axe split his skull, his bowels empting as he fell, releasing a thick cloying stench of faeces.

Telor was now facing the man who had shot an arrow at him, and slashed at his legs with his sword. His opponent pathetically tried to deflect the attack using his bow, but Telor spun around the parry and took the mountain man's head cleanly off with blood spurting from the severed neck. His head rolled over the edge of the cliff, his body swayed for a moment - almost as if it needed time to realise that the head had been cut off. The body hit the floor as Telor called 'three.'

Of the six mountain men remaining, two advanced on Arenwen, but he skilfully held off any attacks they were making, their short knives which were no match for Arenwen's long sword and powerful shoulders. They lunged at him, but he quickly repelled their attacks, making them take a backward step with every move. Repeated stabs were followed by his long blade flicking their knives away as easily as a cow would swat flies with its tail. Lunge, step back, lunge step back.

Durston was embroiled in his battle with one assailant, but was comfortable enough to glance over at Arenwen. He instantly spotted what Arenwen intended as the two mountain men lunged once more, and were pushed back yet again, not realising that they were being skilfully manoeuvred towards the ledge where they had attacked the party below. They were being pushed back, a few inches closer to the drop each time they tried to attack the Celtic warrior. They had stepped too far back, with one falling backwards over the edge. The second man realised too late that he was on the edge, and dropped his knife as he flailed his arms desperately trying to regain his balance. Arenwen moved forward slightly, and gently pushed the tip of his sword in to his opponent's gut. It wasn't meant to be a killing blow but merely a little nudge, and that's exactly what it was. The second man fell screaming over the edge to join his dead comrade on the path below.

Durston refocused on the man he was fighting, and deftly sliced open his midriff. A swell of red blossomed quickly on the waist of his furs as he fell to his knees and looked up as Durston drove his sword into the man's face, shattering yellow teeth. The lethal weapon exited through the base of his skull, instantly severing his spinal column.

Arenwen slid his sword back in to its sheath and joined Durston in watching the remaining melee, his friend wiping his own blade clean on the furs of the man he had just dispatched. The pair of them watched as Telor, Vaughn and Dafydd each played with the last three mountain men, now thoroughly terrified as the twins and their friend teased and played with their opponents before dispatching them.

Dafydd was the first to move as he raised his axe as if to bring down a shattering blow to the man's head, offering his opponent a deceptively easy stab at his ribs. As the man lunged Dafydd expertly reversed his grip on the axe so the handle was at the top and the head at the bottom, catching the man squarely under the jaw with the butt of the haft. He was lifted clean off his feet, and stumbled back as Dafydd swivelled the axe once again. He brought it down on the man's lunging right arm and severed it from the body. The limb flopped to the ground, still tightly gripping the knife. He looked pleadingly at Dafydd and begged 'please make it quick,' the humiliation of his defeat thickening his voice. Dafydd obliged, sinking his axe into the man's neck putting all his considerable strength behind the blow. The cut hadn't quite severed the head, but he'd provided his adversary with the quick death he had pleaded for.

Vaughn swung at his opponent's left leg. The mountain man tried to block the blow with his knife flying from his hand as the sword bit viciously into his thigh. Going down on one knee the last word he heard was 'three.'

Telor smiled knowing that he had the last mountain man. He had purposely danced around this man waiting for his brother to equal his killing tally, and be free to watch his victory. All Telor had to do was to dispatch this man to claim his fourth victim and win this killing contest. Telor raised his sword to deliver the death blow when Arenwen called 'wait!'

Everybody suddenly looked at Arenwen in complete astonishment.

'We need one alive to send back to Felix,' Arenwen said.

Telor considered arguing as the adrenaline was coursing through his veins from the fight, but knew better to question his Lord.

'Cut off his index and middle fingers as well as his thumb from his right hand – that way he'll never shoot a bow or wield a knife again,' Arenwen said.

Telor nodded, he could feel his heart thumping wildly, and his head throbbed as if in time to the rhythmic beating in his chest. Telor took three deep breaths and focused on bringing his heart rate down.

'So how do you want this, the easy way or the hard way?'

The man was resigned to his fate, and knelt down on the ground. He retracted his ring and little fingers leaving the three to be severed. Telor put the tip of his sword on the middle finger and brought the edge of the sword down slicing off the two fingers, screaming again as Telor removed the thumb.

Arenwen ripped one of the dead mountain men's trousers with his sword and tore off a strip of cloth. He threw it at the man bleeding on the floor and told him to wrap it tightly to stop the flow of blood.

The men climbed back down the ridge they had come up earlier, but this time accompanied by their prisoner and descended to meet up with the rest of the men. They caught up with them around the final bend the scouts had told Arenwen about. The leader heard the twins bickering behind him.

'So I won that one,' Telor said to Vaughn.

'How so, we both killed three?' Vaughn asked.

'Yes, but I killed three men, two fingers and a thumb,' Telor said as he playfully cuffed his brother around the back of his head.

'Can't argue with that,' Vaughn said laughing as he punched his brother in the stomach.

The scouts had been very accurate, the track had levelled off and Arenwen thought it had even started to descend, returning to more wooded and temperate surroundings with the right hand side slowly getting wider. The path moved away from the sheer drop to their right and headed more inland, where the few gnarled trees of the mountains were becoming groups of proud upright pines once more. They continued to follow the track downwards for quite some time when one of Felix's scouts waived to Arenwen.

'What is it, more trouble?' Arenwen called.

'No trouble, but follow us,' one of the scouts shouted back as he turned a bend and disappeared out of sight.

Arenwen urged his chariot forward, and broke away from the rest of the advance party. He rounded the bend and drew his team to a halt next to the scouts. He couldn't believe his eyes when he saw the wondrous sight. There below him was a vast plain of rich green fertile land as far as he could see. The scouts let Arenwen drink in the magnificent vista before him.

'You cannot go wrong now Lord. Follow this trail and it will take you to the foot of the mountains. From there just travel south and keep the mountains to your left,' the scout said.

'You have served us well,' Arenwen said as he reached inside the chest to pull out some gold coins which he tossed to the scouts.

The rest of the party rounded the bend, Arenwen heard gasps as the men saw what lay in front of them.

'Head back to your chieftain, and take this wretched scum with you,' Arenwen said to the scouts.

They took the leather strap that was fastened around the mountain man's neck and thanked Arenwen for his generosity. They turned around and headed back to their town on the other side of the mountain. Arenwen's men formed two lines for the scouts to walk between. Some of the men praised the scouts as they went through, while others took the opportunity for one last punch or kick at the remaining mountain man who had tried to kill them earlier.

The men cheered as they knew that this was the land they had come to conquer. This was the land that would make them rich, where they could fight battles that bards would tell stories and sing songs about for many years.

Arenwen turned to his men, outstretched his arms and said 'behold our new land.'

Chapter 14

Camar's Dilemma

Camar left Quintus' villa and looked pitifully down at the wooden gladius he was holding in his right hand. This was a disaster, he had never failed in a mission before, and he could not return to Clusium without achieving his goal. He had risen quickly through the ranks and yes he had family connections, but his rise was predominantly due to his skills. However, the rapid rise had made many enemies in the Etruscan League and they would see this failure as an invitation to destroy him.

He walked through the resplendent streets of Rome, wondering how the fortunes of both capitals and himself had turned. Rome was just a tiny village with a few huts when Clusium had a thriving population, impressive shrines, statues and temples, as well as a very formidable stone wall. Those days were gone now, with Rome in the ascendancy. The wars between their two nations had seen the Latin League of cities being the victors and Rome, as its capital, expand in to an impressive city. The Etruscan League of twelve cities was now eleven as the city of Veli was captured by the Romans during the last war. This was one of Rome's greatest conquests, and they held on to it as part of the peace treaty.

Camar racked his brain for a solution as he headed for the main exit from the city. His two slaves followed behind him, slowly pulling the cart that had transported the urn full of wine. He preferred to walk when he was deep in thought, but he glanced back to check that the slaves had secured his horse to the back of the cart.

Camar's brain was racing widely thinking of possible solutions, and then discounting them quickly as every idea was flawed. Then one thought occurred to him, it was high risk, but he could see no other viable alternative other than to return to Clusium and be branded as a laughing stock.

He threw the wooden gladius in the gutter as he had made up his mind. He would go to where the swords were being manufactured, he would go to Quintus' countryside villa.

He passed Capitoline Hill on his right, and looked straight ahead to one of the main gates that would be his exit route from the city. Camar was no novice at this game, although he had made a grievous error by underestimating Quintus. He would not let that drunken Roman get the better of him, and expected that the senator had sent an agent to follow him. They would report back as to Camar's movements, so he glanced back casually and called for his horse. He did actually want his mount, but that was a distraction to enable him to scan the crowd looking for a probable candidate who might be following.

Camar thought that he would have had a visiting ambassador tailed to track his movements, and ensure his whereabouts. He didn't see anyone out of the ordinary, but any one, or many, of the street traders and commoners could be in the employ of Quintus. Camar knew knowledge was power, and after today's experience with Quintus he expected the slippery politician had eyes and ears everywhere.

The Etruscan mounted his horse and rode it slowly out of the city gates, through the rampart and over the wooden platform. There was a constant stream of people entering and leaving Rome so he didn't want to show that he was checking to see if he was being watched. Camar looked around, but there were far too many people to try and spot an individual.

The ambassador led his slaves along the main road and through the small villages that grew up outside all major cities. The road went straight as far as the eye could see without the slightest deviation. Ahead Camar could see that the mighty River Tiber twisted very close to a part of the road, where people were getting in and out of boats. The river would have been one of his options to head for home as Clusium sat on the river Clanis, one of the many tributaries that fed into the Tiber. It was an easy boat ride down the river which he had considered when planning his route to Rome. There was little need for much effort from the rowers as the current carries vessels along like a leaf floating downstream. It was a different matter on the return journey though, as the oarsmen would have to heave with every stroke home. However, he thought that he would be able to manipulate Quintus into letting him collect a sword from the country estate so taking a horse was the better of the two options.

The ebb and flow of people heading towards and leaving Rome was starting to wane. Camar and his slaves continued along the main road for some time when the ambassador wanted to check behind them. He pulled his gelding to the side of the road and dismounted, handing the expensive leather reins to one of the slaves then headed for a nearby group of bushes.

'Let the horse graze and get it some water from the river. I'm going to relieve myself,' Camar said to his slaves. He spoke loudly enough to ensure that his words would carry on the wind to the closest group following.

He ducked behind a thicket of bushes and went through the motions of hitching up his garments as if to empty his bladder. The bushes were over his head and quite dense, but he had positioned himself so that he had a clear sight of the road. It had been a good summer with significant foliage to cover him scanning the road, but not so thick that he couldn't easily distinguish between the small groups following behind him.

There was a cart being pulled by two oxen. By the look of the empty grain sacks the slave had been ferrying a large quantity of it to the capital. He would have had to lead the oxen on foot with such a heavy load, and had to encourage them further with a whip. No need for a lash on the way back as he sat on the wagon being pulled by the heavy beasts. His weight, to the oxen, was as insignificant as flee to a dog. The cart was of no interest him, it was too slow to keep up with him even if he was at a slow pace.

Camar scanned past the cart a little way further down the road. There was a line of people making their way up the thoroughfare. It was an overseer returning from Rome with a new batch of slaves for his Master. The slaves were bound at the wrists and lined up in single file, joined together with leather neck straps. He quickly dismissed this group as it was too an elaborate setup to be viable.

Looking further down the road he could make out the shape of someone travelling alone. He couldn't determine the gender, but it was a perfect position to track the Etruscan envoy and his slaves. It was far enough back to keep them in sight, and close enough to spot which direction they had to be heading. If he was being followed it had to be this person.

Confident that he had assessed any risk he readjusted his clothing and over exaggerated himself tidying his garments as he came from behind the bush into full view. His horse had been led to the side of the road and was lazily chomping on the grass with a bucket of water to its side. The slaves leapt up from the ground as they saw their Master re-appear.

Camar climbed back on his horse and guided it onto the road. The slaves picked up the handcart and pulled it dutifully behind their Master. The cart was much lighter now that the huge urn had been offloaded in Rome. It now only held a reasonably sized chest with clothes and a small amount of overnight equipment, should they not be able to find a village with suitable accommodation to sleep in.

The afternoon turned into early evening with the sun losing some the heat stored up through the day, but there were still several hours of daylight left. The days were long and the nights uncomfortably hot and sticky this time of year. The highway continued with only the odd small village to break up the view ahead of them, but the mountain range to the right was ever present in the distance. Camar knew that there was a major fork in the road coming soon. He should carry on straight if he was heading back to Clusium, or he would need to fork right if he was to head to Quintus' country estate, which he had planned to do.

The sun was casting long shadows on the ground and Camar knew he had to make a decision. The cart, slaves and mysterious figure all kept them same distances as before. He decided to make camp just north of the fork which would force the hand of anyone, if anyone, was following him. They were a good ten minutes in front of the cart and all three groups edged themselves closer to Camar.

He instructed his slaves that they were stopping for the night just past the fork, and he made sure that they were fussing about, and making an elaborate show that they were setting up camp. Camar looked behind him, past the cart and overseer, and at the figure in the distance which seemed to have stopped. Camar was right, he was being followed. Then the person further back down the road began moving again, and wondered if he was just being paranoid.

The light was growing weak when Camar caught something in his peripheral vision. Someone had quickly sat up from the back of the cart, and Camar just about saw them roll to the side of the road in to the heavy undergrowth that grew alongside the highway. He reprimanded himself as that was the second of two basic errors he had made that day. He had been followed, but his follower had been lying flat on the cart, hidden by the grain sacks.

The cart slowly approached them with the driver smiling and giving a respectful nod as he drove by. The slaves were being pushed harder with the overseer trying to get to his destination before the deep dark of night. Slowly but surely the lone figure in the distance came closer and Camar could see that it was an old woman with an empty basket on her back. She had probably taken some olives for sale in to the Roman capital. She smiled at him with toothless gums as she hobbled by.

'We'll stop here for the night, set up camp and get a fire going for my supper,' Camar said loudly.

More softly he added 'gather plenty of wood to build me a nice big fire, and have my trunk put by those bushes over there.'

Camar had selected an area that would be out of view from where he suspected his follower would be located. If he was watching this camp he would position himself in direct line of sight from where he had seen the figure slip into the undergrowth.

The Etruscan looked up at the moon and saw it was a waxing crescent, which only showed an eighth of its full size. There was very little light as darkness fell as the fire burned brightly. It was the only real luminance for miles around.

As the last shards of light faded in the distant western sky Camar got up and threw a large piece of wood on to fire which made sparks fly up in to the air. He had made sure that he was very visible, and had also forced his watcher to look at the bright light.

Camar had kept his eyes closed as much as possible so he could quickly adapt to the darkness.

Turning away from the fire he stealthily moved from the bright light and into the dark shadows. He moved behind the bush where he had earlier had his trunk stored. The Etruscan slipped out of his bright and garish ambassadorial outfit, and donned a dark brown woollen cloak, pulling the hood over his head to blend into the darkness beyond the reach of the fire light. Camar moved through the undergrowth mentally fixing his target as he moved.

Moving in a wide clockwise arc, he stopped as he reached the part of the road that had forked off to the right. There was no cover available to him so he stopped, double checking for any movement. Camar hoped that the cloak of darkness would provide sufficient cover for him to cross the road unnoticed. He held his breath, checked once more and dashed across the road, into the safety of bushes on the other side.

He couldn't be certain, but thought that he had gone unnoticed. The watcher would have been focussing on the camp if they hadn't already settled down for the night. His only instruction would have been to follow and report back on the direction Camar's party took. With the target having supposedly stopped for the night, the lackey would have no reason but to do the same.

Camar continued on his wide arc and was several hundred feet behind where he thought his target was. He could see the camp fire burning brightly in the distance, so he started edging his way slowly forward using any cover he could as he went. He thought that he saw his target being silhouetted by the fire up ahead, there was a solid dark mass that couldn't be bushes. He slowly moved closer, constantly checking if there was any undergrowth that would snap to reveal his presence. He was close now, and could clearly see that the dark mass had taken shape. It was difficult to see how big his watcher was as they were knelt on one leg watching the camp. Camar drew his knife and as he approached his target, he wondered if his watcher was a boy as the frame was quite small. Man or boy - either way he must die so that no report would go back to Quintus of the direction he would take in the morning.

Camar crept up behind his prey, conscious that those last few steps could give away his approach. He reached around the front of his target and gripped under the nose. He pulled the head back with his left hand as his right hand drew the knife across the throat. The gush of warm blood flowed down over his left hand with the person following him dying quickly and silently. The only sounds were those of the slaves chattering in the distance as they set up camp, the chirping of nocturnal insects, and the faint bubbling of blood as air escaped from the spy's slashed windpipe.

The ambassador rolled the corpse over and searched for anything that might identify the body if it was found at a later date. As he pulled the woollen hood back he was surprised as a mass of long dark hair fell from it. The frame was small not because it was a boy, but because it was a woman. He shivered, he did not like killing at the best of times, but this was the first woman he had ever dispatched to the gods. There was nothing on the woman's body, so if she was discovered she would simply be one of the many unfortunate souls who fell afoul of robbers on this road. He grabbed the ankles of the corpse and dragged the body further away from the well-used highway. Camar wiped his blade clean and headed back to his camp where his slaves would have prepared a meal for him.

He awoke the next morning, but he hadn't slept well that night as he frequently woke from his dreams. He reassured himself that he had to kill the woman or jeopardise his entire mission. He had slept in his woollen robe, and had forgotten how itchy it was compared to his fine ambassador's clothing. Camar wanted to change into his more comfortable clothes, but this garment better suited his needs for his mission today. He ate a light breakfast and pondered what lay in store for him for the rest of the day.

The slaves loaded the trunk back onto the cart and readied themselves for their Master's instructions. Camar was ready but knew that the slaves pulling a cart would be very easy to spot, so he told them to wait there until he returned. He would have to go alone for this part of the mission. The slaves were to say that they were waiting for their Master's return from Rome if they were questioned by anyone of authority, which wasn't too far from the truth. Camar followed the route he had taken the night before, it was much easier in the light of day. He came across the road that led up from the fork further down from the main thoroughfare. He started in the direction of Quintus' villa, but not before cautiously inspecting the road in front and behind him. It was early in the morning, and the road was completely deserted.

He followed the tree lined road for several hours, only stopping and taking cover when anyone came in to sight. Camar noticed how the fields had become more agricultural and had many different types of produce growing in them. He thought that they must be approaching the villa although he couldn't see it. Now he could see there was an increasing number of slaves tending the fields of grain, so Camar thought it prudent to leave the road, positioning himself on the far side of the tree lined road.

The Etruscan ambassador, now turned thief, carried on walking and the villa came into view on his right hand side. Camar decided that he would continue off road until he was much closer to the house, and then see if there was any suitable cover to hide his approach. He spotted several plumes of thick black smoke rising into the sky behind the villa. He thought that he would approach from the area where it was being lazily carried skywards by the gentle breeze that also tickled the hairs on the back of his neck. He recognised the tell-tale sounds of a smith at work, and knew from experience that must be the place where the swords were being manufactured.

Camar used the cover of the tree lined road and continued half a mile past the villa's grand entrance. The road that led to the grand residence was about half a mile long with marble statues equally spread out along the road. The extravagant two story villa could be seen at the end of the long approach to the entrance of the impressive main house of the extensive latifundium.

Once he had gotten safely past the turning to the estate, Camar crossed the road and stopped on the other side. Before he left the cover of the trees he took a quick look to check for any prying eyes. He was satisfied that he was in the clear, and darted into a wheat field that was nearly ready for harvesting. He kept low and walked between the neatly ploughed rows of wheat to avoid leaving any tracks.

As he got closer he saw that there was a large olive grove in the area that the smoke was rising from. Camar made his way to the far end and reached up to pluck an olive from the tree. He squeezed it between his thumb and index finger to find that it was still quite firm. Moving it to his mouth he started to bite in to it until his teeth told him that it was still as hard as a stone. As it was still hard it meant that the olives weren't ripe, so he wouldn't expect any slaves to be in the grove that might spot him. The trees had been planted close together and were in full leaf, providing enough shadow for Camar to conceal himself from the bright midday sunlight.

The Etruscan carefully made his way to the other end of the olive grove and stopped two rows before the end where he could see the three fire pits that were being used. Pairs of slaves were at the base of each one operating huge bellows, while three men removed molten metal from the pits. Camar noticed that one of the men would stop occasionally and go to inspect the other two. This man must be the one in charge so Camar concentrated on him.

He couldn't see clearly enough the actions of the man he thought to be the Master smith, but had noticed that this man was working much faster than the others. The man was taking a lump of molten metal and hammering it into a sword blade every ten minutes while the other two produced one every fifteen minutes. It was too risky to get any closer to watch the weapon manufacturing process up close as there was no cover between the olive grove and the fire pits.

On completion the blades were cooled in buckets of water and left to hang on racks that had been erected to store them. There were rows and rows of racks, each holding one hundred sword blades. Handles hadn't been put on yet, but he knew this wasn't an issue as any of his smiths could finish the sword. Camar decided that he would fulfil his primary mission by making off with one of the swords, and abandon his secondary mission of learning the secret of the manufacture. He could return to Clusium with his blade, and report back about the Master smith. Maybe he could return at some time with a small number of armed men to snatch the smith and take him back to manufacture these swords for the Etruscan League. Once back at his city the man could be offered his freedom and enough money to set him up for life in exchange for his cooperation.

Decision made, there was nothing more for Camar to do now apart from wait until nightfall. He retreated deeper into the olive grove, selecting a spot to have a rest for a while as he had not slept well the night before. He found a suitable place where the tree offered him protection and a little comfort from its shape, then sat down on the floor. He took some food from his small leather sack, ate the slightly stale bread and hard cheese before drifting off to sleep.

Camar woke in a panic; for a few moments not quite realising where he was. He glanced around and settled again as he recognised the olive grove, remembering why he was there. He must have slept for quite a while as the sun was dipping low to the west. A few clouds covered the brightness of the sun, making the sky glow a wonderful red colour. The red sky at night was a good omen for him as it meant it would be a good day tomorrow. He made his way back to the edge of the olive grove which was nearly in total darkness. The three smiths were still pounding away at the molten blobs in an attempt to keep working until the lack of light forced them to stop.

Camar heard a nightingale singing its evening song and knew that night would soon cast its thick quilt of impenetrable darkness over the smiths' work area. He watched as slaves fuelled the fire pits to ensure they didn't go out during the night. The new fuel caught light and Camar watched as its initial burst of brightness settled down in to a faint glow. Two of the smiths left while the third inspected the fire pits to ensure they had enough fuel to sustain them through the night. The third smith must have been satisfied as he soon left.

One of the traits required for Camar to do his job effectively was patience, and that's exactly what was needed now. Acting too hastily at this point could see him discovered by someone returning to the fire pits to collect something they had forgotten. So he waited and watched, and watched and waited, until he was almost certain that he would not be discovered.

He stealthily made his way from the olive grove and across the open area to the racks of sword blades. The fire pits still emitted enough light for him to see and Camar could feel the heat on his cheeks, even from some distance away. His prize was before him, racks and racks of blades.

He carefully made his way down to the rack with blades forged earlier that day, as he suspected the last set could be still too hot to handle. He gave one of them a quick touch to check that it was cool and took it off the rack. The blade would be missed the next morning as all of the end rack was full, but he would be long gone by then. He headed past the fire pits, back into the olive grove, knowing that he would be with his slaves in just a few hours. Camar decided that he would travel through the night until he reached the capital Clusium.

Tomorrow morning he would present the sword to the council. This could be the resurrection of Etruscan fortunes, and finally teach those jumped-up Romans who really ruled this region.

Chapter 15

The Promised Land

The temperature was getting much warmer as the advance party descended the other side of the mountain. The snow on the ground had melted, with the chariots and men turning the track into a muddy mess as the group trudged downhill. Despite the mud sticking to their boots, and everything it touched, the party was in good spirits. They knew they had completed the hardest part of their crossing. Occasionally the caught glimpses of a vast, lush and fertile plain as the track wound around the side of a hill. What were only tiny pinpricks from the top of the mountain were now becoming miniature trees, on a patchwork landscape that showed the land was being farmed.

Arenwen was proud of his men. They had travelled such a long distance, crossed a raging river, and through a mountain pass that few people had ever crossed. The thick mud was now being dried by the warm breeze that rustled through the trees, and was starting to crack on the sides of the chariots. It fell off in large chunks to be ground into dust as the men and horses trampled over it.

The day was drawing to an end, but Arenwen could still feel its warmth gently caressing his face. A small group of clouds formed in front of the sun which made the sky light up a crimson red, and thought contently to himself that this was a good omen, tomorrow would be a good day. The track had been flat for quite some time, and had opened up into a great swathe of trees. Arenwen surveyed the area and spotted a clearing. He decided that they would set up camp there for the night, satisfied that they had come completely descended the other side of the mountain. It would also be a good opportunity to let both his men and horses have a decent rest.

The party settled in the clearing and made camp with Durston and Dafydd put on first watch. They were in a new land after all, and it would surely pay to be cautious. The group organised the camp and a fire was lit. Arenwen was confident the dense undergrowth and the onset of nightfall would mask any smoke that would rise up into the night air.

The horses were unhitched from the chariots and tethered to nearby trees. They munched on the thick green fern leaves that grew in vast quantities around the clearing. The warriors still had plenty of supplies and water, so there was no need to send out a foraging party.

Suddenly there was a movement in the undergrowth behind them. Deborah was first to react by snatching up her bow that she had just off loaded from the chariot. The ferns twitched again as Deborah loosed an arrow followed quickly by a second. A larger area of greenery crumpled to the floor leaving a hole where the tall bracken once had stood. Deborah rushed over to the ferns quickly followed by Arenwen. They looked down, and were very happy to see a young deer dead with two arrows sticking out of its head. They both took a leg and dragged it into the dell. Bakher went over to the dead animal and looked in to its lifeless eyes.

'I will skin this beast as I want to examine the entrails,' he said.

The druid slit the fawn's neck, and collected the blood into a large wooden bowl. The men gathered around him as he cut open the gut with some skill, all the way from the anus to the sternum, pulling out the warm entrails. Bakher reached to the back of the animal's abdominal cavity, and felt the intestine for any lumps or abnormalities. Moving forwards to the chest he felt the large mass of lungs underneath the ribs, and expertly located the heart. Going in with his knife he made small movements with his right hand, and pushed in his left to remove the heart.

Bakher took the heart over to the light of the camp fire and turned it slowly in his hands.

'Well, what are the omens?' Arenwen asked.

Bakher didn't reply, but passed around the wooden bowl of deer blood. Each man took a drink and wiped the excess blood from their lips. Finally after everyone had taken a drink Bakher said 'the omens are good,' but Arenwen knew him very well and could tell that something was troubling the druid.

The men didn't notice the slight frown on Bakher's face, as they cheered and went about the business of butchering the deer; they would eat well that night.

Dafydd and Durston were relieved from their sentry duty after four hours, and happily tucked into the cold roasted venison that had been saved for them. They quietly chatted about what they thought lay ahead of them and for the first time in a very long while, they drifted off to a comfortable, deep sleep without the need for any furs to keep them warm.

Arenwen was woken by the sentry guards.

'Is there a problem?' He asked.

'No problem Lord, but as it is morning, I thought I should wake you,' the sentry replied.

Indeed it was morning and the sun was already peeking over the mountains to the east, flooding the forest with shards of bright light. Arenwen rubbed his eyes and looked around the camp. They had all slept well, but then noticed Bakher and Deborah were not with them.

'Where are those two?' Arenwen said pointing to the places where his companions should be sleeping.

'They left and disappeared into the forest a little while ago,' the sentry replied.

Arenwen knew they would either be gathering something or paying tribute to the gods.

The men began to stir as the embers of last night's fire had fresh wood thrown onto it to bring it back to life. The group went about preparing breakfast and readying themselves for the day to come. All had visited the spot designated as the temporary latrine. Arenwen was glad he had chosen to locate it away from the camp as he had visited the area himself to empty his bowels, and realised how badly it stank.

He pulled up his woollen trousers then headed back to the clearing to find that Bakher and Deborah had returned, and we putting something on Bilhild's chariot.

'What do you have there?' Arenwen asked Bakher.

'Nothing to concern you, but you will be glad we have it later,' the druid replied with a wily look on his face.

'Riddles, more damned riddles!' Arenwen muttered to himself, needled by the druid's puzzles.

The horses had been fed, watered, and hitched to the chariot. The fire was put out and Arenwen surveyed the gap in the woods. There were three tracks not far from the clearing when Durston piped up.

'South, Lord?' He asked.

'Yes, Durston south and on to claim our fortune,' Arenwen replied with a smile.

'Then we should take the middle track, as it heads south,' Durston said cheerily, proud of his new found skills. Dafydd laughed and playfully dug him in the ribs with a punch.

'Take some axes to either side of the trail to mark our direction for the others to follow,' Arenwen said.

The men marked the first five trees on either side of the track. The following army would see that the cuts were fresh, and realise it was a marker for them to follow. Arenwen led the way with Bilhild following behind. The ground was firm, which made it easier for the men on foot who were enjoying the morning light, and the fresh smell of pine as they followed the two chariots.

The group continued along the trail until it opened out in to a wide plain. It was flat as far as the eye could see, reaching from the mountains on the left beyond Arenwen's view to the right. The Celtic leader couldn't see any distinguishable landmarks or buildings so he followed the advice given to him by the scouts as they departed. They had told him to head south and keep the mountains to the left.

The warriors easily crossed the fields as Arenwen scanned the area looking for a road, as roads always led somewhere. With nothing in sight he called Bilhild up to his side.

'We need to get an idea of the lay of the land, and we also need fresh water,' he said to his second in command.

He told the men to carry straight on towards a group of trees in the distance. Bilhild was to scout the western side of the plain, while Arenwen would take his chariot to scout the east. He estimated it was about a four hour journey to the group of trees for the men on foot. Before setting off the Celtic leader informed the others that this would be the area where they all would rendezvous.

'Avoid contact if you can. Kill if you must,' Arenwen said to Bilhild who confirmed with a nod.

The men carried on forward as the two chariots headed off left and right. Arenwen headed towards the mountains and saw several small villages which he gave a wide berth to, so that he did not panic any of the locals. Apart from the occasional small village, there was nothing of interest on this vast fertile plain.

Bilhild's experience was very similar to Arenwen's as he guided his team of horses across the rich land, until he had been going for about an hour. He wasn't too sure what it was at first, but now he recognised the scar on the landscape was a road. It carried on straight in front of him, but more interestingly ran north to south, and there was a small lake on the far side of the road. There was no one to be seen, but they were in unfamiliar territory so Bilhild took Arenwen's advice to avoid any potential contact. To continue anywhere near the road would sooner or later bring him into sight with someone. Bilhild looked to the distance and could make out the group of trees that they had all agreed to meet at.

'Head back to the meeting point, what do you think?' He asked Deborah.

'Yes, I agree, it's too risky anywhere near this road,' she replied scanning the area.

Bilhild slowed his horses down, pulling firmly on the left rein. The geldings turned as instructed, heading towards the meeting point. The terrain was smooth and easy to travel upon. Deborah thought that it was fine land for cultivating, and wondered why no one had planted crops or had livestock grazing. She then remembered the view from the mountains to the swathes of seemingly untouched land, and thought that the local inhabitants must have so much land they didn't need to farm this area at all.

Bilhild and Deborah carried along, and pulled up the chariot next to the men at the agreed rendezvous area. The men were underneath the trees, shading themselves from the heat of the sun.

'Any sign of Arenwen?' Bilhild asked Durston.

'Nothing yet, was there anything over there?' Durston said looking over to the right.

'A few villages that were far too small to be worth raiding, but more importantly a road,' Bilhild replied.

Deborah and Bilhild got down from the chariot and led the horses under the cool shade of the trees. It wasn't long before they saw Arenwen approaching from the east. He came in to join the others and headed straight for the group.

'It's damn hot out there. We can't take the men far in this heat,' Arenwen said wiping sweat from his brow.

'Well we have two options as I see it. One is to wait here for Brennus to join us as we have a good supply of food and water. He was only a day behind us at the river crossing. So if he made good time over the mountains he could only be only a half a day behind,' Bilhild said.

'And the second option?' Arenwen asked.

'There's a big road to the right with a lake next to it. We could easily take one of the small villages to settle in for a day. Have a fresh supply of water and what meagre animals the locals have we will take.

Arenwen considered the two options. He would prefer to take the village and wreak havoc on the locals, but it could stir up a hornets nest. At best they were a small raiding party and that road hadn't been built without reason. A mounted force could descend on them quickly.

'Men, unpack; we'll spend the night here and wait for the main force to join us. Organise yourselves into a watch, but there are to be no fires tonight,' Arenwen said.

Arenwen's mission had been to ensure that the main army had a smooth transition though the Celtic tribes' lands. He had done this and hoped that Brennus would be pleased with his efforts. He had some luck along the way but with all things considered, Arenwen thought he had achieved what his cousin had sent him to do. The druid had overheard the conversation and came over to join the two men.

'A wise decision. There will be plenty of opportunities for fighting,' Bakher said.

Although there were still several hours of daylight left, the group settled down for the rest of the day. They still had supplies of sausage, cheese and plenty of water. It had been a very hot day so the men didn't mind going without a fire to heat up some food. In this land they would be able to live with much less fuel, the land was good for farming and raising livestock. It was clearly going to be another warm night as the company settled in for the evening, a few small groups chatting excitedly about the riches and battles that lay ahead, but the noise soon died down as they all drifted off to sleep in the warm night air.

It was another beautiful cloudless day when the group woke up. A thin, wispy mist lay over the ground, but the sun was already up and starting to burn it off. The sentries had nothing to report from the previous night. Arenwen pulled the group together.

'Today should be the day Lord Brennus joins up with us,' he said.

Arenwen sent out a foraging party, not because they were short of food, but it kept the men busy. He also sent others out to gather wood, as this morning he was in the mood for a good blaze. The men collecting it returned with an ample supply of dry combustible fuel, and set about lighting the fire their leader had requested. The foraging party returned shortly after with three braces of rabbits. There wouldn't be much meat off the six rabbits, but it would add a nice flavour to the food they did have. The fire was well alight as the rabbits were gutted and skinned. The smoke rose into the morning sky like a beacon in the night. Bakher approached Arenwen

'I take it that the smoke is for Brennus' benefit,' Bakher said.

'Yes, it is a signal to let our Lord know our location,' Arenwen said emphasising the word 'Lord.'

'Then if I may, I have something that will make it much better,' Bakher asked.

'By all means,' Arenwen replied wondering what the druid was up to.

Bakher got the men to stand well back from the flame, and also made sure that the horses were moved. He went over to the fire, and spent several moments moving his hands in circles over the flickering flame. He couldn't quite see what the druid pulled from his pouch, but whatever it was, he sprinkled it onto the flames and stood well back. At first the smoke turned green as it continued to spiral in to the air. Arenwen thought this was good as Brennus would know it was a signal from him, but he was amazed by what happened next.

The fire burned purple, orange, green and blue before it shot a hundred feet into the air. Not only was it a frighteningly large flame, but it suddenly took the shape of a great red dragon, the lower part becoming the body, and the higher licking flames forming the fire breathing head.

The smoke dragon danced as the wind took it, and remained for a few minutes before the smoke returned to its original green colour.

As the flame died down and the smoke returned to its normal colour Arenwen approached Bakher.

'That should do it,' the warrior said with a smile.

'Indeed it should, now let's get those rabbits cooking,' Bakher replied.

The signal had certainly worked as just before midday Bilhild noticed a dust plume from the north. He pointed it out to Arenwen.

'It must be a large force to kick up so much dust,' Bakher said.

'Yes you're right, we've got company for sure,' Arenwen replied to his comrade.

The leader called for his chariot, as did his second in command. Their regular companions joined them as they set off towards the dust plume. The chariots crossed the hardened earth at pace and they soon saw what had been making the clouds, it was Brennus and his army. Arenwen urged his horses on with a shout and a flick of the reins to meet his Lord, as Bakher grumbled that they were going too fast. Arenwen glanced over and could see the Druid's knuckles were white as the old man gripped the side rails as if his life depended on it.

The army was an impressive sight, and Brennus was in the centre of twenty five chariots with another twenty five in line behind the first rank. A thousand cavalry flanked each side. Eight thousand of Brennus' foot warriors and the two thousand send by

Galatos followed behind the chariots. In total they were an impressive twelve thousand battle hardened warriors.

Brennus was moving at a reasonable pace to let his foot soldiers keep up, but when he saw the other two chariots approaching he pushed his horses into a full gallop, covering the ground as if they had wings, quickly joining the other two chariots.

'That could only have been you, Bakher,' Brennus said referring to the smoke signal.

'I thought it might catch your attention,' the druid replied with a slight bow.

There was no question that Brennus was the Lord, but druids were a class amongst themselves. The ruling Lords needed their advice and powers, so there was a mutual respect between Celtic Chieftains and the druids.

'You negotiated well Bakher, we had ample supplies and unfettered access right across our cousin's lands,' Brennus said.

'I cannot take all the praise, Arenwen and indeed some of his men made the task much easier,' Bakher replied.

Brennus then turned his attention to Arenwen.

'I knew you were a good choice, cousin.'

'Thank you, Lord but if I may add that Bilhild has been an excellent second.'

Arenwen outlined the result of the scouting mission they had undertaken the day before. He explained how there wasn't much towards the mountains, but how Bilhild had discovered the road with the small lake next to it.

'Then that is where we shall go. A large road will certainly lead us to a large town,' Brennus said with a smile.

Arenwen instructed Bilhild to lead the army to the small lake while he would return the short distance to the rest of the advance party and meet back up with them at the copse. Bilhild agreed and wheeled the chariot around to come to the side of Brennus'. Brennus signalled the change of direction with his right arm, and the army adjusted its direction with almost perfect precision - the far flank pivoting slowly, while the other moved quicker to cover the same ground, it was truly a magnificent sight to behold.

With a friendly wave, Arenwen also wheeled his chariot around and headed back towards his men. By the time he had got there, they were all set and ready to go. Dafydd passed Arenwen a stick with the remaining skewered rabbit as he kicked out the remnants of the fire. Arenwen, in turn, passed the cooked rabbit to Bakher who tore off one of the hind legs and bit in to the succulent meat. Arenwen took the rest of the rabbit and picked his way through the animal until all that was left was the remaining hind leg. He wiped his face clean with his sleeve, and tossed the carcass on to the ashes of the fire.

The warrior led his men towards the road, and could already see small plumes of smoke in that direction. The army had come across some of the small villages Bilhild had told him about. There would be no mercy for any villagers who hadn't fled before the army reached them. The small party made their way across the land and came across the first village that had suffered the ravages of the army. There were no bodies to be seen, but nothing from the simple dwellings was left intact. The small villages had been burned and looted with the remnants of what couldn't be carried away by their owners strewn all over the floor. Large cooking pots had been kicked over and the fires were used to torch the meagre homes of the tiny hamlet.

'I hope this isn't all that's here,' Dafydd said to Durston as they passed through the second village.

'Why, because there won't be much for us to take?' Durston asked.

'No, we're already rich, but I want someone to fight!' Dafydd said and they both laughed.

The group were now coming up to the third and final village that had sprung up by the side of the road. The army was on its far side, by the lake. The villagers must have fished the lake as some of their nets lay scattered around on the ground. As the group walked past the houses Bilhild noticed something moving under one of the nets. He pulled his chariot to a halt and went over to investigate. To his surprise he found a young dog had been pinned by the falling nets. He lifted the weight to find a chocolate brown puppy which shivered, and looked up at him with its deep brown eyes.

'What have you got there?' Arenwen asked.

'A puppy,' Bilhild replied.

'Leave it there, its mother will be somewhere close by,' Arenwen said.

Bilhild looked around, but couldn't see any sign of its mother.

'I'm going to bring it with us,' Bilhild said.

'I've never seen your soft side before,' Arenwen laughed.

Bilhild scooped the pup up in one hand, and looked around to see if there was anything suitable for it to eat. He saw a bowl that had been knocked to one side, but it hadn't been completely tipped over. It had a small amount of milk left in it, so Bilhild carried the pup over to the bowl. He held it under its chest and lent its head towards the milk. The dog's little legs dangled down from Bilhild's hand as its little pink tongue lapped at the milk.

The whole group had stopped to watch the pup drink. As soon as the bowl was emptied, the warrior gently placed the dog under his cloak and safely inside the bole of his tunic, got back onto his chariot, and the party carried on the short distance to the small lake.

Arenwen urged his horses up the small rise and onto the road. He was impressed by the quality of the surface and looked left where it was perfectly straight, unlike the mud roads at home that twisted and turned around any natural obstacle. He crossed the road and down the small slope the other side in search of Brennus. He wasn't hard to find as Arenwen could see that his tent had already been taken off one of the carts, and had been erected close to the lake. Fires were being started and a few Celts had taken some of the fishing nets from the last village and were casting them in to the lake. It looked like they were stopping for the night. Arenwen pulled his chariot up behind the tent and handed his reins to a slave.

'Keep it there, I won't be long,' he said.

The slave nodded as Arenwen went around the front to the tent's entrance. The guards stepped to one side as Arenwen approached, he ducked under the tent flaps to see Brennus standing over a poor wretch. The man was on his knees with each arm being pinned behind his back by two of Brennus' men. A small amount of blood trickled from the corner of his mouth, with a large swelling around his right eye where a richly dark, purple bruise was already spreading.

'Is that all you can tell me?' Brennus said as he punched the man in the face.

'Yes, that is all I know. I am just a simple farmer,' the man replied.

'OK, get him out of here,' Brennus said to his two men who promptly pulled the man out of the tent by his arms as his legs dragged along the floor.

Brennus repeated the little information he had gathered from the villager. The road they were on would, in half a day's march, take them to a very large town called Clusium or as he called it a city. The villager had been there to sell his crops and had seen armed men there, but did not know how many. The villager also knew of other large towns but not their locations, as he had never travelled further than Clusium.

Brennus called for a slave to bring ale and meat.

'Now tell me of your journey here,' Brennus said as the slave returned with two horn cups of ale and a platter of meat.

Arenwen recounted the trip so far on their three month journey. He talked about the feast, the river crossing, how his men had saved Felix's son and the minor skirmish with the mountain men. Brennus sat intrigued at his cousin's exploits along the way. Arenwen was enjoying himself, it had been a while since he had had ale, but he needed to ensure his men were well provisioned.

'May I take my leave and make sure my men are settled?' Arenwen asked.

'Of course,' Brennus said, 'I have kept you here far too long. Go and make sure they are all comfortable,' he said as he drained his horn of ale.

Brennus called his slave again telling him to make sure that a good supply of ale and fresh meat were sent over to Arenwen's men.

Brennus looked smiled at Arenwen and said 'let your men eat and drink tonight, they have deserved it for tomorrow we go to Clusium!'

The army awoke the next morning at first light. Brennus had summoned his senior warriors, of course including Arenwen and Bilhild, to his tent to outline the plan for the day. This was still unknown land and Brennus was unsure what to expect, but still confident that his twelve thousand warriors were a match for anything that could be put before them. Arenwen and Bilhild were to take twenty five chariots, a thousand cavalry and a thousand foot soldiers. They were to approach Clusium and enter into negotiations for land. The force would be sizeable enough to intimidate the population, but Brennus would not show his full might until he absolutely needed to.

'Get them up, get them fed and get them moving,' Brennus said.

The senior warriors bowed and went to ready their men.

Arenwen and Bilhild got their groups organised, as instructed, and the two thousand strong army set off down the road.

Just as the villager had said, after half a day Arenwen saw the very large town the wretch had called Clusium, curious to find out why the villager had called it as a city. Not only was this a new word to him, but an entirely alien concept for someone who had grown up knowing little more than the small town that he had been raised in. As an adult he ruled over great swathes of land, but the dwellings were interspersed settlements, with his being the largest.

As they got closer to Clusium, he could see the locals scattering like ants before them to seek shelter behind the large stone walls. This too was new as the size of the town was at least three times bigger than the one at Andematunnum, and he had never seen a wall made from stone before. So this is why the villager had called it a city, it was massive. As he stood before it, marvelling at the huge walled settlement before them, the thought occurred to him that this might not be as easy as they had first imagined.

Arenwen signalled the senior warrior leading the cavalry. He told him to take five hundred men to the back of the city to cut off any possible escape route. As the mounted force set off at an easy canter, he used the rest of the men to encircle Clusium as best they could. Due the vastness of the city he didn't have enough men to cover the area completely, so he made sure that the front and back were secure, and sent smaller numbers to guard the sides of the town. He corrected himself calling it a town, in his mind, as previously he didn't know any other word for it. Now he knew the name of a town that was bigger than a big town was called a city. Arenwen signalled Bilhild, and they approached the city walls making sure they were out of arrow range. The huge gates had been firmly closed and barred, so Arenwen called up to the men on the walls and told them that he was here for land and riches, asking them to send out an emissary out to discuss the terms of their surrender.

Chapter 16

A Cry For Help

Camar was still tired when he awoke that morning, and would have dearly loved to sleep in until at least midday. After stealing the sword from Quintus' villa he had travelled all night without even stopping once, as he had to report on the success of his mission as soon as he could. He quickly got dressed back into his ambassador's apparel, and made sure that he was impeccably turned out to present himself before the Etruscan government. With one last look in the polished bronze mirror he was satisfied, and then had one heart stopping moment when he couldn't see the blade, before remembering that he had hidden it under his bedroll for safe keeping. He threw back the bed covers and retrieved the stolen property.

Camar went down the stairs of his home, fussing away the slaves who were offering him a morning meal as he didn't have time for breakfast that particular morning. He needed to visit a smith to have the edges of the blade sharpened, and a handle attached before the council was assembled. He wrapped the blade in a cloth and hurriedly left his home. He turned right and made his way down the streets, which were already bustling with traders getting their goods ready for another day's trading in the city.

The ambassador dodged in and out of the outraged merchants as he hurried down towards the end of the street where he knew he would find one of the many smiths that plied their trade in the city. He saw the familiar sight of black smoke billowing in the air, which indicated that at least one smith had already started his working day.

'How quickly can you sharpen and put a temporary handle on this?' Camar asked.

The smith sucked a deep intake of breath through his pursed lips.

'Could get it done by midday,' he replied after he slowly let the breath out. Camar pulled out his purse, selected a silver coin and tossed it to the smith.

'I need it in fifteen minutes,' Camar said.

'This coin feels a bit too light for fifteen minutes,' the smith said holding out his hand.

Camar huffed as he placed another silver coin into the smith's dirty palm.

'One more should do it,' the smith said with a grin.

'That's robbery,' Camar protested.

'There are plenty others in the city,' the smith replied, starting to turn away from the ambassador.

Camar knew that he wouldn't have time to get to any of the other smiths before the government assembled. Begrudgingly he placed a third coin in the smith's palm.

The smith took the blade and immediately went to work. He sat down and locked it into place between his knees. Reaching over to a table he took his whetstone and carefully rubbed it up and down the blade before taking it to his grinding wheel. The smith pumped the foot pedal that spun the giant stone. Sparks flew from the blade as it got sharpened by the spinning stone. When he was satisfied that it was sharp enough the smith took a wooden handle and punched hot rivets through holes to secure the handle to the blade. The handle end of the sword was pushed in to a bucket of water which hissed as it cooled the hot rivets.

'That's cooler, but still hot,' the smith said.

Still sulking about the amount he had been charged Camar carefully wrapped the sword back in the cloth. He thought to himself that the smith would rue the day that he had overcharged an up and coming member of the administration. Who knew one day he might even get elected as Governor. Camar hurried to the government building as he knew it must be about to open soon.

As he entered, he made his presence known to the clerk. The clerk was the person who scheduled the discussions and debates to be held that day. Seeing that Camar had returned from business with an edict issued by the Governor himself, the official scheduled him to be the first to make his address to the noble members. Camar was very pleased with his listing and thought about the red sky he had seen the day before, it was truly a good omen as today he would receive high praise from those in power.

Camar waited patiently as the members of the council, many of them quite elderly and rather slow, filed into the circular chamber. The entire space was brilliant white, further enhanced by a dome above that let an abundance of light in through wooden slats. Everything seemed to have been either inlaid or constructed with immaculate marble, and there were three tiers of marble seats that surrounded the centre circle where the speaker would address the officials.

The clerk took a look out of the entrance one last time to see if there were any other officials arriving. When he saw that there weren't any, he picked up his parchment from his desk and made his way in to the centre of the chamber. The clerk read out the business for the day as Camar sat outside nervously. When he had finished reading the list he called Camar to present himself to the government. He had butterflies in his stomach, with his legs feeling like jelly as he walked past the guards and entered the chamber through the huge brass doors, clutching the precious bundle under his right arm.

Camar fumbled with the cloth that contained the sword before finally managing to unwrap it. The members gasped when he drew the sword as weapons were forbidden inside the chamber. His mission had been known only to a small number of the government, due to its delicate nature, so he needed to address the full body to inform them of what had been requested of him. Camar outlined that there had been a recent report from one of the Etruscan spies in Rome of this new stronger metal. He went on to describe how he had been dispatched quickly to retrieve one of these new swords. There were calls for him and his weapon to be immediately removed from the chamber before the Governor stood up and hushed the other members.

'It is with my special permission that this has been brought before us. I will also permit for a second weapon to be brought in before you,' the governor said as he summoned a guard from outside.

The guard walked gingerly into the chamber for the first time in the twenty five years that he had served the government.

'Draw your sword,' the Governor instructed the guard.

The man would not draw his sword as he knew to do so was punishable by death. The Governor told him to draw his sword again and reassured him that the soldier was under his personal protection. He drew his sword and stood awkwardly not knowing what to do.

'Strike that sword with all your might,' The Governor told the guard pointing at the one being held by Camar.

The guard removed his conical bronze helmet, and laid his circular shield on the floor. His bronze breastplate that went down to his naval was a little restrictive, but he would still be able to strike a fearsome blow. The sword he was carrying was much longer than the one he was to strike, and was almost twice as long. Unlike the straight sword being held by the ambassador, the guard's blade was slightly curved and the tip, its thickness doubled as it got to the hilt because it was primarily designed as a weapon for slashing and cutting. The guard did as he was instructed and raised his sword, bringing it down with an almighty blow onto the short sword. Camar stumbled back with the force of the strike as the loud clang resonated around the chamber. The guard stepped back and looked at the pathetic remnants of his weapon. It had buckled in two whereas the other sword was perfectly intact.

'This was the only safe place I could demonstrate this to you without Roman spies seeing. I beg the government's forgiveness as I hope you agree my actions were necessary,' the Governor said apologetically.

There was a ripple of agreement around the chamber as the guard was dismissed. Camar went on to tell the nobles that he had a plan to acquire a man who knew the ins and outs of this new metal. He had them in the palm of his hand and all his nerves had disappeared. Surely he must be promoted for his actions - any minute now, a noble or maybe even the Governor himself would propose it.

Suddenly the large bronze doors burst open and the clerk rushed in. He climbed the tiers and whispered in the Governor's ear. The colour in the Governor's face drained away until he was a sickly white. The Governor got up and stepped slowly to the centre of the chamber. He gestured to Camar to take a seat and addressed the members.

'Villagers have been streaming in to our city over the last half an hour. They give reports of a large army, exact size unknown, marching towards us,' the Governor said.

There were questions coming in from all directions of the chamber.

'Both gates have been closed. Our soldiers have manned the ramparts, and I propose we send word to our fellow cities of the Etruscan League, as well as our allies in Rome for military support,' The Governor said.

'Seconded,' came calls of support from the chamber.

'Given his outstanding performance, skill and intelligence I propose that ambassador Camar is dispatched to Rome immediately and ambassador Rossi is sent to our city states.,' the Governor suggested.

'Seconded,' came the calls again.

The Governor thought it would be an honour to send Camar to Rome, but he did not know how Camar had acquired the sword. He thought that he would avoid Rome for quite a while, until the matter of the missing blade had blown over. There was no chance that the blade had not been missed from the neatly filled racks. Quintus would certainly know within a day or two of it going missing.

Camar feigned gratitude, but inside he was in a sheer panic.

'Ambassadors Camar and Rossi, go ready yourselves with all haste to bring back reinforcements,' The Governor said.

Ambassador Rossi got up and left the chamber with Camar following behind. Camar made his way back to his home with his head spinning with thoughts of what he should do next. Should he gather as much money he could and escape, but escape to where? There was no viable option other than to return to Rome and front it out. His best hope and worst nightmare was to go to Quintus, and if the subject of the blade was raised, deny all knowledge. If he didn't go to Quintus and went straight to the Senate he was sure that Quintus would use his influence to block any request for military assistance. It was very risky, but he didn't seem to have much choice. It felt like his destiny had been already been decided by the gods.

Camar gathered a few possessions together then called for his horse to be saddled and brought to the front of his home immediately. The slaves ran off to follow their Master's bidding with the horse being made ready and presented. Camar went to the rear gate of his city when he saw Rossi was also ready to ride. Camar shouted for the gate to be opened, but as the soldiers were about to remove the huge wooden bar, that locked the gates together, another voice came down from the ramparts.

'Hold that order,' it was the captain of the guard.

'We are on critical government business, and we carry the orders of the Governor himself,' Camar called back.

'That's as may be, but unless you want to die you had better come and take a look,' the captain shouted above the din of the panicked crowd.

The two ambassadors dismounted and pushed their way through the crowds that had got through the rear gate before it had been barred shut. They climbed up the steep stone steps to the top of the rampart where the captain was standing.

'Take a look,' the officer said.

It was too late as the rear entrance had been cut off by a horde of horsemen who were indiscriminately killing everyone outside the safety of the castle walls.

'I've had reports that there are even more at the front gate, but not so many at the sides,' the captain said.

'I will wait until nightfall and be lowered down a side wall. Then I will slip through their lines to reach our Etruscan brothers,' Rossi said.

A good plan, Camar thought. He would use the cover of darkness to escape down the side wall, but unlike his colleague who needed to go inland Camar would use the river. If he could get to a small boat, the river would carry him to the Tiber and then on to Rome.

The day drew on and Camar heard that the Governor had gone to the front wall to speak to the invaders. After agreeing a truce he left the city to enter discussions. He had been gone some time when he re-entered through the main gate and returned to the council chambers and addressed its esteemed members.

'They have asked for a list of lands and the total amount of gold, silver and coins we have. They have made it quite clear that the list is to be accurate or there will be severe consequences. Once they are in possession of this list they will take half and leave us the other half,' The Governor said.

The nobles rose up in protest with cries of

Preposterous!' and 'we'll see them dead first!'

One of the nobles stood up with the others growing anxious to hear what he had to say.

'And what was your response?' The noble asked.

'I am in utter agreement with you all. They shall not even get the droppings from my horse. However, in order to stall for time I told them that I must take this proposition before you all,' the Governor replied.

The Etruscan leader had asked for forty eight hours to debate the issue. Arenwen had given them twenty four.

As darkness fell the two ambassadors were lowered down the side walls. They could see the camp fires of the invaders, and the captain had been correct in his observation. The army was thinly spread out as they guarded the side walls. The two colleagues shook hands and wished each other good luck at the bottom of the wall, before splitting up and going their separate ways with Camar heading for the river and Rossi heading inland.

The other ambassador scanned the area calculating which would be his best route. Most of the campfires were set so that they were equal distances apart. Seeing that there was large gap between two of the fires, he calculated that this would be the safest option. Rossi hugged the city walls for as long as he could, and used its shadowy darkness as his cover. When he was in front of the large gap he slowly made his way to the escape route. Once through he knew that there would be cover from trees and ditches that would take him through the thin line of invaders that encircled his beloved city. As he got closer to the gap he felt his heart thumping in his chest. Rossi thought that it was now or never and made a break for the gap. He was through, and felt an immense sense of relief before a receiving a heavy blow to the back of his head. He went down to the ground, and fell in to unconsciousness.

Rossi came round, but was still groggy. He could hear two voices.

'You see, that is how you set a trap in a siege,' the first voice said.

'Yep, you were right,' the second voice replied.

'This should wake him up,' the first voice said.

Rossi came to his senses instantly as a bucket of water was emptied over him.

'Yep you were right Dafydd, that did the trick alright,' Durston said smiling.

'Let's get him up and take him to Lord Arenwen for questioning.'

Rossi was manhandled around the side walls to the area at the front of the city where he was dragged in front of Arenwen.

'I have two questions, and if you answer them truthfully you will die quickly. If I think you are lying you will die very, very slowly,' Arenwen said.

'I will tell you nothing,' Rossi spat out.

Arenwen went over to the fire and put his knife blade into the bright flame. He watched the tip turn white and removed it. Wisps of smoke left the blade and swirled into the night air as Arenwen told Dafydd and Durston to hold their captive firmly. Rossi tried to twist and turn, but the two warriors held him so tightly he was unable to move. Arenwen waved the white hot knife in front of Rossi's face.

'Which eye would you like to lose first? Left or right?' Arenwen asked.

Rossi did not reply so Arenwen moved the blade to Rossi's left eye. He held it close enough that the heat was evaporating the water from the captive's eyeball. Rossi bucked again and closed his eyelid, but it was futile. Dafydd and Durston had him in a vice like grip as Arenwen prised his eye lid open.

The warrior moved the tip of the blade so it was nearly touching Rossi's left pupil.

'Alright, alright, what are your two questions?' Rossi blurted out in panic.

'One, how many of you are there?'

'And two, what was your mission?'

Rossi was a realist and knew he was going to die, so he preferred to die quickly. However, while he was no warrior, he was a skilled diplomat and that meant being an accomplished liar. Rossi quickly came to the decision that he did not want to betray his colleague or his city. The captive explained that this was the capital of the Etruscan League and that he was to contact the other ten cities to raise an army to come to the aid of Clusium. He added that he was the only one charged with this mission, and therefore acted alone. Arenwen looked him in the eye as Rossi went through the distance and description of the other cities. Either this was the truth or the man was a great liar, but it wasn't really of any concern to Arenwen as the Celts hadn't shown their true strength.

'Take him away and secure him,' Arenwen told his men.

While this was going on Camar had made his way to the river. He slipped into the water and silently untied a boat. He kicked the small craft into the flowing water, and held on to it from the side with only his head above water. He used the boat to shield himself from the bank of the Celtic encampment. The vessel was caught in the river's current, and was quickly picking up speed when suddenly the area above him was illuminated. A torch had been thrown in the sky as the boat had been spotted. Camar's heart sank as he thought that he had been discovered when he heard some voices.

'What is it?' the first voice questioned.

'Nothing, there's no one in it. Just a boat that has slipped its moorings,' came the reply.

Camar breathed a sigh of relief as he hung onto the craft as it floated downstream. When the invaders camp fires were but a faint speck in the distance Camar hauled himself into the boat and took up the oars. He calculated that he would be in Rome by the morning, and then his relief turned to dread as he remembered the task in hand. He realised that he would have to face Quintus.

The sun rose the next morning and Arenwen looked at the sky and thought it would be another and warm dry day. Breakfast was a much more appetising affair now that they had joined the main army, as both supplies and cooking utensils were plentiful. He went over to one of the large cooking pots and helped himself to some hot honeyed porridge and fresh bread. Having had his fill he, went to the front of the camp and shouted at the guards on the wall to bring the Governor.

The Governor soon appeared on the wall and shouted down to Arenwen that the twenty four hours would not elapse until later that afternoon.

'Correct me if I am wrong, but you wanted time to discuss terms with your government.' Arenwen bellowed.

'That is correct,' the Governor replied.

Arenwen held up his hand and the Governor's jaw dropped as he saw Rossi being dragged to Arenwen. The captured ambassador was kicked in the back of his knees, making him fall to the floor. Arenwen drew his longsword from its scabbard. The longsword only had a small hand grip with most of the weight towards the end of the blade, but once it was set in motion a skilled warrior could twist and turn the long heavy blade with ease. The Celtic chieftain moved the sword around in a figure of eight before raising it above his head. He brought it down in a slashing blow that sliced Rossi's head clean off.

'Negotiation over,' Arenwen said as the body hit the floor.

Chapter 17

Roman Treachery

Camar's calculations were correct, and he had travelled through the night being swept quickly down the river. He pulled his boat up to the landing area, tossing the mooring rope to one of the slaves. He climbed out of the small vessel, it rocked from side to side as he shifted his weight.

'You can't leave that there without paying,' the dock Master called after him.

'Keep it,' he shouted as he ran down the road, knowing he wouldn't need the craft again. Camar was winded, but had to keep going as he passed through the small villages. He slowed down as he approached the main entrance to Rome to recover from the slight stitch in his side, and compose himself for a meeting with Quintus. He crossed the wooden bridge and thought that he would need to be on top form as the shrewd Roman had already outwitted him previously. He passed the steep Capitoline Hill on his left, and headed straight for Quintus' domus.

Camar entered the vestibulum and was immediately attended by a slave on the door. He racked his mind thinking of the name of the overseer when it came to him.

'Go and fetch Aesop,' Camar ordered.

A few minutes went by before Aesop returned and ushered him into the formal entrance hall.

'My Master will be very annoyed at your presence for a second time without an appointment,' Aesop said.

'This is a matter of the utmost urgency,' Camar explained.

'Very well, I shall see if my Master will see you,' Aesop replied as he went.

Aesop announced Camar's arrival to Quintus as he sat in the colonnaded garden enjoying the fresh morning air. Aesop was surprised that his Master had granted the Etruscan ambassador an audience and went off to fetch him. Quintus moved to his office, and was sat down when Camar was brought in.

'Well, I'm surprised you have the nerve to show your face around here,' Quintus said with a scowl.

'How so senator? I thought we had agreed a fair deal,' Camar bluffed.

'Let me give you my account of the facts. One of my little birds did not return to her nest after she followed you from the city. Secondly, I had a report that one of my new blades has mysteriously gone missing. Put two and two together and I get you,' Quintus said accusingly.

'I must strongly protest senator. I know nothing of either matter,' Camar lied.

'I returned immediately to Clusium, following our agreement, and set about having the scabbard manufacture started. Why on earth would I do such a thing and return before you now?' He added.

'Why indeed?' Quintus puzzled.

'I have come on the orders of the Etruscan government,' Camar explained.

He went on to tell Quintus about the invading force, and that he had come to Rome to ask for military assistance. Knowing that the authorisation to dispatch the army would require the Senate to sanction it Camar hoped that, after their dealings, Quintus would put forward favourable representations from the Etruscan League.

Camar thought he had delivered the performance of his life as Quintus seemed to believe him. Quintus even accepted the charge of delivering a recommendation to the Senate that an army must be dispatched. The Roman senator called Aesop and told him to have two horses ready at the front of the domus immediately. Quintus put his arm around Camar as they strolled through the house, and headed for the front exit. Camar paused as they entered the atrium and flattered Quintus on the likeness of his marble bust. The ambassador was much more relaxed and confident, now that he was certain he had gotten away with his deception. He knew that he had hit a soft spot when Quintus went on and on about his bust, where it had come from, how long he had to pose and how much it cost.

The pair crossed the atrium and went outside where Aesop had a slave hold the horses. Camar rode slightly behind Quintus as they made their way through the streets of Rome. They barged their way through the plebeians, who were on foot, and the pair were soon crossing the Forum to the Curia Hostilia, where the Senate would be sitting.

They dismounted, Quintus leading Camar up the steps into the Curia. They both waited patiently until the current speaker had finished speaking and the next debate that followed. As the latest debate finished the next speaker started to make his way down the steps to begin his monolog about water provision, when Quintus took the floor. There were protests from his fellow senators, but they became silent as Quintus slowly waved his arms.

'My fellow senators, please forgive this interruption and breach of formalities, but I bring before you a matter of great importance. An invading army has encircled the city of Clusium and is holding it under siege. I present to you their ambassador who has asked permission to address you,' Quintus said.

Camar bowed and took his place in the middle of the Curia.

'A barbarian army currently lays siege to our capital city. I have been tasked by our governor to seek armed support from our allies, the great city of Rome. I respectfully asked Senator Quintus Fabius Ambustus to advise you on what I have told him,' Camar said.

A murmur went around the Senate which died to a silence as Quintus took centre stage.

'Indeed I have been informed of the invading force. Indeed the Etruscan League is our ally,' Quintus said.

Camar was pleased with Quintus' opening, and now expected him to endorse the call for military support, but then his expression changed completely.

'We have no idea about the size of this force, which may be no more than a large band of raiders. I propose that the Senate commission a trio of honourable men to identify and negotiate with this so called army,' Quintus said.

Quintus had deceived him yet again.

The treacherous Roman had no intention of asking for the army to be dispatched. He had bigger ideas as to the expansion of Rome. If the Etruscans were weakened then there would be an opportunity for Rome to further expand its territory. Furthermore, individual Etruscan cities might look towards Rome for protection, and willingly pay the high price of permanent occupation.

'I propose that I and my two honoured brothers are tasked with this important mission,' Quintus went on as the curia quietened.

The large portion of Quintus' family seconded the proposal and the Senate voted to dispatch Quintus with his two brothers, Caeso and Numerius. Camar stood dumbfounded and couldn't see why Quintus had not requested troops.

Camar followed Quintus out of the curia when Quintus turned on him.

'You are nothing but a worm boy! You killed my little bird and stole one of my blades, now you and your city will pay the price. Get out of my sight before I have you killed,' he hissed.

Camar made himself scarce as the senator sent messengers to his brothers, inviting them to join him at his domus.

Quintus was having a goblet of wine as Caeso arrived first, followed very shortly after by Numerius. Quintus told his brothers how he had tricked the Etruscan ambassador to get them sent to negotiate with the invading army. Quintus had his sights set on the Etruscan capital as the latest city to join the Latin League.

'We are in no rush, brothers. It is a full day's ride so I suggest we dine and spend the night here before we set off tomorrow. We'll let the Etruscans become a little more desperate for our help,' Quintus said with a smile.

The three brothers spent the evening reminiscing about their childhood. Quintus drank himself in to a stupor before he was helped to bed by Aesop.

'We leave at first light tomorrow, Aesop, so make sure my brother is up and ready,' Caeso said.

Aesop understood what that meant. The only way to raise his Master early was to wake him and suffer his wrath while plying him with wine. After all, the best way to avoid a hangover was to stay drunk.

They set off the next morning, and Aesop was as good as his word in getting his master ready. Quintus was still slurring his words as they left Rome, and insisted on drinking more wine from a skin he had slung over his saddle. The ride went reasonably well with Quintus only nearly falling of his mount once. The trio continued along the road most of the day until by late afternoon they could see the walls of Clusium, but as they got closer six riders approached them at speed.

As the mounted warriors pulled up next to the three brothers, Quintus held his hands up to show they were no threat. The newly promoted Roman senator explained that they were there to negotiate with the leader of the invaders. The three brothers were taken just outside the camp so they couldn't asses the strength of the invading force. The Romans were guarded by four of the six horsemen while the other two went to inform Arenwen of their diplomatic visitors. Quintus swigged more wine from the skin and offered it to his brothers, who both declined. Arenwen and Bilhild arrived shortly on foot to show that there was no show of force, which was to be expected when entering into peaceful negotiations. To show that he respected the diplomatic truce, Arenwen sent the horsemen away so that they could start the arbitration. He expected the three Romans to dismount but they didn't, instead remaining in their saddles with one of them seeming extremely agitated.

'I am Quintus Fabius Ambustus, senator of the mighty Latin League and from its jewel and capital Rome. My two noble brothers are also high ranking officials, and we are here to negotiate with you,' he slurred.

Arenwen realised that the man was not agitated, he was drunk!

'What are you here to negotiate?' Arenwen asked.

'We are allies of the city you have laid under siege and we are here to pay you to go away. All we need to agree is how much you want. Then go away you certainly will as you have no idea of the might of the Republican army; they will wipe you off the face of the earth,' Quintus threatened.

Bilhild laughed, to which Quintus responded by moving closer towards Bilhild and buffeted him with the side of his horse. Bilhild stumbled back, but managed to stay on his feet. Arenwen protested and reminded Quintus that he was here to negotiate, and as such neither side would receive any threats of violence. Quintus sneered and said 'there is nothing to negotiate here, you are nothing but a bunch of barbarians who pose no threat to us,' he said as he spat at Arenwen.

Bilhild took a step forward obviously offended by the insult. Caeso pulled up his horse alongside his brother in an attempt to control his outrageous behaviour. They had received clear instructions from the Senate that they were to open negotiations. Caeso had seen his brother like this many times before, and knew that he needed to calm his sibling down. As Caeso moved closer to his brother Quintus nudged his horse closer to Bilhild.

'Treat a dog like a dog,' Quintus said as he drew his sword and in a quick movement slashed Bilhild across the throat.

Caeso and Numerius looked horrified. Their brother was a nasty drunk, but neither of them expected him to break a peace oath given by all who enter into negotiations. Numerius moved forward and grabbed Quintus' horse by the reins and dragged it away. The horse responded with Caeso following quickly with them.

'By Saturn, what have you done?' Numerius asked Quintus.

'Teaching them a lesson,' he barely manged to say through his cloud of wine.

It had all happened so quickly, with Arenwen not having a chance to react. He was now screaming for the guards as he cradled his friend in his arms, with blood pulsing from his neck. Bilhild looked up and mouthed softly 'look after my family.'

Arenwen assured him that he would as Bilhild closed his eyes and slipped into the next world in the arms of his friend and comrade. The six horsemen had heard his calls and quickly galloped to his aid. They didn't need any explanation when they saw Bilhild dead on the floor and raced after the Romans.

Despite the Roman's horses being much smaller they had got a good head start before the Celts started after them. The three brothers were pushing their horses as hard as they would go. Caeso glanced over his shoulder to check for pursuers, but couldn't see anyone.

'Are you out of your mind?' Caeso said to Quintus.

After a while they checked again and couldn't see anyone following so they slowed their horses down in to a trot.

'We must go to your villa and get you wife. You can guarantee they will lay waste to the whole area,' Numerius said to Quintus.

'Wives are easy to get by men of my power. Just because you can't see anyone behind doesn't mean they are not too far away. You get my wife if you want, I'm going to the safety of Rome,' Quintus slurred.

Caeso looked at Numerius and rolled his eyes. The point had come to turn off to Quintus' villa or head straight on for Rome. Two of the brothers headed for the villa while Quintus rode straight onto the capital.

The horsemen returned to Arenwen and told him that they were unable to see where the three Romans had gone. The warrior looked up and roared his grief at the sky, as tears rolled down his face.

'I must go and inform my Lord Brennus of this treachery,' Arenwen said to no one in particular.

Arenwen ensured that Bilhild's body was taken to a place of rest before mounting his horse and heading the few miles to where Brennus was camped. He arrived at the camp, but couldn't remember a single part of the journey. He was a warrior and was used to death, which usually comes on the battlefield or occasionally of old age, but never during a negotiation. Arenwen dismounted and entered Brennus' tent. The chieftain was pleased to see his cousin, but the smile left his face as he saw the blood on Arenwen's clothes, and the grim expression on his face.

'What is it?' Brennus asked.

'They killed Bilhild. They approached in peace to discuss terms, and they killed Bilhild,' Arenwen said.

Brennus flew in to a fit of rage, Bilhild had been one of his senior warriors and they had grown up together.

'Do you know who they are?' Brennus asked.

'Oh yes, the one who did it introduced himself as Quintus Fabius Ambustus, and his two brothers came from a city called Rome,' Arenwen said bitterly.

'Take a thousand men to this place Rome. Demand that all three are turned over to you immediately, and then we will discuss how much money they will pay for this treachery,' Brennus said instructed.

Arenwen bowed and left the tent to summon more men. Within a short space of time he was heading south, he thought that must be roughly the direction the three Romans had come from. Arenwen pushed his horses a little harder than he should have to enable the men to keep up with him, but the story had ripped through the camp. There were no complaints from the Celtic warriors as they jogged behind the chariot mile after mile. The battle hardened men were conditioned to run over mountainous terrain so the straight, flat road posed no problem to them.

The highway got wider as a fork joined it from the left. Arenwen could see a large river to his right, and in the distance he could make out a long wooden wall that he thought that had to be the defences of Rome. He could also see that across the river there was another large settlement with a stone wall like Clusium. The small villages ahead lay abandoned as they got closer to their destination until the war band stopped a short distance in front of the entrance to this city. It was protected by a large ditch, wooden walls and wooden gates that had been barred shut.

Arenwen pulled up his chariot at a safe distance to ensure that the treachery would not be repeated again, this time with a storm of arrows as their welcome. The warrior shouted up to the guards on the walls.

'Is this Rome?' Arenwen called.

'Yes,' came the reply from somewhere behind the wooden defence.

'Then fetch me someone in charge,' the Celtic warrior yelled up to the hidden guard.

'I'm just a captain of the city guard. It will take a little while to fetch someone of importance,' he called.

'I'll wait,' Arenwen called back calmly.

He used his time wisely to examine the wooden palisade. The warrior drove his chariot up and down the walls that surrounded Rome, the city being nestled on a series of hills. He couldn't identify any specific weakness, but this wall was not anywhere near as formidable as the stone walls of Clusium.

The Celtic warrior saw movement and heard a voice he recognised. The mere sound of it made his blood boil.

'What do you want barbarian, have you not had enough lessons for one day? Do you want more?' It was Quintus.

'We demand you and your brothers are handed over to us to face whatever punishment my Lord decides. We also demand payment for your perfidy, your breach of faith,' Arenwen said.

'Punishment? You make me laugh! I have reported to the Senate and they have granted us honours, land and the title of Tribunes for our dealings with you dogs,' Quintus mocked.

Arenwen wanted to storm the wall right there and then, but controlled himself. He was not going to waste the lives of his men crossing a ditch, and directly assaulting a heavily manned high wall. Quintus stood on top of the defences and looked down.

'As for payment, this is all you will receive,' he mocked as he hitched up his toga, reached inside his loin cloth and pulled out his cock. He proceeded to piss in Arenwen's direction waving it left and right in a spraying motion, with the urine bouncing off the wooden bridge and down in to the trench.

Arenwen had seen enough and wheeled his chariot around. He would take his men back to his Lord, and report the further insult that had been made by this man who supposedly represented Rome. As he turned away Arenwen heard Quintus call out.

'That's it, turn and run like the dogs you are.'

The Celtic warrior did not want to show how much the man had irritated him and didn't give the Roman the satisfaction of looking back, but as he drove away he vowed that it wouldn't be long before he returned. The men were livid at the Roman's actions and they followed behind Arenwen, but many of them dropped their trousers to bare their arses at the Roman. The pace back was a little slower as Arenwen worked through the options.

The war band passed the besieged city of Clusium and made its way to Brennus' camp. Arenwen found Brennus outside his tent with a group of senior warriors.

'Their response?' Brennus asked.

'They pissed on us,' Arenwen replied.

'As if I didn't need any more motivation; we will avenge Bilhild's death by making the land run red with their blood,' the chieftain said.

Brennus gave orders to his senior warriors to break camp. The army was already on standby following the news of Bilhild being murdered. They quickly moved to the city of Clusium where Brennus ordered the siege to be lifted, with the two thousand warriors instructed to join the main army. The Clusium guards just stood in amazement and with a sense of relief as the invading horde headed south.

The army marched until the city was a distant object. Arenwen was to the right of Brennus who called over to him.

'How far is this place Rome?' Brennus asked.

'Less than a day, Lord,' Arenwen replied.

'Then we have time for what we need to do,' Brennus said.

Arenwen knew exactly what that meant. There was still plenty of the day left but Arenwen signalled for the army to make camp. They would be set in a circle around a pyre, it would be Bilhild's funeral pyre. Groups were sent out to gather wood while others set about butchering animals for three purposes. One of the reasons would be for the feast tonight. The second would be that some would have their fat trimmed and placed on Bilhild's body, and the third purpose would be so the carcasses would be added to the fire. Brennus went over to Bakher.

'He died without a druid being close,' Brennus said.

'He did, Lord but we can speak to him,' Bakher replied.

Bilhild's body was washed and prepared in a death shroud. He was ceremonially placed on the pyre that had been laid out. Four of his personal slaves wailed and moaned not only about the death of their Master, but also that they would be killed and placed on the pyre just before it was lit. It was tradition that dogs and horses would also be burned with their owner, but Brennus decided the pup was too young to die. So it would only be the two chariot horses would join his funeral pyre.

Other fires were lit to cook food for the feast. As dark descended, Bakher followed his orders and found several barrels of ale. Carefully prizing them open, he placed a henbane leaf in each before securing the lid. All was ready as night fell with the whole camp trying to get as close to the pyre as possible. The slaves and horses were killed and laid around Bilhild, he would need them in the next life. Each man filed past the body taking a horn of ale, and placing coins next to the body for the afterlife. Finally Arenwen and Brennus gave their respects and the fire was lit. The animal fat that was smeared over Bilhild's body caught light quickly and blazed on the fire. Bakher nodded to Deborah who stood next to the blazing fire, seemingly unaffected by the heat. She drank a horn of the ale with the henbane leaf in it, raised her arms in the air and went into a trance.

'I have been wronged,' the words came from Deborah's mouth, but it was not her speaking it was Bilhild's voice.

Everyone knew that Deborah could talk to the dead, but this was the first time many had seen it. They stood in silence too afraid to drink their ale. Deborah turned and looked directly at Brennus, all that could be seen was the white of her eyes, and her pupils had vanished. She walked over to him as the fire roared behind her. Deborah placed both hands on Brennus' shoulders and said in Bilhild's voice 'avenge me,' and then she fell to the floor.

Brennus replied 'I swear, by all that is dear to me, I will.'

A few minutes later she came round and looked up.

'I have guided his spirit to the other side, and he was happy knowing you would punish those who had insulted him,' the necromancer said.

Brennus looked up at his men and addressed them.

'Honour Bilhild at this feast tonight. Eat and drink, for tomorrow we go to battle - tomorrow we are bound for Rome!'

The cry was taken up by the army and spread to the outmost parts. The fires burned, ale was drunk and food was eaten until slowly one by one the men went to sleep.

Next morning they awoke, and knew they would be going into battle that day. It was customary to drink the henbane infused ale before conflict, so the warriors drained the ruminants of the open barrels from the night before. The druid had made sure that there were an ample supply of barrels left to consume before combat. With the ale in them they were invincible and would charge at any foe that dared get in their way as the hallucinogenic effects of the leaf coursed through their bodies. By midday they would be at the gates of Rome.

The chant from the night before sprung up and was sung again. 'Rome, Rome, we are bound for Rome!'

Chapter 18

The Battle of Allia

18th July, 390 BC

An emergency meeting of the Senate had been called, and the senators filed in to the curia even before the sun had risen. Quintus took the floor of the Senate and addressed the gathering.

'Only but yesterday did a thousand ragged barbarians stand at our gate and demand recompense for the actions of a senator of Rome.'

'This is nothing but a band of thieves and robbers that have stumbled into our lands. I say we let the mighty Republican legions send them back to where they came from with stories of what to expect if any others dare follow!' Quintus roared.

He was a skilled orator and continued amassing support from the listening senators. There were a few dissenters, but they were in the minority and were being shouted down by others lapping up Quintus' words. He wound up his speech that had gone on for over an hour with a suggestion; 'I propose we send four legions to eradicate these vermin.' Echoes of approval rippled around the forum as the vote was passed, almost unanimously. General Sulpicius was summoned to the curia where he was issued with his orders. He was to assemble four legions, march and wipe out the invaders in the field. Sulpicius accepted his orders from the Senate and left to discuss his tactics with his cohort commanders. Each legion consisted of heavy infantry, the legionaries, but also auxiliaries who provided cavalry and skirmishing troops. Sulpicius was confident that the sheer might of Rome would crush the rabble that had dared trespass on their lands the day before. He thought one legion would be enough, but having four legions at his command made him feel very comfortable. Three of them were veterans with the last one having been recently formed. With that in mind he thought he would keep the new legion in reserve as the three legions could easily deal with a thousand barbarians.

Sulpicius led his twenty four thousand men plus a large number of auxiliaries through the streets of Rome to the pleasure of the locals, who cheered and threw flowers as they marched past on their way to a heroic victory. Although it was still early morning the masses thronged the streets eager to see their loved ones in all their military glory. The many hours of drill formations in the vast area of Villa Publica had paid off as they marched in step and in perfect formation. Young boys tried to keep up as they mimicked marching in step along the ranks of the heavily armed soldiers. Rome was happy and Rome was sure that this would be yet another victory as it had been for hundreds and hundreds of years. The Roman army was magnificent with all of the men immaculately turned out. They all wore a red tunic as an undergarment, then leather body armour, which was reinforced with a bronze chest plate. The infantry had their heads protected by their cassis, that most considered their most important piece of armour. The bronze helmets were very difficult to make, it took a highly skilled armourer to beat the single piece of bronze into the exact shape. They all held their rectangular shield on their left arm which was curved to protect them from an attack from the front as well as the sides. Most of the heavy infantry were drafted from the regular citizens of Rome. Two thirds of the ranks held the long spears, which had been adopted from the Greeks, while a smaller group carried the newer weapons. These had been copied from the Samnites and consisted of two pilum spears, a shield and a short gladius sword. The armour was heavy but invaluable in combat, and as each man had to supply their own armour they purchased the best they could afford. The nobles rode in front of the infantry on their horses, but the difference in the body armour was significant. The detail in their bronze full torso armour was impressive and had scenes of the gods or animals intricately moulded into the ornamental breastplates that slaves had polished to a mirror shine.

Sulpicius knew the land well and planned to confront the horde at the river Allia – really not much more than a brook this time of year, and was one of the many small tributaries that fed the mighty Tiber. He had laid out a map of the area (Map 2) and discussed the battle plans with his senior commanders. Sulpicius identified the small hill to the south of the river. This would be where he would anchor his army by placing his reserves on the raised area. The hill would also offer an excellent view of the battlefield, and so he would place one of his commanders there to send runners with messages about enemy movements. A large bend in the Tiber would secure his left flank, while it would also offer protection from the rear. So the commanders were confident that they could not be outflanked from either side, or attacked from the rear. The smaller barbarian force must meet them head on and when this happened on an open field, the larger force won by sheer strength of numbers.

The mighty Republican army made its way out of the city and onto the road that would take them north to the river Allia. There was still an early morning chill in the air, but it was slowly starting to wear off. The sun began to burn off the mists rolling in from the fields that lay on either side of the road. Peasants from the villages, which clung to the great city like limpets to a rock, stopped their busy lives to see the troops march by. They had never seen anything as spectacular as this in their lives. The war with the Etruscans had been old stories passed down from generation to generation. The Hernici tribe to the east had sued for peace after Rome's mighty army had repeatedly defeated them in battle. The Aequi had been vanquished with their leaders now being slaves in Rome. Only the Volsci still troubled them, but any conflicts had reduced to small raiding parties or minor skirmishes for decades.

The army travelled swiftly up the road and moved into formation. Sulpicius was sure that their quick deployment would catch the raiding party off guard, and that the sheer size of his force would be enough to make them turn and run, but he would not allow them to get off so lightly. He had two plans, one was to harass the retreating barbarians all the way back to the mountains, hopefully killing as many as possible. However, if his preferred plan played out as expected his cavalry would ride behind them and force them to face the mass of his superior army.

With his four legions in full formation he signalled for his senior officers to join him. He had set up a field command tent just behind his centre, and one by one the four legates and their chief officers entered the tent. They found Sulpicius sitting on a stool sipping wine as he surveyed the map he had shown them earlier. Each commander took up a goblet of wine while Sulpicius discussed battle orders for the day. The Roman discussed how he expected the barbarians to turn and run when they saw the numbers they were facing. The three legions were to advance in close order with the fourth following behind. The cavalry was to flank the enemy and herd the war band to their deaths. The three legions would need to move forward quickly, so the men would have to be ready to advance on their commander's orders.

One of the commanders protested, respectfully reminding Sulpicius the strength of the hoplites was their long spears and close formation. They would need to raise their spears vertically to move forward with the speed not being very fast as the hoplite formation was nine men deep. Sulpicius dismissed the man's concerns as he wanted speed; these barbarian scum would be stupid to attack such a superior force. The other commanders nodded in agreement, and so the battle lines were drawn. Before sending his commanders back to their legions Sulpicius asked his officers if there were any further questions, only one legate spoke.

'As we have time, I suggest we fortify the camp and dig entrenchments at five hundred meters behind our lines, so we can fall back in to a defensive formation if required. I also recommend sending out scouts to look for the enemy,' one of the commanders said.

'Fortifications, defensive entrenchments and scouts, what is the matter with you? We vastly outnumber them, and have no need to think about anything else than our complete and absolute victory!' Sulpicius yelled angrily, veins protruding on his temple and a slight nose twitch that only appeared when he was annoyed.

'I meant no offence, but it is standard battle procedure,' his commander replied.

'Be damned with procedure, we will not need it today. Now if there is nothing else return to your men,' Sulpicius said stubbornly.

The commanders returned to their units, and relayed the orders that would eventually filter down to the infantry through the normal chain of command. The Roman lines stretched for miles as the cavalry were given their instructions on how they were to turn the enemy. Everything was ready for the Romans to show their military might and achieve a glorious victory.

Brennus had fought too many battles to even begin to remember, and had years of experience in warfare. He had been told by Arenwen that the walls of Rome were tall but wooden, unlike the solid stone fortifications around Clusium. Wooden walls could be easily burnt so he suspected that Rome would not sit behind them, as the Etruscans had, but sally out and meet him in combat. With this in mind he had dispatched scouts well in advance of the main army in a wide arc in front of him scanning for enemy activity. It was these scouts that now returned to report to Brennus. They had seen the Roman army deploy about a mile ahead of them and reported their numbers, formation and troop composition.

'Were you seen?' Brennus asked the scouts.

'No, they wouldn't have been able to see us through the mist, and they haven't sent out any scouts,' the warrior replied.

Brennus brought his army to a halt, with the wagons carrying the last barrels of henbane ale brought forward. Word was spread around the camp that the enemy had been sighted and the men were to prepare themselves for battle. They dipped their horns into the ale and took hearty gulps as they readied themselves. Most stripped to the waist while a number of the warriors stripped completely naked. Small groups began to form as the men organised themselves into their fighting units. The numbers ranged from pairs to groups of four, but it was impossible to spot when in full combat as the group members moved gracefully from side to side and forward and back. Durston and Dafydd as well as Telor and Vaughn agreed to work in pairs. They would act as independent units, but also keep a watch on their closest pair on either side of them. This is how the whole Celtic battle line would be formed. To an opposing enemy it would seem like there was no logical formation, but it was a very effective killing machine.

The first thing the Romans heard was a long harsh haunting note that carried across the land towards them. It was like nothing they had ever heard before and then they saw what was making the unsettling noise, the Celtic carnyx. The ghastly heads of bronze towered twenty foot in to the air. Heads of dragons, snakes and boars all floated through the air of the morning mist calling a haunting deep low note that sent shivers through the Roman lines. As the Celts drew closers to their enemy, the Romans could see that the haunting instruments appeared to be floating. It was a straight bronze pole with a mouth piece bent at one end, and the horn bent into a creature at the top. The horn blower held it to his mouth with one hand, while the other supported the long pole above his head.

The horns continued to sound as they got ever closer to the Roman lines. The deep note resonated through the bodies of the Roman soldiers, before the rest of the Celtic army slowly stepped silently out of the mist like a mass of ghosts. The Romans watched on in amazement as more and more men seemed to materialise. They were told there was only a thousand, but vast numbers were before them, increasing as every moment passed. The Celts parted as their Lord and leader came through the centre. Brennus was resplendent in his battle armour and drove down to the Roman formation. He pushed his horses along the lines of the Romans, just out of reach of the hoplites' long spears, but as he passed by one of the cohorts carrying pilum they launched a volley. Brennus didn't even look in their direction, totally impervious to the threat as each spear went harmlessly past him. He went along the line until he turned his chariot around at the hill on his left. Drawing his sword he raced past the line roaring just one name.

'Quintus Fabius Ambustus,' he bellowed, challenging the enemy force as he went down the line.

The Romans were stunned by the ferocity of the warrior, and the Roman cavalry stood frozen instead of riding out to cut him down.

'I am here to kill you Quintus Fabius Ambustus, come and meet me in single combat,' Brennus roared.

A lone voice called from the ranks as Brennus reached the far right of the Roman line.

'I am Sulpicius, and I command the mighty Republican Roman army.'

Brennus focussed on the area he thought the voice had come from and spotted Sulpicius by the grandeur of his armour.

'Then come and fight me, man to man,' Brennus called.

Sulpicius was an experienced commander, and was beginning to regret not ordering defensive fortifications, but he was no warrior. He could command men into battle but thought that one on one combat would only bring his death.

'I will not fight you barbarian, come bring your rabble to us and we shall wade in your blood as you die on Roman spears and swords,' Sulpicius called back from the safety of his lines.

If this had been a Celtic tribe he was facing the chieftain would have accepted his challenge, but these cowardly Romans had no honour so Brennus turned his horses and headed back to his line. He was significantly outnumbered, but his challenge had given him the opportunity to closely inspect the enemy line. The silent Celtic horde now howled and cheered as their Lord returned, roaring defiance and selecting their targets among the enemy forces while the Romans simply stood watching. The wall of noise was almost deafening as the Romans closed their ranks tighter, locking their shields and holding their spears steady.

Brennus jumped down from his chariot and went to where he had previously assembled his senior warriors. He was going to launch his attack using the fifty chariots. They were to be used in a shock and awe tactic that would run parallel to the hoplite line, throwing spears and shooting arrows as they went up and down past the Romans. Brennus pointed out where the volley of spears had been thrown at him, and told his senior warriors to warn their men of this. The thousand strong cavalry were to keep a close formation in case of a counter attack from the Roman mounted force, but from his recent experience he did not consider them a threat as they did not want to engage him, even by himself. The reality was that the Romans did not use stirrups, and the role of their cavalry was very unlike the Celts. The Romans would engage with the enemy, throw a hasta spear and then dismount to join the infantry with their short swords. However the Roman nobles would have to abandon an expensive horse to do this, so they preferred to fight against other cavalry. The nobles observed their opponents' mounts and saw that the barbarians' horses were much bigger. They would be at least an arm's length lower on their smaller horses, and be equipped with only their short swords. Unlike the long blades that the Celts wielded with such careless ease, and therefore the Romans rightly noted that they would be at a significant disadvantage.

Brennus thought little of the enemy's numerical superiority, but the hill on the north-eastern edge of the field of battle was causing him some degree of concern. He had not been able to scout behind the raised ground, and was worried that additional reinforcements were being concealed, which could emerge to try and outflank his army. Arenwen was pleased with the decision to have the chariots lead the charge, as he would be one of the first to assault the Romans. With Bilhild murdered by the Roman politician's treachery, he would take Deborah as his chariot partner who would be a formidable opponent to the enemy. His heart skipped a few beats as Brennus said that all chariots would lead the assault except Arenwen's.

'You won't be in the first attack, Arenwen,' he said.

'Have I offended you, Lord?' Arenwen asked.

'Not at all, I want you to take the hill,' he smiled as he pointed to the legion positioned on their left.

The warrior beamed at his leader, knowing he had been given a great honour by attacking a large number of enemies with a potential reserve waiting to trap him.

'See those pretty lines? I want you to make them messy. Take the hill, Arenwen, and make sure the bastards don't outflank me,' Brennus said.

'Consider it done, my Lord,' Arenwen replied.

Orders were relayed and, half the men spread themselves thinner along the line in an attempt to match the length of the line in front of them. Others surged to their left to join Arenwen's attack. Chariots raced at the Roman lines in a single file as the Romans steadied their long spears for a full frontal attack. The Romans were confident that the horses would die on their long spears, and then they would move forward to kill the occupants. When the lead chariot was a few feet away from the first hoplite spear, it turned sharply, racing on a parallel down the Roman line. The other chariots fell in behind like the body of a serpent following the head. The forty nine chariots ravaged the Roman line while Celtic slingers took shots at anyone who raised their head above their shield. The Romans were terrified as the chariots wheeled away and circled to begin another attack. The only Roman response was the second volley of pila which took one horse in the hind but it kept running, the shaft bouncing up and down with the animal's movements.

The second wave of chariots inflicted more physical damage, but it had put doubts in the minds of the enemy as to their chances against such an army. Sulpicius was shouting orders for his men to hold as the second wave of chariots wheeled away towards their own lines. The Romans breathed a sigh of relief, but then, the chariots suddenly stopped and the warriors dismounted. Others joined at their sides and the howling began again as the Celts moved closer. They were shouting abuse and challenging individual Romans to step out of the line to fight. This was no feint as the warriors were buzzing from the effects of the drugged ale, and the urge for a killing frenzy rose so that it pounded in their heads.

Arenwen led his men in a wide arc, (Map 3) his force was free flowing and extremely mobile, unlike the Romans who were restricted by heavy armour and rigid, tight formation. The Roman legate on top of the hill saw the left flank of the Celts move as one around the base. He barked orders at his men to re-adjust their positions to face the oncoming threat, but it was too late. The forth legion on the ridge were reserves, and were not as well drilled as the other three. They attempted the repositioning manoeuvre, but the men on the outside ranks were dropping as their exposed flanks were being ripped apart by axes, arrows and spears. The legionnaires who were further inside the hoplite formation couldn't see what was going on, but could hear their comrades scream and see their long spears topple to the ground like so many felled trees. Arenwen and his men smashed into the side of the legion which sent shock waves through the lines. He was chopping down at the enemy as they fell before him while Deborah's legs dangled over the front of the chariot, having wrapped the reins around both feet to keep her hands free for killing. She loosed arrow after arrow into the backs of Roman soldiers. She steered them away from a direct assault on the legion as she guided the chariot behind the rear line of Romans. They raced up the rear killing and maiming indiscriminately with Arenwen chopping down, splitting helmets in two.

Dafydd and Durston constantly swapped and interchanged places with Telor and Vaughn as they hacked their way through the now thoroughly panicked Romans in a much practiced dance of death. Telor looked over as Vaughn floored a Roman by striking him with the flat of his blade, knocking the loosely strapped helmet off his opponent. This was followed by a head butt that made the man's nose explode like a ripe fruit, spraying blood as he dropped to the ground. The twins killed, counted, and then moved on to repeat the slaughter. The four were just a small part of the Celtic killing machine as they wielded their long swords, slashing through the armour and into the soft flesh beneath. It was being repeated all around them by other groups of dancing Celts as the killing frenzy was on them. They gave no mercy as they hacked their way through line after line of Romans, helplessly trapped in tight formation. Their shields were locked to that of the man on their left which would normally provide them protection, but now it just brought their death. Rank after rank started dropping their weapons until entire cohorts were in full flight down the hill, splashing through the streams of blood from their brutally butchered comrades. Arenwen had routed the entire left flank of the enemy, and as they tore through he was pleased, and a little relieved, to discover that there weren't any reinforcements hidden behind the hill. Legionnaires were tripping over their own dead as they scrambled down the hill for safety. Those at the bottom of were horrified to see their comrades fleeing, but the sight of streams of blood was nothing compared to that of heads being tossed down the hill. The remaining Romans were being decapitated as they tried to escape, with the Celts were hurling the heads down onto the troops below.

Sulpicius looked on in horror as his right wing completely collapsed, a quarter of his army was now in sheer panic, and it was quickly infecting the other legions rank by rank. Then he looked forward to see that the Celtic leader had unleashed the rest of his army, who were running at him armed with long swords, spears and double headed axes. The oncoming Celts were running at the Romans utterly consumed by battle frenzy. The long spears of his phalanx were designed to protect against formed attackers but they were heavy, too slow for the Celts who nimbly pivoted around the spears and chopped them down. The blows forced the Romans to dip the tips of their spears, so before the defensive line could react the Celts had broken through the tight formation, and were flooding through the front lines with their short axes and long swords. This was the last the legions could take as they were already panicked by the losses on their right flank; they were being attacked from the front while half the Celtic army was streaming down the hill, and scything down their right.

The Roman army broke along the entire length of what was left of the remaining three legions. The Tiber that had until now, offered protection on three sides, but now it had become a trap. The only fortunate thing was there weren't as many Celts as there could have been, so gaps opened up for some to escape. The few Romans who had miraculously not been slaughtered on the hill managed to escape and headed for Rome, discarding their armour and weapons as they ran for their lives. Many of the defeated Roman soldiers thought that the city of Veli, with its stone walls, offered better protection than Rome and started to cross the Tiber. Hundreds of them were dragged to their deaths by the weight of their precious armour as they refused to discard it. It had cost more than five years work to pay for the armour, but now it cost them more, it cost them their lives. On seeing the heavily laden men drown others decided that their lives were more important, and tore off anything that would way them down before swimming to the far shore. The cavalry had not engaged in any of the battle, and were now being chased from the field by the Celtic horsemen. Sulpicius regretted his decision not to fortify his camp or build a defensive fall-back position. His most experienced men surrounded him and step by step edged their way to the river as the Celts hacked and beat them down. They had all abandoned their long spears, and were trying to fend off the attackers with their short swords. This was a futile task as the Celts stood back and smashed at their shields with their longer weapons. Defender after defender fell as the Celts came howling at the Romans, until eventually

Sulpicius was felled with a savage blow to his thigh which tore straight through his left leg. He fell to the floor with blood pumping from the severed artery. He looked up and held his hand up for mercy, but only heard 'ninety six,' as Telor snuffed out his life and took his head.

The Celts had inflicted a humiliating defeat, the Roman army having suffered horrendous losses with the majority who were still alive taking shelter at Veli. Some of the Roman army had managed to make it back to their capital city utterly dejected. Brennus let his men work through the killing frenzy, and by mid-afternoon it had turned into picking the spoils from the dead Roman bodies. He summoned his senior warriors together to assess their losses, going through each getting reports of few deaths and then turned to Arenwen 'how many dead?' Brennus asked.

'None, we had a few injuries, but none are fatal. We were on them before they could turn into us,' Arenwen replied with a smile on his blood splattered face.

Brennus instructed his senior warriors to treat the wounded, honour the dead and reward the living.

'Get them rested, for tomorrow we are bound for Rome. Then I want you to return to me as quickly as you can,' Brennus said to his cousin.

Arenwen went to see that his men had everything they needed and found them in good spirits as they shared out the loot they had captured that day, recounting tales of their kills as they ate and drank.

'Take it easy tonight as we move on Rome in the morning,' Arenwen said to his men, and then returned to see what Brennus had in store for him.

'I have another task for you cousin, and perhaps the most dangerous yet,' Brennus said.

'Whatever you need, Lord,' Arenwen replied.

'Go and find the best fit of Roman uniform you can. I want you to get into Rome tonight as a returning soldier,' Brennus said, but the task of finding a Roman uniform would be difficult to fit over Arenwen's huge frame.

'Here is some coin. Get in to Rome and find that snake Quintus Fabius Ambustus as I'm sure he will try to slip away when we approach,' Brennus spat.

Arenwen nodded and headed off to search for a suitable dead Roman who he could strip of his uniform. He managed to find a reasonably close match, it was still very tight and some of the straps did not do up fully, but it would serve his purpose. He wondered how men could possibly fight in these tight constraints that offered no flexibility as it felt like being wrapped tightly in a blanket. He made his way south to Rome and as darkness fell he approached the main gate. A voice called down to him from the wall. Arenwen feigned an injured arm, and gave a loud groan as he limped closer to the main gate. He expected that he would be challenged or worse have spears thrown down at him but none were forthcoming, so he walked through the open gate and into Rome.

Chapter 19

The Sacking of Rome

The day of the battle the few Roman soldiers who managed to escape back to the city told tales of the defeat to the barbarian horde, and their ungodly practices. Fear spread through the streets, which quickly developed into a widespread panic. Some of the survivors were summoned before the Senate to confirm the rumours the senators had heard. Quintus was among the ones who sat in silence as they were told how four of their legions had been resoundingly beaten. Unlike the previous day Quintus made no speeches to the gathering, and tried his best to avoid any eye contact with the senators sat opposite him. There is one burning question that they all wanted to know. How many men remained alive to defend the city? The beleaguered men looked at each other and shrugged their shoulders. They had seen men escaping to the far bank of the river, but in all the confusion they were unable to place an accurate figure on their number.

The captain of the city guard was summoned, given instructions to close the gates at dusk, and take a roll call to get an accurate picture of the remaining forces. The officer was to report back the next morning, and with that there was nothing left to do other than wait. The senators discussed options that would hinge on the report the next morning, then brought the session to a close. Quintus left the curia and didn't care what the next morning's report would bring as his little birds had already told him that no more than two thousand troops had returned from the battle. If that number were fresh and armed it still would not be enough to garrison the walls of the great city. However, all they actually had were predominantly unarmed soldiers who had been crushed on the battlefield. Most of the survivors were either wounded or without weapons, all despondent following their humiliating defeat. He was going to return to his domus and gather as much of his wealth that he could. The plan was to get out of Rome the next day, but he would need the cover of night to conceal his exit.

Arenwen made his way through the streets of Rome, and gazed in amazement as to the size and grandeur of the buildings. He didn't know how the Romans had built these structures that towered above him, to then have statues twice the size of a man placed on top of them. He slipped in to one of the side streets and spotted a likely candidate who might part with the information he needed. She was sitting in the gutter wearing little more than worn and tattered rags.

'Old woman, I am looking for the house of Quintus Fabius Ambustus,' Arenwen said.

She looked up and was surprised to see a Roman soldier, something didn't seem right, but she couldn't quite put her finger on it. It was not unusual for army members to come from different countries so it wasn't the accent, but she just couldn't figure out what it was.

'Never heard of him,' the old woman replied.

Arenwen took a silver coin from the pouch Brennus had given him and rolled it through his fingers.

'Oh well, never mind. I'm sure I can find someone to tell me where he lives,' he said.

'For that coin I won't just tell you where he lives, I'll take you there,' the old woman said as she slowly creaked up from the gutter.

'How can I be sure you aren't lying now you've seen my silver?' Arenwen asked.

'I know him, just made senator, but he is a drunken fool. I have seen him several times and followed him as he barely hangs onto his horse. He gets so drunk he doesn't hear his coins fall to the floor that I gather.

The warrior didn't know much about the man, but this seemed an accurate picture of the dog that had killed Bilhild. He tossed the coin to his guide, she deftly snatched it from the air. She used her rotting teeth to bite down on it and was satisfied that it was real, so she tucked into her dirty clothing.

'Follow me.'

The old woman led Arenwen through the twists and turns of Rome until she came to a stop at the end of one of the streets.

'That's the one,' the old woman said pointing a filthy gnarled finger at a house.

Arenwen thanked her and slipped into the shadows. He would watch the house for a while to assess if there were any guards. He had all night as Brennus would not be advancing until the next morning. He was getting hungry and wondered if there was anywhere he could get food, but thought better of it. It was too risky to wander the unknown streets, but then all thoughts of eating went out of his mind. A horse pulled up outside the house he was watching, a servant rushed out to attend to the new arrival. The rider moved into the light of the torch being carried by the attendant, Arenwen recognised his face instantly. It was him, the man he was looking for - Quintus Fabius Ambustus.

Marcus heard his father rush into the house and call Aesop to his office. The young lad edged up as close as he could to try and catch a little of what was going on.

'I will be leaving Rome tomorrow night. I need all the valuables, including the bust of me, loading on carts!'

'Yes Master, I shall have everything ready for your departure. I shall inform your wife's servants to ready the mistress' and your son's possessions?' Aesop asked.

'Don't worry about them, they are not coming with me. Now go and do as I say. Fetch wine and my brothers,' Quintus shouted.

Marcus had heard the slaves whispering about the defeat of the Roman army, though he didn't believe it at first. He pondered what else could have panicked his father so much? Then his father's words hit him.

'Don't worry about them they are not coming with me.'

By the gods, his father was planning to leave him and his mother behind! The teenager skirted his father's tablinum, and rushed to his mother who was sitting in the colonnaded garden at the rear of the house. Marcus told her what he had overheard and she listened, astonished that her husband could leave them both to the mercy of the barbarian horde.

'You have done well, my son, but it is obvious we must look after ourselves now. Try and listen to the conversation when your uncles come to try and find out more. I shall go and prepare for our departure,' Lucia said.

Marcus remembered his experience after the gladiator fight, and how the back streets of Rome quickly became a dangerous place. So if they needed to go off the main streets the young lad thought that they would need protection. Knowing that it would take a little time for his uncles to arrive he went in search of Lucius. It was likely that at that time of the evening he would be in the slave quarters, and that was exactly where Marcus found him. His young master briefed him on the situation and told him to be ready to move at short notice, maybe it would be tonight, perhaps tomorrow.

It wasn't long before Quintus' brothers arrived at the house. They were shown straight to the office so Marcus returned to his listening position. He eavesdropped as his father outlined the dire situation.

'Twenty two thousand soldiers are dead or missing. We don't have enough soldiers to man the walls when the barbarians arrive let alone defend the city. Rome is lost,' the senator said quietly.

Marcus couldn't see the expressions on his uncles' faces, but they went silent for a few moments.

'Then what are we to do?' Numerius asked.

'We will attend the Senate tomorrow morning as dutiful citizens of Rome, but when you leave here prepare your household to move out at nightfall tomorrow,' Quintus replied.

'Won't that be too late?' Caeso asked.

'The barbarians will be raiding the countryside for days. I don't expect anything to be left of my villa, but it will buy us time as they search for plunder,' his brother replied.

Quintus and his two siblings finalised the plan that would see them safe from the invading barbarians. Marcus' uncles left shortly after, with his father shouting at the slaves to bring more wine.

Arenwen saw the two men leave and noticed that they bore a striking similarity to the one he was seeking, sure that they had to be related. He checked that the coast was clear, slipped across the road and into the house. The slave who had been undertaking the duties of doorman was not there, Arenwen looked in amazement at the picture on the wall of a dog in chains. He had never seen a picture made from very small pieces of coloured pottery. There was a movement from up ahead, so Arenwen darted into one of the side rooms. He peeked from behind a curtain where he could see it was the slave who had been at the door earlier. Arenwen drew his short Roman sword and crept up behind the man. He slipped his left hand over the slave's mouth and raised the sword in his right hand at the slave's throat. Arenwen tilted the man backwards which forced the slave to bend his knees in an attempt to stay upright.

'Do as I say and live, don't then you die. Nod if you understand, and be sure I will slit your throat before you even begin to scream,' the warrior said menacingly.

The slave nodded slowly, so the Celt released his grip on the slave's mouth. Arenwen spun him around and put the tip of his blade on the man's Adam's apple.

'I am looking for Quintus Fabius Ambustus. Nod slowly if he is here.'

The slave nodded, Arenwen quickly took a look around to check if there was anyone else who might raise the alarm.

'Take me there and remember, one sound, and you're dead. Do you understand?'

The slave nodded once more so Arenwen removed the sword from the slave's throat, moving it into the small of his back. He pushed the tip of his weapon into the man's spine and saw the skin form a dimple around the sharp point. They moved straight on, hearing a lot of noise coming from some of the side rooms, but there wasn't any other activity. Arenwen was led deeper into the house and wondered if all Romans had a small pool in the middle of their houses. The slave stopped at the end of the atrium and signalled head.

'You'll find him in that room,' the slave said quietly.

'Stay silent now or I will find you,' Arenwen said as he pushed the man back towards the main entrance. The slave stumbled as he fell forward, but quickly regained his feet and ran straight out of the house not caring what happened to his cruel master.

Arenwen burst in to Quintus' office with his sword drawn.

'Remember me, Roman?' The Celtic warrior hissed in utter contempt at the man before him.

Quintus jumped to his feet, and reached for his newly made iron sword.

'I remember you, barbarian dog,' Quintus spat.

Arenwen launched himself at Quintus, kicking him squarely in the chest with the ball of his foot. The senator was sent flying backwards, smashing a table as he fell on it. Marcus came running in to find out what all the noise was, as it sounded different to his father's usual drunken antics. Lucius followed in closely behind to find a huge legionary in extremely ill-fitting armour towering above Quintus. The intruder was distracted as Marcus entered the room, in that split second Lucius had taken a sword off the wall and attacked. Arenwen turned and parried his assailant's blow, his opponent was smaller, but certainly skilled with the short blade. Arenwen struggled as he was not used to the confines of fighting in armour, and the short weapon he carried was not much longer than a dagger to him. Lucius flicked Arenwen's sword to one side and lunged at his chest, but the blow wasn't deep enough to penetrate the body armour. This only served to enrage Arenwen into a full attack, and he repeatedly smashed Lucius back until he was down on one knee, defending himself from a torrent of blows. Lucius knew it was pointless to resist anymore, and threw down his sword to accept his fate. He looked up into Arenwen's eyes and waited for the death blow, but Quintus had gotten back to his feet and launched a sly attack from behind the intruder.

'Look out!' Marcus cried as his father brought a slashing blow down, aimed at Arenwen's head.

The Celt had just enough time to wheel around and block the blow, but as the two swords met Arenwen's sword shattered while Quintus' barely had a mark on it. The Roman laughed evilly. Marcus picked up the sword that had been dropped by Lucius and saw the look of astonishment in the intruder's eyes not understanding how his sword had disintegrated.

'Behold the might of Rome,' Quintus said as Marcus got closer to the two of them.

'Now my son and I will finish you off together,' the senator said imperiously as he flashed a confident grin at his son. Quintus seemed pleased, obviously expecting that his offspring was going to help him. Marcus looked at his parent, not remembering if his father had ever smiled at him before. The teenager edged closer to the intruder who had put an arm behind him, trying to feel his way out of the room. Arenwen reached for is belt where he would have normally retrieved his short axe, but only grasped empty air, as of course he was wearing a Roman uniform. The warrior's eyes darted around the room looking for a weapon or an escape route, but could find neither. Quintus moved closer as Arenwen raised his arms in an attempt to defend himself when Marcus noticed the tell-tale scars that he had seen on Krasper. The burn marks meant that this man had to be a smith! The senator nodded at his son and went for the kill. As he did Marcus drove his sword under his father's lower rib, and twisted it up into his body. The man who had persistently bullied and tormented his wife and child fell to the floor, Marcus had delivered a mortal wound. As he lay there dying, blood trickled from the corner of his mouth and he gasped 'why son, why?'

The teenager pulled the sword out of the man on the floor and said

'I am no son of yours.'

The teenager turned to Lucius and told him to go fetch Lucia, then turned to the man who had come to kill his father and asked 'who are you?'

'My name is Arenwen, and I am a senior warrior of the Celtic tribes that defeated your army. Your father started this trouble by not honouring peaceful negotiations. My Lord's army will be in this city tomorrow, but you do not need to fear that, as I owe you my life,' he replied.

Lucius returned with Lucia, who glanced down at her husband lying on the floor in a pool of his own blood.

'Good riddance to him,' she hissed icily, her voice laced with years of unreleased venom, and spat on his lifeless body.

'Grant your protection to me, my mother and everyone in this household. In return I can show you how to make swords like the one that shattered yours,' the teenager said.

'How do you know how to make these? You would not work in such a trade,' Arenwen asked.

Marcus rolled up the sleeves on his toga, and showed him the scars that the teenager got while forging swords with Krasper, the ones that he had so carefully hidden from his mother.

'I have been trained, and I can make you those swords. The metal is called iron and is much stronger than bronze,' the young man explained.

'Then I extend my protection as you wish,' Arenwen said.

The next morning Caeso and Numerius waited at the entrance to the Senate for their brother. They could wait no longer as the great bronze doors were about to be shut, so they went in without their sibling. They thought that he had spent another night drinking, and would join them later when he managed to get out of bed. As they sat the captain of the City Guard took the floor to make his report.

'It is with regret that I have to inform you that we have fewer than two thousand men, which you will know is not enough to defend the city. I have two proposals for the Senate to consider,' the captain offered.

A murmur went around the Senate, the officer waited for it to come to a hush before he continued.

'Option one is the complete abandonment of the city, move all our remaining force and government to the city of Veli. Its stone walls and extra men will offer a greater protection.'

The murmur rose again, but his time the captain did not wait for it to die down.

'Option two is moving all fighting men to the Capitoline Hill where two thousand men could defend the single point of access up the steep slope. As we all know the remaining sides are totally impassable. We will hold the hill and wait for reinforcements from our allies. Any man who is not capable of fighting should withdraw to the safety of the Latin or Etruscan cities. May I respectfully remind the Senate that time is of the essence.'

The Senate discussed both options and when the votes were cast. It was a very close thing, but the Senate had voted to take option two and defend Capitoline Hill. Orders were given to evacuate non-combatants, any man of fighting age was to arm themselves and join in the defence of the steep hill. Many had already started streaming from the south gate of the city, joined by those not able to fight. All that was except six elderly senators.

'We will not bow down to barbarians. They will not dare harm us, so we will sit here and reason with them,' they said to the other senators. They didn't pay them any attention as they either left to join the fighting men, or with any others deemed too old to fight.

A few hours later Brennus arrived with his army, expecting some form of resistance, but couldn't believe it when he got to the city. The walls had no defenders on them and the gates were wide open. He feared a trap so they sent in a small exploration force. They went in and quickly returned to report that the city was empty apart from one well defended hill. The Celts flooded in to claim any prize they could. The magnificent city of Rome was put to the torch. A band of Celts went up to Quintus' domus to find Arenwen standing guard at the door.

'This house and everything in it belongs to me, but before you go I want one of you to go, and get my men,' Arenwen said.

The men recognised him from his assault on the hill at Allia. They obeyed his instruction to get his men and didn't argue, as there were still vast quantities of spoils to be had.

Another band had made its way across the Forum to the Curia Hostilia, and pushed open the two heavy bronze doors. They entered the large building, noticing that the many rows of seats were empty, apart from six men wrapped in what the Celts thought were white blankets. The six senators remained seated with the red stripes of their toga showing their status. The long swathes of white cloth was draped over their left shoulders, and wrapped around their bodies, the end having been carefully placed over the left forearm. They sat motionless on their stools, and waited for the warriors to come to them. The war band edged cautiously closer, expecting some form of trap, but as they approached one of the senators raised a hand. The group immediately formed a defensive circle and waited for an attack, but none came. They slowly turned to face the six men sat at the end of the Curia.

'There is no need to worry, I assure you that you will come to no harm. Now let us discuss terms,' one of the senators said patronisingly.

'We will discuss terms the Roman way,' one of the Celts replied.

The Senators relaxed, pleased that they were correct in thinking that the barbarians would not dare attack them.

'This is how the Romans negotiated with our Lord Bilhild,' the Celt said as he pivoted his long sword from side to side and up and down in a fluid movement.

The five remaining Roman politicians looked at each other in horror as the senator who had spoken had his head separated from his body in a single stroke. The rest of the war band stepped forward with the remaining five senators quickly meeting the same fate. Their bright white togas were now stained red as blood pumped from their decapitated bodies.

Bands roamed the city looking for plunder and slaves. All but one small part of Rome had fallen to the Celts, plumes of smoke billowed into the warm summer afternoon sky as Rome was sacked.

Chapter 20

Vae Victis - Woe to the Vanquished

Brennus had taken the city without losing a single man. He had placed a large force at the bottom of the steep Capitoline Hill, sending scouts around it to be told that the other three sides were sheer rock. Three days later he was still receiving reports of more riches being found in newly discovered parts of Rome. There were temples full of gold and precious jewels everywhere!

Arenwen stood on guard at what was the entrance to Quintus' domus, and had discarded as much of the Roman uniform that he could. As time went by he wondered if the Celts he had sent to fetch his men had not followed his instructions, but then he saw some faces he recognised. Deborah rounded the corner driving his chariot with Bakher behind her, severed heads tied to the frame by the hair swaying on the side of the chariot. The rest of his men dutifully followed, and raised a cheer as they saw their Lord. Dafydd ran to the back of the chariot to fetch Arenwen's weapons and proper clothing.

The warrior stripped off the remaining parts of the Roman uniform, relieved to pull on his woollen trousers, tunic and cloak. He especially enjoyed strapping his belt around his waist that carried his long sword.

'This house, everything and everyone in it is under my protection. This is where we shall make our base while we are here,' Arenwen said and went inside, followed by the band of men. Deborah tethered the horses and followed Bakher inside the house. The men looked in awe at the pictures made from thousands of tiny tiles covering some of the walls and most of the floor. Telor and Vaughn stripped completely naked, and lay down in what they thought was a pool in the middle of the atrium. The brothers looked down into the shallow water and laughed at the picture of a she wolf suckling two baby boys.

Arenwen found Marcus sitting in the colonnaded garden at the rear of the house with Lucia and Aesop.

'Aesop, you are to give these men anything they ask for,' the mistress said.

The slave nodded and went to attend to the new guests, but was shocked to see the stark naked twins in the atrium. He shielded his eyes from the shameless exposure, and ran off to fetch towels to cover their nudity.

Arenwen spoke to Lucia, and told her that he would need to take her son to his Lord, a chieftain called Brennus. She was initially concerned, but the Celt assured her that the young lad would be safe, and that his men would ensure the safety of her and the household.

'Grab that sword of yours and come with me,' Arenwen said to Marcus.

The young lad had already picked up the iron sword, which had lain by the side of his father's dead body, and had not let it out of his sight since. Walking past the tablinum, the teenager noticed that his father's body had been removed. The blood and the broken furniture had been cleaned away as if nothing had happened. Lucia insisted in accompanying her son to the door, and froze as she entered the atrium. Marcus was shocked too at the naked men in the shallow impluvium, a drain pool to catch the rain water from the opening in the atrium. However, this was not what she had reacted to. She was staring intently at the bust of her dead husband, oblivious to the twins. Lucia walked slowly over to the object, wrapped her arms around it, and staggered back as she lifted the full weight off the plinth. Her son rushed over to help her.

'No, I will do this alone,' she said and struggled towards the door.

She shuffled forward and adjusted the weight a few times as she went. Marcus followed closely behind just in case she couldn't take the weight any longer, but there was no need as she made it to the outside. Arenwen followed behind as they exited the house to see what she was going to do next. Marcus had no idea where his mother got the strength from as she raised the bust above her head and threw it at the ground. The marble split in two as it smashed on the ground.

'There, I never have to see that face again,' Lucia said, then she turned around and went back into the domus.

Arenwen looked puzzled as to why a wife would react with so much venom, but then remembered that the man had been killed by his own son. The warrior decided it was best not to ask. He untethered the horses and climbed onto his chariot. It was so different to the ones Marcus had seen used for sport in the Circus Maximus. The teenager jumped on the back and Arenwen showed him where to hang on. They went slowly through the streets of Rome, many of them thick with acrid smoke from the burning buildings. Groups of Celts sat on the sides of the road swigging plundered skins and amphorae of wine, or brawling in the streets.

Arenwen was asking the men where Brennus was, and he was directed to a part of the city that Marcus knew well. The warrior got off the chariot and handed the reins to a slave outside one of the big buildings at the bottom of Capitoline Hill. The chieftain had taken the temple at the bottom for his new residence; the temple of Saturn to be specific. He used the building for his accommodation, and as he went in Marcus got his first glimpse of the fearsome leader. The furniture had been piled to the side of one of the walls and he was sat, cross legged, on a mass of furs on the ground. His long blond hair was in plats that went down past his chest, with his horned helmet placed next to him.

It looked like not everybody had managed to escape the city as a number of scantily clad women sat around him. By the looks of their clothing they were Roman, and as Marcus approached one in particular stared at him as if she knew the young man, but then quickly glanced away. Marcus noticed she had looked at him, and racked his brain trying to see if he had met her before, but couldn't place her. Even sitting down the lad could see she was tall with her long black hair falling down her tanned shoulders. Most striking of all were her deep blue eyes but no, he was sure that he didn't recognise her.

To the left of Brennus, in the corner of the room, there was a large pile of gold, interspersed with jewels and other valuable objects. Brennus looked up as smiled at Arenwen.

'We have done well cousin. We have taken most of the city with only one hill holding out,' Brennus said.

'Capitoline Hill, my uncle lives or should I say lived up there,' Marcus chipped in as he popped his head around from behind Arenwen's large frame.

'This pup saved my life, but more importantly has something very special to show you. Show my Lord what you have,' Arenwen said.

Marcus took the sword out of its scabbard and presented it to Brennus.

'It is a very pretty toothpick, but I have no need for another one,' the chieftain laughed.

'It is made from a new metal that the boy calls iron. Let me show you,' Arenwen said.

The warrior drew his sword and told Marcus to strike his blade. As the lad stepped forward to hit his sword he pulled his own blade away.

'Just a minute, I'll be right back,' Arenwen said as he sheathed his sword and went outside.

Brennus looked at his young visitor puzzled, but Marcus had no idea what was going on. Then Arenwen came back in, holding another sword that he had taken from one of the drunken men outside. The teenager then realised what he had done. He didn't want to risk any damage to his own personal sword so had gone and got a substitute.

'Right, try again,' Arenwen said raising the borrowed sword in the air.

Marcus brought the iron sword down onto Arenwen's long sword, and as it had done previously the bronze sword bent while the iron sword remained straight. Brennus was taking a gulp of wine when the swords struck and spluttered a mouthful out at the sight of the bronze sword buckling.

'What is this called again?' Brennus said this time paying more attention.

'Iron,' Marcus said and then added the word 'Lord.'

'Ambrosia, bring us more wine, we have much to discuss,' Brennus said.

The woman who had looked at me earlier got up and headed for the big clay amphora. It was nearly as tall as me with its pointed base supported by a metal frame. They must have had drunk a lot already, as Ambrosia had to dip her arm deep into the storage vessel before she could scoop out any of the liquid.

'They have found the main wine store, so the men won't be fit for anything for days,' Brennus laughed.

He gestured for the two new arrivals to sit down next to him, and Marcus handed him the sword as they sat. He took the sword and flicked it back and forth, judging its weight and balance.

'Tell me about this iron and tell me about this hill. Are your armies equipped with such swords?' Brennus asked the lad.

'No, there is only one of these in Rome, but I would estimate there may be a large quantity in a villa north to the city.'

Marcus explained to Brennus that the manufacture of iron had only come recently from a Thracian who was tasked with making enough of these iron swords for the whole Roman army.

'They won't need many now,' Brennus laughed and slapped the teenager so hard on the back it rocked him forward.

The lad sat back upright and went on to say that the process had only just started. The army were equipped with bronze swords and armour, but the teenager could lead some of Brennus' men to the villa to capture the newly manufactured weapons.

'I'm not worried about those short swords as they won't get close enough to hit us. Were there any spear tips, arrow heads or armour made from this?' Brennus asked.

Marcus reassured the chieftain that the manufacture of iron had only just come to the knowledge of a select few in Rome, and there was no further production other than the gladii being produced at the villa.

'Tell me about the hill,' Brennus asked.

'It's steep, very steep. I rode my horse up there not too long ago, and it must have taken five minutes for the horse to get to the top, and it really struggled,' the lad said.

'Yes I guessed as much as we have sent men up the hill, but they cannot get far without being beaten back,' Brennus said.

'This pup holds the knowledge of how to make this iron. I would like to start making our weapons with this new metal,' Arenwen added.

'With your knowledge and skills in weapon making that would be a good idea,' Brennus agreed.

We left the Lord drinking and in the company of his ladies while the pair headed back to Quintus' domus although, it was now belonged to Arenwen's.

The weeks went by with Marcus enjoying spending time with Arenwen and his men, as did his mother. Marcus helped scour Rome for rudimentary tools, and Arenwen had sent his men out looking for the raw materials needed to manufacture iron. They came back empty handed, but they weren't really sure of what they were looking for. So by the end of week three Marcus convinced Arenwen that everything they needed was at the villa.

A group set out early one morning with Marcus riding on the chariot with Arenwen. His men had commandeered two oxen and a heavy wagon. They also had a handful of men sent by Brennus to help, but also to scout the local area for supplies and any sign of Roman reinforcements. The teenager was pleased to have gotten out of the city as the stench of death hung heavy in the air. Most of the Romans who got caught in the city now lay dead where they had fallen. A small number had survived, and were now slaves to the new Masters of Rome.

There was no one to be seen as the small group travelled along the cobbled road. The villagers had gone at the very first approach of the Celts, and now either took shelter in towns far to the south or had crossed the Tiber to the hills. The going was very slow because of the ox cart, but it was a warm sunny day, and

Marcus was feeling like a great weight had been taken off my shoulders. Even his mother seemed very happy as she saw her son off from the house.

They took the right fork in the road, and headed towards the country villa. The teenager was surprised that the surrounding area still looked as it had in the previous weeks before the invaders arrived. The crops were a little riper, but no evidence that the Celts had touched any of the land or buildings as they headed to Rome. Marcus pointed out the villa as they got closer and showed Arenwen where the lands that his family used to own stretched from and to.

'One family had all this land?' Arenwen said surprised.

They headed down the long driveway, with its marble statues untouched, and Marcus was amazed to see the villa was in perfect condition, as if nothing had happened. Slaves came out to lead the chariot away. Marcus looked at them in surprise.

'Have you not heard about Rome?' He asked.

The slave nodded and smiled 'but where else is there to go, Master?' The slave replied.

As Marcus made his way through the house he noticed that some of the slaves had made off, and he was told that Krasper was one of them. The teenager smiled as he had got to like the smith who had been so patient with him. The young lad led the group to the area that lay just before the olive groves, and before them was everything they needed. All the tools, charcoal, iron ore and one of the big bellows were all untouched. The cart was brought round and loaded up. Marcus surveyed the area and was sure that the villa and the surrounding area would not remain so untouched once the scouts reported to Brennus the vast quantities of food available. Arenwen gave his orders to his men to accompany the cart back to Rome as he and Marcus would be going on ahead.

They went back to the front of the house to find that the horses had been fed and watered. Arenwen and Marcus climbed on to the rear of the chariot, but as the teenager stayed towards the back Arenwen told him to come and stand at the front. The warrior passed the reigns and let the young Roman drive the chariot. Although it appeared that the teenager was driving Arenwen stood behind him showing the teenager how to guide the animals. By the time they had reached the fork in the road they had gotten up quite a speed; Marcus laughing as the wind blew through his hair and the speed bringing trickles of water from his eyes.

They covered ground very quickly and dashed past the Tiber, bereft of any boats that would normally be ferrying both goods and people to another busy day the capitol city. As the chariot entered the city one of the guards on the gate signalled for them to stop.

'Lord Brennus wants to see you,' the guard said.

Arenwen took full control of the chariot, and drove to where Brennus had taken residence. He was in discussions with some of his senior warriors when Arenwen came in with Marcus following closely behind.

'You wanted to see me, Lord?' Arenwen asked.

Brennus looked up from a parchment.

'I have lost too many men trying to assault this cursed hill, without any success at all,' he said referring to Capitoline Hill.

'But our luck has turned. One of our guards has found what looks like to be a track up the back of the hill. It looks recently used which suggests they are sending messages in and out. I want you to climb the path and gather information on their numbers and provisions,' Brennus said.

Arenwen bowed and followed the guard who had spotted the track marks on the side of the hill. It was still light and the soldier pointed out the likely footholds and hand holes that showed signs of recent use.

'You wait here,' Arenwen told Marcus.

Night fell and Arenwen started up the cliff face, feeling for grips and foot holes as he climbed. The scout was right there; there was certainly a way up that wasn't immediately obvious from the ground below. Arenwen edged up the side of the hill and paused as one of his feet lost purchase and slipped a little, a small sprinkling of dirt rolled down the face of the rocks. Luckily it hadn't alerted anyone at the top, so the warrior kept climbing. He could see the top now and paused to check if there were any guards patrolling the area. If there were they would have to be dispatched quietly; if reports were correct there were two thousand troops on that hill and Arenwen didn't want to get trapped up there. As he approached the top the Celt heard snoring, and ran the thought through his head that the guard must be asleep. As he flipped over the wall, at the back of the hill, he found the guard was indeed fast asleep. The soldier was using the wall to support his back while two dogs curled up tightly around his feet. He considered slitting the guard's throat, but thought better of it as it may disturb the dogs; best let sleeping dogs lie. Arenwen edged further away from the guard and headed for the shadows to start his reconnaissance mission.

Marcus was tempted to climb up to join the Celt when all hell broke loose. All the lad could hear from the top was honking geese and men shouting. Marcus hung his head, cursing himself for forgetting about the geese of Juno. Arenwen turned and knocked down the guard who was groggily getting to his feet, and leapt over the wall. He had climbed up very carefully, but now it was a combination of climbing down, sliding and controlled falling as he tried to get purchase on anything to slow his rapid descent. Torches and spears were being thrown at him as he tried to get back down to safety. He slid the last twenty feet, hitting the ground hard with a thump. Arenwen shook his head slightly dazed and got up.

'Well that didn't quite go as planned, did you know about those geese?' he asked.

Marcus very sheepishly apologised, and honestly told him that he had completely forgotten about them. His father would have berated and punished the lad, but Arenwen simply ruffled the young Roman's hair and said with a smile 'no harm done.'

The warrior went in search of Brennus to report what he had briefly seen, with Marcus dropping in behind him, as he had been accustomed in doing. When they got into the light of Brennus' temple Marcus could see that Arenwen's arms, and one side of his face were badly scratched where he had slid down the cliff face. The top surface of skin had been scraped off by his rapid decent, and now blood ran from the open wounds.

'Report,' Brennus said.

'From the brief look I had Lord, they are in a very bad shape. The guard I floored was thin and emaciated, but I'm confused as to why they haven't eaten the geese,' Arenwen said.

'They won't eat the geese. They are sacred and belong to the goddess Juno,' Marcus said.

'Then I will not waste any more of my men, we'll starve them out,' the chieftain said, satisfied with his cousin's short outline.

Two further weeks went by which the group mostly spent in the house. The streets were becoming disease-ridden, the dead bodies now bloated to the point of bursting open, riddled with yellow maggots and huge black flies. Marcus noticed that his mother seemed very happy to spend her time with Arenwen. Dafydd made his way through the house and informed Arenwen that there was one of Brennus' men at the door asking for him to join the chieftain immediately. The Celt got up and went straight to Brennus as instructed. As usual Marcus followed him while ignoring the cries from his mother who wanted her son to stay in the relative safety of the domus.

They made their way through the dirty streets, it was clear that the Celts were not city dwellers as the routine daily hygiene tasks were not being done. The invaders had no idea of what needed to be done, as they had never lived in such close proximity to others. The slaves who would have normally undertaken the tasks had fled the city or died in it. Arenwen and Marcus found Brennus outside his newly adopted temple.

'The commander on the hill has made a proposition,' the chieftain said.

'Are they to be trusted?' Arenwen asked.

'Looking at the man I sensed no trickery. The officer was so weak he could barely stand up straight,' Brennus said.

'What are they offering?' Arenwen asked.

'Gold, lots of gold,' came the reply.

Brennus recounted how he had had a conversation with the commander. He also factored in that the Celts were dying from illness, and if he remained within these walls he would lose many more.

'I've agreed a price, or rather a weight,' Brennus said.

'I'm sure you have negotiated well Lord, but may I ask how much gold?' Arenwen asked.

'One thousand pounds in weight,' Brennus grinned.

Arenwen was amazed and wondered if one thousand pounds of gold actually existed.

The deal was done and Brennus allowed Roman messengers to leave the city to return with the agreed amount from the neighbouring cities. The carts started to arrive a few days later, and just kept on coming from all directions. Two of the people who came down from the Capitoline Hill were Marcus' uncles, Caeso and Numerius. The teenager was pleased to see that they were alive, but ducked out of sight so they couldn't see him. Every wagon that came in was offloaded and weighed on a set of huge scales that Brennus had found in one of the temples. Although he had the scales he did not use the weights that were recovered with it, instead he had his own made. Numerius was placed in charge of overseeing the ransom, and sat there as the carts were offloaded, weighed and loaded again. Numerius noticed two large solid gold statues that had been put onto the scales, but the scales barely moved. He went over and picked up one of Brennus' weights, able to tell instantly that they were much heavier than they should have been. Numerius protested and demanded to see the chieftain immediately. A few minutes later Brennus appeared to see what all the fuss was about.

'Your weights are not true,' Numerius complained.

Brennus looked very serious as if the Roman's protestations were a matter of concern to him, then paused before bursting out laughing. Numerius went silent not understanding what was happening.

'Put the weight back on the scale,' Brennus commanded.

Marcus' uncle did as he was told, and the slaves continued loading the gold back onto the other side. Brennus unbuckled his long sword and threw it on the side of the weights, which made that side heavier and said 'Woe to the vanquished.'

Now it was the turn of his men around him to burst into laughter as the Romans had been clearly tricked into giving even more gold than they had agreed. Numerius was powerless to do anything else but to watch in silence. The deal was done and Brennus sent word to his men to be ready to leave in two days. The remaining time passed quickly, and Marcus thought about the joy that he had experienced with the Celts, they were full of life unlike his boring Roman lifestyle. The teenager approached Arenwen in the house.

'So you are leaving tomorrow,' he said.

'Yes, it appears so,' the warrior replied.

'But you need me to show you the secret of iron.'

'I was just thinking that, and how it could still happen,' Arenwen said.

'It's easy, take me with you,' Marcus beamed a smile.

'What would your mother say to that?' Arenwen asked.

'Without my son there is nothing for me in Rome, so take me too,' Lucia's voice came from behind them.

And so it was agreed that Lucia and Marcus would travel with Arenwen to his home, wherever that was, to make iron and seek out new adventures.

Author's Notes

I've created the notes as I crafted the story so they should read chronologically like the story itself. As I came across little things that weren't historically accurate I made notes of the changes for the folk who would no doubt correct me. However, I hope you allow my slight adjustments as the changes allowed the story to flow.

The timing of the transition between the Bronze Age and the Iron Age varied depending which part of the world you came from. It reached central Europe approximately two hundred years before this story is set, but here I will take the liberty of quoting a well-established author; 'never let historical facts get in the way of a good story.'

The Forum Boarium was the location of Rome's meat and fish market. In the story I describe two small temples. The small round temple was originally thought to be the Temple Of Vesta, where the famed vestal Virgins resided, but in fact was the Temple of Hercules. The second temple was thought to be the Temple of

Fortuna Virilis, but was actually the Temple of Portunus the god of keys, doors and livestock. The Forum certainly would have been present during this period, but the temples were built approximately 200BC, one hundred years after our story takes place, although the Great Altar of Hercules stood in the spot 600BC before the temple was built. Both temples still exist today in modern Rome, and like most of the remaining ancient ruins, they owe their existence to the fact that they had been consecrated as churches in the medieval era.

The age of the gladiatorial games significantly varies depending on which ancient scholar you read. Livy wrote that the Campanians, an area in the south of Italy whose capital today is Naples, held games as early as 310BC. Other historians place them at 1BC, but we know that a gladiatorial contest took place in Rome in 264BC as part of an aristocratic funeral. It was a tribute by Marcus Decimus Junius Brutus Scaeva and his brother Decimus in honour of their dead father.

The Etruscan name for Clusium was Clevsin. So if you do come across any maps showing cities from this period you might not see it listed as Clusium. I have used the newer name on the map outlining the Etruscan and Latin Leagues for the ease of the reader. I also took a slight liberty with the city of Veii and named it Veli as three vowels in a row are a bit hard to get your tongue around. While we're discussing the Etruscans the title camthi means magistrate, but it is reasonable to assume that this would have been a senior position and could double up as an ambassador.

There is no formal record as to why Quintus killed the Celtic chieftain that I have called Bilhild in my story, but portraying him as an arrogant bully and a wife beating, heavy drinker suited my purposes. Whatever the reason for this true event, it was clearly a breach of all agreed standards of neutrality that would be respected during negotiations. We are also unclear if this was the trigger for the attack and sacking of Rome. It may have been the reason but equally the Celts, having defeated a large Roman army, saw Rome was there for the taking and took it.

Quintus Sulpicius was the roman leader at the Battle of the Allia. I have stuck with only using his surname Sulpicius, as another Quintus might have been confusing. The actual happenings of the battle is historically correct. The outnumbered Celts attacked the left flank of the Roman's, and smashed through their defences. The Roman historian Livy actually drew a map of the battle and the starting formations, so over two thousand years later – thanks Livy as they were the basis for my maps. The Roman general did indeed flout standard battle tactics, and didn't build the usual fortifications before the conflict. The Roman army at the time was very different to the one that we know in modern times that conquered the known world. During this period they still fought using mainly the Greek phalanx, and were not the well-oiled fighting machine that created the Roman Empire. The army was made up with nobles who commanded their own mini armies, and lightly trained peasants, but this is not to take away the achievements of the Celts who were heavily outnumbered. When researching the battle it was difficult to calculate actual numbers. Roman historians state that the Celts significantly outnumbered the Romans who were made up of a hastily assembled army. However, we have to remember that the Celts did not keep much note of their history, and history is written by the victors. So although the Celts won this battle, the Romans ultimately won the war, and hid their dramatic defeat with spin from historians such as Livy. The 18th of July was considered to be an unlucky day, very much like our modern Friday 13th, for many hundreds of years after the battle of Allia. Other non-Roman historians combatant figures range widely, but the numbers I have used in the battle of Allia are, I believe, to be a fair reflection of what actually took place.

And finally Vae Victis - Woe to the vanquished can also been translated as Woe to the conquered. I hope you've enjoyed my Celtic tale, it is the first of many where our heroes will travel across most of the known world at the time, getting into scrapes and battles.

The first chapter of The Empire Of White Gold – Book 2 in the 'Iron Sword Series' is included at the end of this book. I hope you enjoy it, and go on following the adventures of our Celtic warriors.

Book 2 Empire of White Gold

Chapter 1

The Journey Home

Brennus had promised Arenwen a quarter of all the new land that they conquered after they had crossed the Alps, but following the treaty with Rome they were to return home. Brennus had extracted well over a thousand pounds of gold from the Romans, and made sure that Arenwen was suitably rewarded with a quarter of his share. This instantly made the warrior extremely wealthy, and was satisfied that when he returned home to the Silures tribe he would lead a very good life. But something was troubling him.

'May I ask you a question cousin?' Arenwen said to Brennus.

The chieftain noticed that Arenwen had called him cousin, and therefore it was a personal matter he wanted to discuss.

'Go ahead,' Brennus replied.

'Bilhild died in my arms, and I promised I would make sure his family would be looked after.'

'I have also been giving thought to my promise that I made him about his share of land,' Brennus said.

'And so I shall honour his family with his rightful portion, a quarter of the gold,' Brennus added.

He also assured Arenwen that the wife and three daughters of his senior warrior, killed by the Romans, would be well looked after and want for nothing.

In the midst of it all, a teenager born to a rich noble Roman family, from a villa a few miles north of Rome, accompanied by his mother had been willingly adopted by the Celts. The army had crossed the Alps and invaded Roman lands, easily defeating the mighty Republican Roman army.

'So what is your tribe called again?' Marcus asked Arenwen, who was the chieftain of the band of men him and his mother were travelling with.

They were towards the front of nine thousand warriors all heading north, although twelve thousand had made their way across the Alps at the start of the campaign. The Celts lost more men through disease and sickness than they did in battle. This was the primary reason that Brennus had accepted the huge ransom to leave, and head back to his lands.

'My tribe is called the Silures, young Marcus,' Arenwen said to the teenager.

He tried to pronounce the strange word.

'Seel-oor-es,' he said to himself, rolling the unfamiliar name around his mouth, trying to pronounce it correctly.

There were three of them on the chariot, with the third person being an old man called Bakher. He held the title of druid, but Marcus didn't really know what that was. His mother, Lucia, followed behind on another chariot driven by one of Arenwen's warriors called Deborah. The rest of his men followed behind on foot, and while they looked very threatening Marcus had come to like their rough exterior, knowing they had a softer side to them. One of the softer sides was being displayed by one of Arenwen's men, and brother to Deborah. The war band had adopted a young puppy on their travels, and it was struggling to keep up so Dafydd scooped it up and put it inside his cloak. His best friend Durston saw him pick up the dog and gave him a shove, playful by Celtic standards, but it would have been enough to knock most Romans flat.

They travelled along the road that ran mostly parallel to the great Tiber River. It was a road that Marcus had travelled frequently over the last year when he made his visits to Rome. He had travelled it but only as far as one of the major forks, where he would have gone right to his family's villa with its corresponding estates. The teenager knew the road still carried on further north, but that part of the road would be new to him. Arenwen had told stories of his journey from his home, though the names of the lands were alien to Marcus. The warrior said he was chieftain of the Silures tribe in a land called Cambria, one of the many countries on the isle of Britannia. He crossed the sea to Gallia to see his cousin and mighty Warlord Brennus, and happened into an adventure that led him across raging rivers, high mountains. Marcus often wondered how his life would have evolved if the Celts had not turned up. He pondered, would he have killed his father, or would he have just grown up a rich noble in the great city of Rome? No, the teenager was sure, one way or another he would have certainly killed his father for treating his mother so badly. That seemed a lifetime ago now, and the young lad had never seen his mother so happy, catching her smiling at Arenwen several times.

The weather had been very warm for quite some time, and Arenwen could see Brennus up ahead signalling him forward. He guided his chariot off to the side of the road, and clicked his reins for his horses to speed up past the troops. He pulled up next to Brennus' chariot and asked 'what is it, Lord?'

'It is a day and a half to the mountain pass, so I would like to make camp here,' the chieftain said.

'Good idea Lord, that way we will start crossing the mountain range in two days with plenty of light.'

'I'll head to the ground on the left to make camp. Follow me and get close to the river,' Brennus instructed.

Arenwen nodded, pulling his chariot around to head back down the line to take his original position. He passed the orders to his men, who in turn relayed it down the line. All of the nine thousand strong army pulled over to the left side of the road and headed for the Tiber, providing them with fresh water for the night.

Arenwen led his small band to an area that hadn't yet been occupied by the river bank. The horses were unhitched from the chariots, while Deborah went about getting buckets of water for them, making sure they were going to be comfortable for the night. The slaves got the fires going, not that it was going to be a cold night, but because they were preparing hot food for the warriors. Animals had been slaughtered in Rome and preserved with salt for the long journey back to Arenwen's homeland. The slaves hoisted a slaughtered pig onto the spit, rotating the carcass slowly. It would be several hours before it was ready, but there was an ample supply of fresh vegetables, freshly baked bread and a round circular thing that Marcus had been told was a sausage. The ale was rolled out as the fat from the pig dripped onto the fire, making it sizzle and shoot flames up to lick the flanks of bubbling skin.

Arenwen and his small party sat in a circle on the cool grass, many of them recounting tales of their exploits in battle. Marcus was sat next to Arenwen when Lucia came over and squeezed into the small gap between them, forcing her son to shuffle over. The men were getting a little rowdy, but as Marcus had spent nearly two months with them he knew this was nothing unusual. The teenager had come to expect some sort of contest going on between the twins Telor and Vaughn, and best friends Dafydd and Durston frequently ending the night arm wrestling.

By the time the group had eaten the sausages, bread and vegetables the night had closed in, and the sky was lit with a twinkling array of stars. At last the pig was ready, with the slaves slicing slabs of meat and serving them to the warriors. Arenwen was presented with one of the hind legs, he bit into it taking a big chunk before he realising it was too hot and reached for his ale to cool his mouth down. Lucia laughed at his stupidity with Arenwen bursting out laughing too. The night wore on, songs were sung, and ale was drunk. Marcus watched how his mother played with Arenwen's long dark hair and giggled like a young girl; now that she was away from the oppressive behaviour of her dead husband.

The Celts ate a lot more meat than Romans, but Marcus was getting used to it, he particularly enjoyed the roasted pig. True to form, Dafydd and Durston started their wrestling, but this time they had decided they would test leg strength, so they lay on their backs in opposite directions and raised their right legs. They locked their ankles together and began the contest. Whoever was the stronger would make the other perform a backward roll, with their legs ending up over their head. The men gathered around and swigged their horns of ale, Marcus noticed that some of them had acquired fine Roman goblets.

It was an even contest with Dafydd going ahead then Durston pulling a few back. The teenager was enjoying the carefree life style of his new family. The entire group were all enjoying the contest when Marcus noticed that something was troubling Arenwen.

'You seem deep in thought,' the young lad said to Arenwen.

'Yes, it is something that I heard while in Rome,' he replied.

'Anything I can do to help?'

'What do you know about the ships on the coast?' he asked.

'I know that Rome couldn't produce as much food as the city needed, so grain and other things were imported from many different countries. The port is about twenty one miles away,' Marcus explained.

'I thought as much,' Arenwen said as he got up, leaving his men to make wagers on who would win the next leg wrestle.

The warrior went off to speak to Brennus, and made his way through the campfires that lit up the dark area by the river. He found his cousin sitting outside his tent with some of his senior warriors eating and drinking. By the smile on his face Brennus was pleased to see Arenwen, and moved one of the senior warriors to one side to make room for his visitor.

'Cousin, it is great to see you,' Brennus said as he called for slaves to bring meat and ale for his guest.

Arenwen gratefully accepted his hospitality, and waited for the right moment to address what was on his mind.

'Come on then, I can see on your face that this is not a social visit,' Brennus said.

'You know me well, cousin,' Arenwen said with a smile.

'I've been thinking about all the gold we have,' the warrior said.

'Yes, we are rich beyond our wildest dreams,' Brennus said slapping Arenwen on his back.

'We will have difficulty getting it over the mountains, and after that I have much further to travel than you, including another sea to cross,' Arenwen said.

'Hmmm, I had thought about the mountain crossing and made sure there is rope and blocks to help get the carts up the steep mountain sides, but I hadn't thought about your journey home. So what do you propose?' Brennus asked.

Arenwen told Brennus of the huge quantities of grain and other goods that came into a port about twenty one miles to the west. The warrior thought that the ships must be quite large to carry all that weight and wanted Brennus' permission to brake off from the main army. He wanted to try to secure passage for his small party on a boat and avoid the mountain crossing. As well as circumventing the mountains Arenwen wanted to get as far up the coast has he could to shorten his journey home.

'That works on two levels, cousin. You may find a shorter route for us when we come back, and I'm sure we will come back now we know the wealth here. We will let them refill their treasury, and return to empty it again. Secondly it should reduce your journey time home, and with the amount of gold you have you could buy a fleet of ships,' Brennus laughed.

'The only concern I have is that once we leave the safety of the main army we are open to attack in lands we do not know, but I'm sure my men would be up to the task,' Arenwen said.

'It is agreed then, rest here tonight then when we continue north you will go west to the coast,' Brennus said.

Just as Arenwen was about to go Brennus added 'send Durston to me.'

Arenwen returned to his men to find that they all had now entered into competition of leg wrestling. Dafydd and Durston stood and watched as they drank their ale. Arenwen darted in between the competing pairs on the floor, jumping over Taylor and Vaughn to where the two friends were standing.

'Who won between you two,' Arenwen said.

'A draw,' they both said together then laughed.

'Durston, Brennus wants to see you,' the chieftain said.

Durston handed Arenwen the horn of ale as he went off in search of Brennus. Dafydd was wondering why his friend had been summoned, but thought he would soon find out when he returned.

Durston waited outside Brennus' tent until he was summoned inside.

'Durston, it is good to see you,' the Warlord said.

'And you too, my Lord,' he replied, going down on one knee.

'I have a question for you,' Brennus said.

Durston waited while his sworn Lord took some ale from a highly decorated golden goblet, which was encrusted with rubies and sapphires.

'Arenwen will be leaving us in the morning, looking for a ship to transport them back to Cambria,' he explained.

Durston's heart sank as he knew that one day he would need to part from his friend as he was bound to his Lord Brennus, but he thought he would have a few more weeks of Dafydd's company before they needed to go their separate ways.

'I have seen you and Dafydd in combat, and in friendship, so it does not sit well with me to break up such a bond,' Brennus said.

'You are right, my Lord, he is my brother from another mother,' Durston chipped in.

Brennus nearly choked on his ale as he tried to swallow, spluttering a laugh at the expression.

'Yes, yes, I couldn't have put it better. So I need you to accompany Arenwen and travel to his homelands. Spend some time there, when the time is right return to me and report on the journey from here to there,' Brennus said.

Durston dropped to both knees as he had been released from his vow to serve Brennus, but at the same time the wise leader had left the option for him to return whenever he wanted to.

'Thank you, Lord,' Durston said taking Brennus' hand and kissing it.

'Be off with you now, and be careful of those Cambrian women if Dafydd's sister is anything to go by,' Brennus said giving him a playful kick to the backside as Durston made his way out of the tent.

By the time he had returned to the camp the leg wrestling contests had turned into a 'winner stays on' system. The last two were pitting their strengths against each other. Arenwen, the reigning champion and to Durston's surprise; Deborah. The crowd chanted 'three, two one!' and the tussle began with both of them straining their legs, neither yielding an inch. Arenwen would take an advantage and then Deborah would pull him back, her flame red hair falling on either side of her head. Arenwen pulled again and Deborah took the strain and pushed harder as she rolled Arenwen over. The men cheered and raised their ale in celebration. Arenwen got up, dusted himself off and reached out a hand to pull Deborah up. She had no need to take his hand as she athletically flipped up onto to her feet. Arenwen took her arm and raised it in the air.

'The best man in the party,' he said.

The ale continued to flow, with Arenwen gathering the party together to tell them of the plan.

'In the morning we are to carry on north until we find a bridge or ferry crossing. We will cross the river and head west for the coast to hire, buy or steal a ship,' Arenwen explained.

He turned to his druid, Lucia, and Marcus saying 'it is uncharted territory for us and I do not know what it brings. I cannot guarantee your safety so you have the option to stay with the main army, and join us in Cambria when you can.'

Bakher turned to the two others.

'I don't know about you two, but only the gods know what will happen to him without my protection, so I'm going,' he said.

'Me too,' Marcus said.

'Me three,' Lucia added.

Dafydd's face dropped as the realisation hit that his best friend must follow his sworn Lord.

'And me four,' Durston said as he explained what Brennus had told him.

Dafydd launched himself at Durston, gripped him in a bear hug as the friends bounced up and down with joy.

'So it is settled. Tomorrow we will follow the river bank while the main army heads north east to the mountain passes. Now eat and drink and rest,' Arenwen said with a broad smile.

Nearly everyone had a little more food and ale except Dafydd and Durston. They carried on drinking until the early hours, with the occasional boot being thrown at them as a signal to keep the noise down.

They awoke the next morning, and gathered supplies from the main army which consisted mainly of heavily salted meats and round cheeses. The group covered the riches being carried on the wagon with furs, and then loaded the food on top to hide the treasure from any prying eyes. They had their morning meal of fresh bread and porridge, and packed up the few belongings they had on to the wagon. The main army set off at the same time, Arenwen's group travelling with them for a while until the road headed north east. The party turned off and followed the river looking for some form of crossing.

The small party travelled all morning without sight of any ferry or bridge, being careful not to follow the river too closely as some of the twists and turns nearly wound back on each other. Eventually one of the men thought he spotted something up ahead in the distance. Arenwen asked Bakher to move to Deborah's chariot with Lucia. Deborah was to hold her chariot back and to remain with the men while Arenwen and Marcus pushed on to check what his man had spotted. Although they were off the road the grass was flat and firm, so the going was easy. They covered about half a mile when Arenwen pulled the horses to a halt. It was much clearer to see now, it was a wooden bridge across the Tiber. Arenwen passed the reins and told Marcus to hold the chariot there. He jumped off and went ahead to see if the bridge was guarded. As he got closer he saw that there were two guards on both sides that would have to be dealt with if they were to make it undetected to the coast.

The Celtic chieftain made his way back, and jumped back on the chariot.

'Two guards either side of the bridge, but I have got a plan,' he said.

Marcus passed the warrior the reins, and he wheeled the chariot around to join the rest of the small war band. Arenwen gathered everyone together, and made sure everybody knew exactly what they had to do. Bakher needed to step down from the Deborah's chariot. The warrior pulled the hood of his cloak over his head, and sat down at the front of his chariot, his legs dangling over the edge, with Marcus standing. Deborah did the same with Lucia taking position at the rear of their vehicle. The men were to follow, but would not be involved, because as soon as the bridge guards spotted a small band they would run and sound the alarm. Lucia and Marcus were still in their Roman clothes, the quality of which would show that they were from a noble family, even at a distance. As they approached the bridge the two guards on the closest side spotted them, not knowing what to do as they were not familiar with the chariots, but saw and heard the two ex-Romans as they made themselves very conspicuous by waving and calling to soldiers. They eased their stance as the chariots drew closer, spotting what they thought were two nobles being transported by their slaves. Deborah brought her chariot up close enough for guards to address Lucia. Arenwen was to her side, ready to rush past when he made his move.

'Salve, you should be careful traveling alone. The barbarian horde is not too far away, but reports say the scum are heading to the mountains,' one of the guards said.

Marcus' mother had had many years of abuse, with her confidence being knocked out of her by her violent husband. However, a mother is like a lioness when it comes to protecting her children so she stood straight and calm. Arenwen glanced over to check that Deborah was ready, she acknowledged with a nod that she was.

'Now!' Arenwen shouted as he jumped from his chariot and threw back his hood.

'Hold on,' Deborah said to Lucia as she cracked the reins. The horses responded by galloping across the wooden bridge. Marcus watched his mother holding on tightly as the wheels bounced up and down on the wooded trunks of the bridge floor.

Arenwen had hidden his long sword under his cloak, and unsheathed his weapon before the first guard could raise his spear. He thrust the weapon under the man's jaw and out through the back of his skull, putting his foot on his victim's stomach to push him off his deadly blade, but no matter how hard he tugged it was lodged firmly in the man's skull. The second guard rushed at the warrior and tried to impale him, but Arenwen let go of his sword with the dead guard falling to the floor. He spun around the spear, pulling out his short axe from his belt. With a leap and a deathly scream he crashed the weapon down on the second guard's head, splitting through his helmet, crushing his skull.

There was only a few seconds in it, but it gave the guards on the far side enough time to see what was happening, readying themselves for Deborah's chariot that was charging at them. The soldiers took a low crouching position, and kept their bodies behind their large rectangular shields. They stuck one end of the spear into the ground, angling it at forty five degrees to impale the horses on to the tips of their spears. Every soldier knew that horses wouldn't crash into a man wielding a spear. Deborah saw their intentions, and took out a spear from the side rack. Marcus watched in awe as she steered the horses with one hand while throwing the spear at full speed on a bumpy surface. The teenager would have thought it an impossible shot if he had not seen it made with his own eyes. The spear took the guard on the right through his exposed shoulder, pushing him backwards to the floor. The second looked in horror at his comrade rolling in agony with the spear lodged deep in his shoulder. The second man steadied himself for the impact, but just before she reached the guard Deborah brought the horses to a halt just in front of the soldier. These were battle trained horses, so when Deborah pulled back on the reins they reared onto their hind legs and crashed their hooves down on the guard, who's only option was to let his shield take the impact of the horses' stamping feet. He looked around in panic, looking for an escape route, but couldn't see any viable option that wouldn't result in him getting killed. Deborah brought the horses to a complete stop, they stamped their hooves in front of the guard.

'Run,' Deborah said calmly.

The guard looked confused, as if he didn't understand what she was saying.

'Run,' Deborah said again.

The man dropped his shield and spear, then started running down the road away from the bridge. Deborah watched as he ran and slowly picked up her bow. She popped her right index finger in her mouth to wet it. She slowly raised her finger in the air to judge the wind strength and direction. The guard was still running for his life and was a significant distance from the bridge, but dared not look back as he expected the sound of hooves to be behind him any second. Deborah tossed her head to one side to flick the hair out of her face, and notched an arrow onto the bow string. She drew back the cord, making a slight adjustment in the upward angle of the bow and loosed. It flew up in the air, stalled for a split second, then the arrow hurtled towards the ground striking the guard cleanly in-between his shoulder blades. Deborah told Lucia to hop off the chariot, then rippled the reins to make the horses move into a gentle trot. She headed for the guard, who was desperately trying to crawl away. Deborah pulled the chariot next to the man, and jumped off the back. She pulled the arrow out of the stricken man, him screaming in agony as the head ripped through his flesh. With one knee on his back she grabbed his hair and drew back his head.

'I gave you a fair chance,' she whispered in his ear as she took out a knife and slit his throat.

Deborah tied the man's feet to the back of the chariot and dragged his body back to where she had killed the other guard. The bodies of all four men were concealed under the bridge, with Arenwen signalling for the men to come up the river bank to join them.

'That's us across the river, now on to the port,' Arenwen said - they headed west.

Printed in Great Britain
by Amazon

19063056R00200